£23.00

D1789409

JRO
24/4/2010

SELF PSYCHOLOGY AND DIAGNOSTIC ASSESSMENT

IDENTIFYING SELFOBJECT FUNCTIONS THROUGH PSYCHOLOGICAL TESTING

SELF PSYCHOLOGY AND DIAGNOSTIC ASSESSMENT

IDENTIFYING SELFOBJECT FUNCTIONS THROUGH PSYCHOLOGICAL TESTING

Marshall L. Silverstein
Long Island University

www.routledgementalhealth.com

Reprinted 2009 by Routledge

Cover design by Kathryn Houghtaling Lacey

Cover art by Vladimir M. Pechanec

Library of Congress Cataloging-in-Publication Data

    Self psychology and diagnostic assessment: identifying
selfobject functions through psychological testing / Marshall L.
Silverstein
       p. cm.
Includes bibliographical references and indexes.
ISBN 0-8058-2280-1 (hardcover : alk. paper)

    1. Self psychology. 2. Projective techniques. I. Title.
RC455.4.S42S55 1998   98-27593
616.89'075—dc21   CIP

10 9 8 7 6 5 4 3 2 1

For my devoted parents,
Jack
(1891–1963)
and Gertrude
(1915–1998)
who, despite all odds,
provided the kernel for a resilient self
and for Marian Tolpin, M.D.,
who fortified it

Contents

Preface

A patient delivered projective test responses that included a Rorschach percept of a well-made but faded shirt, a Thematic Apperception Test (TAT) story about a depressed woman tied to her parents and unable to strike out on her own, and a drawing of a person described as hunched over or defeated. These responses suggested depression. Inquiry revealed that the patient elaborated these responses by commenting that the shirt was thrown away and that because the depressed woman could not make her mother understand her dilemma, she gave up her aspirations and was too beaten down to leave her parents. The patient also stated that because the hunched-over figure was laughed at, the person hid in shame. Statements about depression or even low self-esteem might be applied to this patient. But such descriptions fail to go far enough.The responses richly depicted a diminished and devitalized self. The patient felt depleted and unable to turn to the world with confidence or pride. Such a person cannot expect others to understand in sufficient depth these feelings of being underpowered or to respond with some recognition that the person needs to be made to feel intrinsically worthwhile.

Another patient produced Rorschach responses of "a high priestess delivering a blessing to her subjects," "the gods discussing humanity among themselves," and "a warrior from heaven dressed in full regalia." On the TAT, this patient described "a surreal representation of Noah's ark and how he saved the animals from destruction." These responses seemed to convey vigor through an emphasis on exalted states, vitality, and power until the patient elaborated these images on inquiry by commenting that the warrior was defective, the ark might be destroyed in a storm, and the gods discussing humanity were impotent.

These two patterns represent self states of devitalization and their resulting *self disorders*, to use Heinz Kohut's term to describe such conditions. The first patient seemed unable to summon resources to effect a repair of the self disorder and was prone to give up and wither. The second patient revealed some degree of resilience, at least to the extent of hoping that through idealization there was a chance to reinvigorate a depleted self. Although the patient might have tried to establish a compensatory structure as a pathway toward some restoration of a diminished self, however, the attempt was unsuccessful. The initial appearance of grandiosity was only a thin, defensive veneer exposed as such on a sufficiently probing inquiry, and the patient's responses concealed a self state just as injured and devalued as that of the first patient.

This book is about understanding clinical material of this nature. I am particularly concerned here with three problems: clinical identification of the predominant psychological patterns (self states) such as the devitalization or idealization shown in these two examples; patients' attempts to repair an injury to the self, to restore self-esteem by developing compensatory structure (such as turning to a strong or vibrant source for idealization when an underlying state of devitalization is prominent); and clinical manifestations or sequelae of these disorders of the self (disintegration products such as narcissistic rage and affect states such as empty depression or chronic boredom and lack of zest).

The preceding vignettes portray clinical phenomena of self disorders as revealed on several projective tests, and the interpretations of these disorders encapsulate some seminal contributions of Heinz Kohut's psychology of the self. The vignettes serve as a springboard for the conceptual and technical discussion of psychoanalytic self psychology, particularly of the selfobject functions of mirroring, idealization, and twinship.

This book attempts to meet two difficult and unpopular goals: first, to provide a thorough, accurate, and sophisticated presentation of self psychology; second, to demonstrate that interpreting content on projective psychological tests promotes a deep understanding of self states and their resulting disorders.

My first goal, stating the views of self psychology, is difficult because the material is not simple and easy to appreciate without the clinical experience of working with patients in this framework. Self psychology has sometimes been considered a theory of pathological narcissism, but it is not. Self psychology has been misunderstood partly because narcissistic personality and behavior disorders are definable (in the sense that they are described in the *Diagnostic and Statistical Manual of Mental Disorders* [4th ed., DSM–IV]), whereas self disorders are not unfortunately clear-cut and easily comprehended. Indeed, Kohut began his attempt to understand self disorders as forms of narcissistic pathology more than 25 years ago

(Kohut, 1959, 1966, 1971), but his broadened and expanded views (1977, 1984) about the self and its disorders extended well beyond narcissism. The inherent confusion of this situation makes the discussion of self psychology unpopular because it can seem conceptually unclear despite being clinically palpable and vivid.

My second goal, using content analysis of projective test findings to characterize self states, is also difficult. Phenomenologic data are always vague and do not lead to clearly agreed-on interpretations of clinical meaning. The analysis of test content and sequence analysis is unpopular at a time that psychologists rightfully expect and can achieve psychometric sophistication. Some clinicians may find the study of content distasteful because the results of this approach are unverifiable and therefore logically unsupportable and may even appear scientifically regressive. These practitioners of psychodiagnostic testing are satisfied with nothing less than valid and reliable empirical scores and should expect nothing less. Although content analysis cannot provide this degree of rigor, it is valuable in a different way if clinicians follow the highest standards of logical inquiry and practice careful, clinical inferential thinking.

I intend to combine the rich insights of self psychology with an honest attempt to approach content analysis with restraint and logical rigor. I strive to make the best use of suboptimal clinical material to reveal deep levels of the painfully experienced affect states that Kohut's psychology of the self has managed to explain. My discussion of psychoanalytic self psychology does not disappoint in its complete and often painstaking accuracy about central concepts, including transmuting internalization, compensatory structure, empathic understanding, and, of course, the crucially significant selfobject functions. This book is not an "easy read"; it sacrifices nothing of self psychology's complexity and nuances. Thus, the book is not everyone's "cup of tea"; certainly it is not for the faint of heart.

ORGANIZATION OF PARTS I AND II

One way of thinking about the convergence between the psychology of the self and projective testing is by asking: What do patients convey through projective test content about the self state, about its vitality or weakness and its attempts to recover from injury? How do people use Rorschach percepts, the characters described in TAT stories, and drawings of human figures to convey feeling competent, whole, buoyant in contrast to feeling brittle, undermined, devalued, and consequently unable to recover from vulnerable states of disrepair? These basic questions I address in this book.

In Part I, I trace the development and major concepts of Kohut's psychology of the self, including his crystallized view about the central role of a cohesive and buoyant self in achieving psychological well-being. Although Kohut's views were originally firmly anchored in the predominant drive theory and ego psychology of classical psychoanalysis, I detail the evolution of his thinking beyond its representing an extension of ego psychology in chapter 1. In chapters 2 and 3, I discuss the major concepts of self psychology; chapter 3, in particular, is devoted entirely to the concept of selfobject functions.

The chapters of Part II contain clinical illustrations of projective test content indicating self states and their associated selfobject functions. I present self psychological interpretations alongside more familiar or conventional ego psychological interpretations of these projective test responses. The self psychological viewpoint, as formulated by Kohut, offers a compelling basis for understanding projective test content. In many cases, I argue that a self psychological view offers a more phenomenologically accurate picture of the personality than does a conventional framework.

Chapter 4 provides a systematic, detailed review of the principal approaches to content analysis in the clinical interpretation of projective tests. I specifically advocate the content analysis approach to reveal important aspects of the self, notably its cohesion or vulnerability and mechanisms to repair self-esteem in the face of injury. The case for using content analysis is based on principles first laid down by Rapaport and Schafer. I apply it here to promote a clinically reasonable means to augment empirical scores on psychodiagnostic tests that are otherwise insufficient to describe self states such as devitalization or depletion.

After establishing this groundwork, I consider the convergence of self psychology and content analysis in projective testing. I then demonstrate the clinical and conceptual characteristics of mirroring (chap. 5) and idealization and twinship (chap. 6) by providing ample illustrations of projective test responses. These examples reflect the principal features and subtleties of expression of these three major selfobject functions. Chapters 7 and 8 contain complete projective test protocols of two patients for further understanding a self psychological viewpoint.

CONCEPTUAL AND CLINICAL OBJECTIVES

People have commonly revealed sentiments of shame and feelings of diminished abilities and compromised self-worth through projective test responses. These responses can include percepts such as faltering objects, unflattering human figure drawings such as a hobo, or TAT stories about characters feeling incompetent. Many patients can more easily make up a story about a failure than talk about similar feeling states in themselves during a clinical interview. When a major depressive episode or dysthymic disorder is acute and feelings of worthlessness predominate, such affect states are to be expected and are common, but in many other clinical conditions, diminished self-esteem is not typically experienced close to the surface. Clinicians may therefore miss the self state altogether, particularly if a patient manifests a superficial bravado or defensive minimization of a self disorder.

Although self-esteem is certainly an important characteristic of the sense of the self and self-depreciation is a frequent consequence of a self disorder, a more crucial consideration involved in a psychological understanding of the self is its resilience. Resilience usually appears in people's capacity to repair injuries on their own or, more typically, to turn to another in expectation of appropriate, empathic responsiveness for help with revitalizing the self. Injuries and rebuffs occur frequently in life and become less devastating when not too recurrent, intense, or traumatic. More important than the severity of the injury for an understanding of the self is the capacity of an accurately responsive environment to take note that an injury has occurred.

Kohut regarded this capacity as the most crucial characteristic of selfobject functions. Such optimal responsiveness promotes a self's sustaining or restorative capacity to be invigorated, robust, and cohesive. Narcissistic injuries in and of themselves are not necessarily pathogenic, but selfobject failures in an already compromised or vulnerable self state produce either a narcissistic personality disorder or a narcissistic behavior disorder. Mild disturbances can appear as subclinical disruptions of self-esteem interfering with the vitality that supports a person's ability to reconstitute. This quality of resilience is the measure of self-cohesion.

As it is in the clinical history, so it is in the analysis of diagnostic testing material: Somewhere in the test protocols is a representation of the patient's attempt to bring about what he or she needs to repair an undermined self state. A Rorschach response of an injured butterfly incapable of flying, a wilted flower, a carcass left to decay in the hot sun, or a similar percept describes the self state as less than optimally intact or vigorous. Equally important, such responses that typically receive morbid codes as special scores guide the search throughout the remainder of the test protocol for the restorative selfobject function needed to repair this devitalized self. From the standpoint of psychodiagnostic testing, a person's response of a decaying leaf, for example, may not be important by itself. What may be more crucial is the person's ability to respond next, on either the same Rorschach card or the following one, in a manner that does not continue the theme of devitalization. Being able to "bounce back" from the injured self state indicates some degree of resilience of the self.

Among the most typical examples of disturbances representing impaired cohesiveness of the self, the psychodiagnostic testing manifestations of depleted energy, emptiness, and devitalization are the most readily elicited. Thus, for example, test responses with references to something broken, split open, lacking power or strength, looking drab or ragged, or appearing dirty, mention of a skeleton or of something beautiful but obscured by junk are typical manifestations of this aspect of human experience. Many morbid Rorschach percepts convey the unique quality of a devitalized self state. Thus, responses with morbid contents such as an object bleeding or left to die or decay, something old or rotting away, or a faded object (such as a photograph, leaf, or even a person) are good examples of this phenomenon. All or even most morbid percepts on the Rorschach test are not by definition aspects of compromised self-esteem, but a clinician can empathically grasp a great many responses of this type from the standpoint of an unmirrored self as described by Kohut. Thus, it is useful to consider a self psychological interpretation to enhance the clinical meaning or relevance of such percepts.

Particular projective test responses may also suggest the disintegration products that characterize many self disorders, such as perversions, addictions, or overt fragmentation phenomena. Disintegration products, representing desperate attempts to sustain self-esteem in the face of threatened loss of self-regulating structures, can be represented by responses indicating states of an incapacity to experience an object or person as solid or tangible or a breakdown of firm boundaries. Imagery from the TAT and figure drawings may also characterize a self state of appreciable distress, a state that fails to hold its own or is incapable of restoring corrective functions. Examples can include stories of people unable to hold themselves up or experiencing devastating loss from which they do not recover, and drawings of a person, tree, or house in midair without grounding or roots or blown apart by the elements. Such imagery is also characteristic of psychotic or psychosis-prone states, borderline personality disorders, or transient fragmentation phenomena. Comorbid psychopathology or other theoretical views about the primary disturbance do not, however, preclude the role of a vulnerable self in disrepair. The self state and its selfobject needs are important influences on severe as well as on nonpsychotic conditions.

Restorative selfobject functions do not necessarily appear in the *response proper*, such as those previously noted. More typically, what is needed to repair the devalued self emerges from *elaborations* of the central response. Thus, it is important for clinicians to unobtrusively elicit verbalizations that extend the primary response, such as an injured bird needing someone to attend to its broken wing or a wilted flower waiting to be watered. Sometimes, these indications do not immediately follow the response suggesting an undermined self state but occur later during the test or on another test. Often there may be no indication about the self state on a popular projective test, such as the Rorschach, but the particular "pull" or character of an instrument like the TAT or figure drawings may be more revealing. For example, a person may tell a story about the young man on Card 7BM of the TAT as distressed over a disappointment and turning to confide in the older man. The person may describe this latter figure as listening attentively (mirroring selfobject function) or offering advice that the younger man eagerly accepts from admiration for the older man (idealization) or from a desire to be exactly like the older man in his resolution of the problem (twinship).

On occasion, clinicians can distinguish the projective test content of somewhat better compensated patients in overabstract, distanced, or philosophically detached responses, which include obsessional preoccupations with ideas or depersonalized images of great figures that are mythical or from the distant past. Other examples are mystical, abstract, human-like content, typically coded (H) or (Hd) in Exner's (1993) Comprehensive System, such as "Valkyries images" or, on figure drawings, "a woman from the Elizabethan court." Examples like these may represent attempts to establish a connection or bond with an idealized mythic figure; such responses are frequently preceded or followed by responses signifying injury or devaluation. Responses about grand or powerful images also demonstrate the unique role of psychodiagnostic tests for identifying compensatory structure, one of the less well-known concepts of the psychology of the self.

ACKNOWLEDGMENTS

I have chosen to discuss only the classical version of self psychology associated with Heinz Kohut. This version is both sufficiently encompassing and difficult to comprehend that a discussion of other outgrowths of self psychology (such as intersubjectivity) only diffuses my primary objective. Although I never knew or studied with Kohut, his views have substantially infused my own clinical practice and my thinking for more than 25 years.

In preparing this book, I have benefitted from the helpful comments of many colleagues, most of whom are at the Chicago Institute for Psychoanalysis, Michael Reese Medical Center, and Long Island University. The preparation of this book was facilitated by a sabbatical leave from Long Island University and by a grant from the C. W. Post Research Committee of Long Island University. Irving Weiner, Susan Milmoe, Nadine Simms, and the production staff of Lawrence Erlbaum Associates provided steady guidance and clarity during the production stage. I am particularly grateful to Joanne Marengo, Michael Simon, and Marian Tolpin, for reading several drafts of the manuscript and for their enduring support of this effort.

I trust that my thinking about psychological testing will enrich the ongoing study of the psychology of the self, and I also believe that the contributions of self psychology will foster a deepening understanding of personality as revealed through psychodiagnostic testing.

Part I
Psychoanalytic Self Psychology

1 The Shift From Classical Drive Theory To Self Psychology

In the introduction to the final installment of *The Search for the Self*, the definitive collection of Heinz Kohut's papers and letters, Ornstein (1990) succinctly captured one of Kohut's principal contributions. He wrote: "Kohut maintained from early on that there were areas of human experience that could not be adequately explored with the aid of drive psychology and ego psychology and considered this fact as one of the most compelling reasons for introducing self psychology" (p. 9).

In this statement, Ornstein conveyed that self psychology had evolved to become a theory in its own right, one that was more than an expansion or development of classical drive theory. Nevertheless, it is difficult to think of another conceptual system in psychoanalysis that is as incompletely understood as is the psychology of the self. Nevertheless, self psychology has achieved a position of importance despite criticisms of its most central features. This chapter and the two chapters that follow outline the progression of self psychology.

In the present chapter, I describe the development of Kohut's thinking, beginning with his initial formulations about narcissism and the clinical phenomena that gave rise to his ideas about the selfobject functions of mirroring, idealization, and twinship. In Chapter 2, I discuss Kohut's formulations of the crucial concepts of empathy, compensatory structure, and transmuting internalization. Chapter 2 also includes Kohut's reformulated understanding of dreams and the oedipal situation and his attempt to define the self and its properties as a mental structure. Finally, the third and final chapter on the central principles of self psychology is entirely devoted to a comprehensive description of the selfobject functions, which represent the conceptual anchor for the self psychological approach to diagnostic psychological testing, the chief focus of the remainder of this book.

THEORETICAL ORIGINS OF SELF PSYCHOLOGY

In his initial formulation of narcissism, a formulation that he subsequently developed into an expanded psychology of the self by 1977, Kohut (1971)

3

viewed his ideas as an extension of the predominant drive (id) and ego psychology of the day. This view was particularly prominent in his earliest writings on narcissism, beginning in 1966 and culminating in *The Analysis of the Self* (1971).

The 1971 book was Kohut's first comprehensive statement about the analytic understanding and treatment of narcissistic personality and behavior disorders although Kohut's important 1959 paper on the empathic-introspective method of obtaining analytic data and on their clinical understanding foreshadowed the book.

In several respects, the impetus for Kohut's views came from shortcomings in classical analytic treatment, which Kohut believed was limited in its ability to reach major areas of patients' distress and internal experience. (Ornstein's [1990] statement, quoted previously, addressed exactly this point.) Kohut thus discovered that an enfeebled self needed to be acknowledged or responded to in a way that was more accepting of people's discomfort and that did not leave patients feeling undermined by analytic treatment, including analysts' interpretations that patients perceived as assaults or criticisms.

Kohut (1977) believed that although clinical improvement occurred, at least from the patients' viewpoint, many people often felt unfulfilled or dissatisfied with their lives so that some aspects of the experience of the self were left essentially untouched. His well-known paper *The Two Analyses of Mr. Z.* (1979) is an excellent illustration of exactly this problem. In this paper, Kohut described in detail the outcome of an analysis, conducted in a traditional manner, followed 5 years later by a second period of analysis informed by a self psychological viewpoint. Despite an otherwise successful treatment that produced substantial amelioration of symptoms, Kohut maintained that the first analysis could not have produced the results that the second analysis had.

Kohut's (1971) early thinking about the self emphasized clinical description of narcissistic personality disorders and the ways that psychoanalysts treated these conditions. The description of the transferences that emerged in treating such patients became the centerpiece of Kohut's attempt to understand this form of psychopathology. His theorizing extended the idea of separate lines of development from classical drive theory to include a developmental line for the self based on his new view of narcissism. Kohut saw his views as a natural extension of drive theory, an "adjacent territory" as Ornstein (1978, p. 98) put it, rather than a variant of the object relations schools.

Kohut maintained this position throughout his career, although he substantially broadened his views about the differences between self psychology and ego psychology. As he increasingly came to realize, his contributions came into focus as an independent theoretical system, often at variance with some of the central tenets of mainstream psychoanalysis. Kohut recognized the inevitability of his views' standing apart from drive theory formulations, notably that of the oedipal conflict.

Other therapeutic advances, such as that pioneered by Melanie Klein (1935/1975), laid the groundwork for contemporary British object relations theory. Kohut considered, however, that using these theories did not help analysts to effectively mobilize patients' needs for self-cohesion or self-esteem. In his view of the self, people crucially needed an empathically attuned responsiveness to provide the basis for feeling psychologically invigorated and energetic. Whereas Kohut considered Klein's emphasis on aggression as extreme ("Klein's essential attitude is that the baby is evil ... a powder keg of envy, rage, and destructiveness" [Kohut, 1996, p. 104]), he preferred to think of aggression as an understandable reaction to unresponded-to "rightfully expressed wishes" (Kohut, 1996, p. 104).

One criticism of self psychology has been that Kohut failed to account sufficiently for the clinical and theoretical importance of aggression. This criticism is related to another—that Kohut ignored the viewpoints of major object relations theorists such as Fairbairn (1941), Balint (1968), and Winnicott (1953). Kohut dissociated his views from object relations theories, as well as from Mahler's (1968) and Bowlby's (1969) work, not because he ignored these theorists' work but rather because his own views were at a variance with the object relations and instinctual drive emphases of some of these theories, including their views about aggression.

According to Kohut's view of how self-cohesion is interrupted, ego psychology could not sufficiently account for a weakened or unresponded-to self. Kohut (1977, 1984) came to believe with increasing conviction that analysts who emphasized drives had only limited success in treating disorders of the self. Because Kohut regarded drives as secondary to a fundamental disturbance of cohesion of the self, his view was that injury to the self was more crucial than were libidinal or aggressive impulses. Kohut departed from the structural theory formulation of the drive (impulse) that produced anxiety, which then gave rise to defenses resulting in symptom formation. Instead, he considered disruptions of self-cohesion and diminished self-esteem as the primary psychopathology, which appears clinically in disorders of the self. He saw ego deficits or weaknesses as defensive reactions to destabilization of self-cohesion (Kohut, 1977, p. 74).

In Kohut's view, the self disorders resulted from chronic or pronounced failures to respond to a person's need for mirroring or idealization. These failures predisposed people to depression, anxiety, rage reactions, and a variety of behavior disorders that attempt to relieve intolerable tension states associated with compromised self-cohesion. In this interpretation of symptom formation, the threat to the cohesiveness of the self, not unacceptable drive states or impulses, is the fundamental core of psychopathology.

Kohut began with the problem of analytically treating people with disorders that did not respond well to interpretations based on standard theoretical principles. He referred to such conditions as narcissistic personality disorders and the narcissistic behavior disorders. He described two transference patterns, mirroring and idealization, which originated from different sectors of the self, the grandiose-exhibitionistic and the idealized parent imago poles (the bipolar self). This view permitted a comprehensive clinical understanding of the psychopathology on the basis of his new understanding of these narcissistic disturbances. From this formulation, Kohut (1971) established a basis of therapeutic action for disorders of the self.

Kohut's psychology of the self continued to develop beyond the scope of narcissistic pathology; Kohut first set forth this enlarged view in *The Restoration of the Self* (1977) and crystallized it in *How Does Analysis Cure?* (1984). Self psychology came to constitute, in Ornstein's (1990) phrase, "a new continent." Kohut himself wrote in the 1984 book:

> Self psychology is now attempting to demonstrate, for example, that all forms of psychopathology are based either on defects in the structure of the self, on distortions of the self, or on weakness of the self.
>
> ... Self psychology holds that pathogenic conflicts in the object-instinctual realm—that is, pathogenic conflicts in the realm of object love and object hate and in particular the set of conflicts called the Oedipus complex—are not the *primary* cause of psychopathology but its result. (p. 53)

Kohut understood that oedipal dynamics could masquerade as disturbances of a self state. He was careful not to confine his understanding of clinical observations to one or the other position in isolation. Kohut stressed the importance of careful listening to the appearance of oscillations in clinical material. Thus, he commented in a lecture:

The more one knows, the more you have a grasp of the totality of the life histories and of the basic disturbance in the personality, the more you will be able, with a variety of configurations in your mind, to watch and see and find out what area the pathology finally falls into. All these variants do occur. If I have contributed something to analysis, it is not just to have replaced one conceptual thing with another....Such individuals do sometimes secondarily retreat from these oedipal positions into narcissistic vulnerability. That is perfectly true. But the secondary narcissistic vulnerabilities or the secondary oral dependency attitudes you see in some individuals are a defense against the deeper going, more deeply situated anxieties of the oedipal period. (Kohut, 1996, pp. 118–119)

In reference to development, Kohut did not argue against the presence of in-phase drives to assert oral, anal, or phallic-oedipal wishes or urges. He did consider these drives as secondary, however, to mothers' responses to these stages in development. For example, mothers might welcome and encourage or display out-of-step rejection or unawareness of their children during the various stages of psychological development. Mothers might show a depressive incapacity to respond encouragingly to such steps and might display outright thwarting of children's expressions of autonomy and accomplishment. Rage reactions to these and similar kinds of empathic unattunement did not represent, therefore, primary aggressive or hostile wishes. Instead, rage or withdrawal or devitalization–depletion reactions by children reflected disappointment over mothers' faulty, unempathic responsiveness. This situation provides a good illustration of selfobject failure.

In Kohut's view, children at each developmental stage endeavored to "show their stuff" and sought to produce a "gleam" in their mothers' eye. Normal children seem to say "look at me" or "look at what I can do"; they act in ways that seek only to be regarded as lovable, worthwhile, or competent. It is a normal expectation that mothers respond in keeping with their children's needs. It is also normal that children respond with anger when their legitimate needs go unmet, in the same way that it is normal for children to feel injured when told that healthy urges are unwelcome or should be inhibited.

Referring to the remobilization of drive derivatives in transference, Kohut said:

The patient's rage is not the manifestation of aggressions directed outward against the analyst who by his correct interpretations seems to be on the side of the dangerous drives and has to be defended against. The patient's rage is "narcissistic rage."

... Concretely speaking, whenever a patient reacts with rage to the analyst's interpretations, he has experienced him, from the point of view of the archaic self that has been activated in analysis, as a nonempathic attacker of the integrity of the self. The analyst does not witness the emergence of a primary primitive-aggressive drive, he witnesses the disintegration of the preceding primary configuration, the breakup of the primary self-experience in which, in the child's perception, the child and the empathic self-object are one. (Kohut, 1977, pp. 90, 91)

It is not difficult to see that this view represents a significant reformulation of the childhood experiences crucial for sustaining a vigorous and cohesive self. Self psychologically informed analysts or psychotherapists attempt to understand that there has been an injury to the self and then to explain this circumstance to their patients. This understanding also influences techniques of interpretation. It is one thing to tell patients that they are angry; it is something else to explain to patients that they are angry because a need has been misunderstood. Treatment proceeds more efficaciously if therapists do not interpret patients' wishes as defensive derivatives of infantile drives that should be abandoned or rechanneled.

Kohut also believed that patients perceived the excessive reserve or underresponsiveness of traditional analysis, based on preventing contamination of transference, as unempathic unless tempered with "emotional undertones and overtones, which, arising from the depths of the analyst's psyche, make themselves heard despite the analyst's conscious theoretical convictions" (Kohut, 1977, p. 258). Treatment, however, need not *necessarily* be amicable or friendly, although casual observers may sometimes misinterpret treatment in this way. On the importance of empathy, Kohut maintained that "man can no more survive psychologically in a psychological milieu that does not respond empathically to him, than he can survive physically in an atmosphere that contains no oxygen" (Kohut, 1977, p. 253).

One consequence of therapists' customary reserved stance is the remobilization of patients' disappointment, rage, or withdrawal in the face of what they frequently perceive as unempathic responsiveness. This experience can re-expose patients to the very conditions that produced the problems for which they sought help in the first place. Such a reaction can be particularly pronounced in patients who experienced a chronically underresponsive or understimulating parental environment. Thus, an overly reserved therapeutic stance can iatrogenically provoke rage or withdrawal reactions. If these reactions are incorrectly interpreted as manifestations of drive derivatives, patients can continue to feel misunderstood, and treatment is often undermined. It was Kohut's impression that therapists whose treatment approach was influenced by a conflict–defense model only imperfectly understood pathological self-esteem and the causes of the self disorder. Thus, they rarely interpreted this disorder to therapeutic advantage.

SELF PSYCHOLOGY: EARLY CLINICAL CONSIDERATIONS

Selfobject Functions and Mirroring

Kohut's (1971) reformulations took shape in his attempts to understand why conventional transference interpretations seemed to be particularly inappropriate for several of his patients. He reported the analysis of a female patient, Miss F., who maintained a long period of intensely angry refusal to hear anything other than a repetition of her own statements about herself. Treatment centered on interpreting unyielding resistances. Eventually, Kohut reconsidered the transference meaning of his function for this patient and decided that he had become an impersonal function rather than an object of love and hate in her transference.

In modifying his understanding of the genetics of her anger, Kohut could explain to his patient how her re-enactment with him revived an attempt to cope with an unresponsive, depressed mother. Thus, Kohut discovered that her stubborn resistance was not fundamentally a negative therapeutic reaction or a defense. Instead, he reconceptualized what at first appeared to resemble a defense as an attempt to obtain an echoing or approving response from the analyst. Genetically, this attempt represented a transference revival of parental failure to respond to the patient's desire to simply be heard or listened to. This function of being attentive as an echoing presence, of affirming and admiring, is what people need to sustain a cohesive self. It is the mirroring selfobject function; its mobilization in treatment becomes the mirroring transference (described in greater detail in chap. 3).

Kohut realized that many patients' internal experiences of the self and the ensuing self-esteem problems that these gave rise to were not understood accurately or in depth in traditional analytic or psychodynamic treatment. Unable to effect a genuine therapeutic result in patients like Miss F., Kohut realized that the principal reason for treatment failure resulted from misinterpreting mirroring by using a conceptual framework based on regressions from oedipal conflicts and libidinal and aggressive drives. He discovered that a revival of mirroring in treatment fulfilled the usual criteria for a genuine transference: inappropriateness to the ongoing work, its function as a resistance, and its genetic basis. Accordingly, Kohut believed that mirroring represented a transference reaction that could be analyzed without modifying standard technique. The meaning of the transference reaction, of course, had to be broadened to include a mirroring need rather than what was formerly considered a transference revival of libidinal or aggressive wishes.

From clinical material such as his work with Miss F. and his observations in other analyses, Kohut formulated the concept of the selfobject function. The transference represented the way that selfobject functions appear clinically; thus, he proposed the term *selfobject transference.* An analyst or psychotherapist had to perform a particular function for the patient's weakened self that could not carry out this function. The selfobject function is first and foremost a mental representation of what the undermined self requires to restore optimal functioning. This function is perceived and responded to as a needed or vital extension of the patient. One important feature of the selfobject, therefore, is its restorative nature: It exists for repairing devalued or injured self-esteem. The selfobject can refer to the person who serves or fulfills the function, and it is usually experienced in reference to another person. The person who provides the needed self-reparative function is not the selfobject, however, this person embodies the *selfobject function.* People do not experience the selfobject as having its own center of initiative with its own wishes and needs and they do not react to it as an object of love or hate.

A selfobject transference may be detected in experiences such as an analyst's or therapist's sense that there is only one person in the room. In this experience, a therapist's presence is felt to be mostly incidental to a vulnerable patient's need for someone to be there listening. The therapist is not experienced primarily as a person with his or her own needs; he or she does not really matter much beyond affirming some vitally needed function to buoy up or vitalize the patient who experiences vulnerable self-cohesion. The patient is not, however, oblivious to the analyst's existence. Indeed, quite the reverse: Intense affects often surround the therapist's lapses or absence. The need is clearly present, but it is not reciprocal; it goes in just one direction. It is similar to casual or everyday experiences in which two people converse, and one person feels incidental or irrelevant beyond the other's need for a responsive, listening presence. The interaction is one sided and unreciprocated: One person exists not in his or her own right, but only insofar as the other person needs him or her.

If this description resembles the conventional definition of selfishness or feeling "used," it is merely coincidental. Selfobject functions rarely represent self-preoccupation or self-aggrandizement. The appearance of selfishness or neglect of another's needs or feelings may accompany but does not define what is fundamentally a need for the other person to shore up a deeply felt disturbance of self-esteem or self-cohesion.

As conceptualized metapsychologically, selfobject transferences are differentiated from classical transference neuroses in that the selfobject is not cathected with object libido. Kohut (1971) regarded narcissism as a separate line of development in contrast to that of object love. It should be remembered that Kohut's (1971) original work emphasized selfobject functions to explain narcissistic pathology. With the extension of his discovery of the narcissistic transferences to encompass the structural neuroses as well, Kohut (1977, 1984) subsequently preferred the concept of selfobject transferences or functions over that of narcissistic transferences.

It is important to avoid confusing the concept of narcissistic transferences or selfobject functions with egocentricity or with the Egocentricity Index from the Comprehensive System for the Rorschach (Exner, 1993). The meaning of self-focusing or self-preoccupation for Exner's index is neutral with respect to selfobject needs or functions, in the same way that it is neutral for general psychological traits of selfishness or grandiosity.

Idealization

The second major selfobject function that Kohut identified was the idealizing transference. In an early case, Kohut (1968, 1971) reported the treatment of a patient, Mr. A., who turned repeatedly to older men or senior male colleagues for signs of approval and praise for his work. This praise was necessary for Mr. A. to feel capable and whole, and his search for approval was re-enacted in the transference.

Although the patient sought treatment because of disturbing homosexual preoccupations, these were thought of as secondary. Fundamentally, the patient turned to men for a feeling of invigorated self-esteem. This behavior had apparently met with welcoming acceptance by Mr. A.'s father, and it was revived in the transference as well. Mr. A. had however experienced disappointment when circumstances in his father's life failed to support the patient's idealization of the father. This experience left him prone to depression and rage. In the transference, prolonged periods of haughty isolation were precipitated by feelings of disapproval or of being insufficiently understood. At such times, it was difficult for Mr. A. to work effectively.

In another example, Kohut (1971) described his work with another analyst engaged in treating a patient. During a brief period in the analysis of the woman, Miss L., she experienced being flooded by intensely felt tension states early in treatment. At this time, she also reported dreams about an idealized priest whom she had known during her adolescence. Although it was too soon to understand her potential for fragmentation at this early stage, the analyst commented to Miss L., in reference to one of her dreams, that he was not himself Catholic. His reason for this revelation had to do with the patient's tenuous reality testing at that point. The analysis was at an impasse for 2 years, at which point the analyst consulted with Kohut about Miss L.

In the course of the consultation, and in light of other evidence, it became clear that, at the early stage of treatment, the analyst had not recognized that the dream signified the patient's need to revive an idealizing selfobject transference. The analyst had inadvertently failed to see the dream as a wish to bring forward the patient's need for a figure toward whom she could again feel awe and admiration. The patient subsequently understood the analyst's failure as a rebuff of her initial and tentative transference step representing her wish to revive an idealized good and healthy version of herself.

Instead, she submerged the idealizing transference, and treatment was essentially at a stalemate for some time. Not until the patient's idealizing selfobject need was recognized and understood analytically could treatment proceed. Ornstein (1978) elaborated further on the consequences of misunderstanding budding attempts at idealizations as reaction formations against hostile impulses and noted that blocked analyses leading to stalemates were an inevitable result of this error.

Kohut (1971, 1984) also believed that attempts to prematurely interpret idealization only inhibited the full emergence of these needs, particularly early in treatment. Consequently, the need for idealization remained unanalyzed and misunderstood, a situation predisposing to lingering, diffuse feelings of dissatisfaction or lack of zest even in an otherwise successful treatment.

Another example of an idealizing selfobject transference illustrates what happens when the person to whom the patient turns for idealization is psychologically incapable of providing this function. The patient, Mr. K., expressed strong admiration toward the analyst, a reaction repeating an intensely felt admiration of his father (Kohut, 1971). The patient had turned to the father when his mother withdrew from him at age 3 after the birth of his brother. The father had apparently been unable to comfortably accept this idealizing need; he rejected the boy's admiring overtures and belittled and criticized the boy's attempts to attach himself to him.

Mr. K. reattempted to repair this injury to his self-esteem at the hands of his father by turning again to the mother through athletic accomplishments, which his mother had previously fostered. Thus, shifts can and do occur in the unfolding of these transference patterns: A renewed intensification of the grandiose-exhibitionistic self can occur after a traumatic interference with attempts at establishing an idealizing parent imago selfobject function. Kohut regarded this development as a secondary mirror transference and thought it best understood as a protective measure to guard against potential injury to self-esteem when the central idealizing transference becomes mobilized. This development also demonstrates oscillations between mirroring and idealization when a redirection of idealizing wishes goes unrecognized or is ignored.

CLASSICAL TRANSFERENCES
AND SELFOBJECT TRANSFERENCES

In the development of the psychology of the self, transferences were generally thought of as selfobject functions (Kohut, 1977, 1984). (In chap. 3, I describe in greater detail the central characteristics of mirroring and idealization.) These transferences represented the central features of Kohut's (1971) understanding of narcissistic personality and behavior disorders. Later, Kohut (1984) proposed that a particular subtype of the mirroring transference, twinship, was more correctly differentiated out of mirroring. He considered twinship as a third predominant constellation in its own right. (I also describe twinship in greater detail in chap. 3.) These mirroring and twinship selfobject patterns, together with idealization, may be differentially predominant at particular phases of treatment. Kohut believed that the transference representing the most urgent selfobject need emerges earliest in treatment, although he did not presume that one selfobject function was more primitive or archaic than another.

Kohut developed his formulations of self psychology by attempting to analyze patients who were characteristically difficult to treat, but he came to believe that his theoretical views could be applied just as readily to treating the usual patients who sought analysis or psychotherapy. According to this point of view, therapists could also clinically understand patients with a structural neurosis and could treat them according to the principal concepts of self psychology. Therefore, Kohut's formulations about selfobject functions could be applied to equal or superior advantage in patients with no prominent developmental arrests or propensity for regression and with the capacity for object love.

The cohesiveness of the self is the crucial clinical problem in the differential diagnosis of narcissistic disorders (currently usually referred to as *self disorders*) and structural (oedipal) neuroses or borderline disorders. The issue of evaluating the robustness (cohesion) of the self as a mental structure entails more than simply distinguishing prominent clinical characteristics such as diminished enthusiasm or zest (Goldberg, 1978). Self-cohesion is judged or assessed by the stability of the self in the face of regression. Clinical manifestations are important considerations in this determination, including the degree of devitalization or emptiness, the presence of perverse activities and addictions, and the severity of transient fragmentation states (M. Tolpin, 1978). It is the evaluation of cohesiveness that remains central.

For example, dependency in the transference can mean something other than oral longings or fear of object loss. It can represent reliance on a selfobject to sustain self-cohesion. The patients whom Kohut originally studied and treated, those with narcissistic personality disorders and narcissistic behavior disorders, were markedly dependent on the analyst's responsiveness or presence despite high levels of functioning. Such patients appeared independent in many external aspects of their lives, however. A clinging quality to their dependency was either absent or not prominent. These patients were prone to react with rage, subsyndromal depression, or sometimes haughty or cold withdrawal occasioned by even minor empathic failures. Their sensitivity to feeling slighted extended to interruptions of appointment or vacation schedules as well as to the therapist's imperfect memory for details about the patient's life. Kohut saw these patients as different in kind from those with dependency–passivity as conceptualized in drive theory or ego psychology.

Differential Diagnosis

The clinical appearance of severe self disorders can be indistinguishable from that of borderline disorders or psychotic presentations. Kohut's decisive test was observing a patient's reaction to the therapist's preliminary or trial interpretations of defenses (Goldberg, 1978). Either the emergence of oedipal material, for example, or self-protective measures to rescue an injured self from fragmentation or regression normally decided the issue.

Verbalizations are diagnostically noncontributory; a self disorder can readily be mistaken on the surface for what appears to be a phallic-oedipal conflict when a therapist assumes one-to-one correspondence between verbal contents and specific meanings. On interview, a therapist can catalog descriptions of symptoms much as Kernberg (1975) did for borderline pathology. Kohut (1971), however, preferred to wait for the decisive transference configuration to emerge clearly and thus to minimize unreliable or premature diagnostic closure. The same caution applies to interpreting surface contents of projective test responses, particularly when the inquiry was too conservative or insufficient. For example, on the Rorschach, a percept of blood sometimes represents rage, sometimes guilt, and at other times devitalization of the self. Only a larger context extending beyond the level of specific or discrete responses ultimately settles the issue.

Goldberg (1978) also cautioned against premature decisions about transference interpretations because a patient can perceive incorrect appraisals of the nature of the transference made too early as narcissistic injuries. The patient may then conceal the true selfobject transference. This reaction intensifies defenses iatrogenically and sometimes gives rise to sexualizations or other externalizations outside the treatment proper. The early appearance of a mirroring transference can also quickly give way to a predominant idealizing transference—another reason to view early transference manifestations as tentative or preliminary. Therapists must wait for the central transference pattern to become established and should offer minimal interference.

This point is also pertinent in reference to the use of diagnostic psychological testing to identify selfobject functions. Because several selfobject needs can often appear, examiners must consider the total protocol to determine the predominant pattern without forgetting that multiple selfobject functions are frequently present in many patients. For example, a helmet percept on the Rorschach can suggest a vigorous self seeking admiring, mirroring selfobject responsiveness. Alternatively, the helmet can represent an idealizing longing or a devitalized self seeking protection. Naturally, examiners must carefully study the full protocol to best resolve this type of diagnostic decision.

Specifying Selfobject Functions

In addition to the main selfobject functions of mirroring, idealization, and twinship, Kohut and Wolf (1978) and Wolf (1988) described other clinical forms of self disorders, including merger-hungry and contact-shunning personalities. Lachmann (1986) contributed the adversarial type, and all of these were added to the mirror-hungry, ideal-hungry, and alter-ego personalities that were already somewhat familiar from Kohut's previous writings. Kohut (1984) derived the alter-ego personality from his impression that the twinship or alter-ego function was properly a separate and distinct selfobject function bridging mirroring and idealization, rather than a subtype of mirroring.

Kohut perhaps had some reservations about categorizing or subtyping the selfobject functions in a way corresponding to these new personality types, which also included Wolf's (1988) further categorization of syndromes of self disorders that he described as overstimulated, understimulated, fragmenting, and overburdened. Kohut believed that these syndromes had heuristic value, much as Abraham's (1921/1927) descriptions of oral and anal characters had to an earlier generation of psychoanalytic theorists. Kohut and Wolf (1978) and Kohut (1984), however, expressed concern about the potential for oversimplifying by devising convenient categories or typologies that might, in the end, only impede scientific progress.

Nevertheless, although the eventual status of merger-hungry, contact-shunning, and adversarial personalities remains to be determined, Kohut did not want his final statements to close off further inquiry in the evolving psychology of the self. Goldberg (1988) also stressed this point. Kohut was clearly mindful of the problems arising from the disputes among Freud's most fervent defenders and others who also wished to further the development of psychoanalytic theory, but sometimes in different directions. Particularly with reference to delineating selfobject functions, Kohut (1984) allowed for additional possibilities beyond his own contributions. He regarded his collaborative work with Wolf as one good example of a useful heuristic direction, although he did not necessarily consider this work as a final statement.

SELF PSYCHOLOGY AND CONTEMPORARY
PSYCHOANALYTIC THEORY

By 1977, in *The Restoration of the Self*, Kohut considered self psychologically informed views about psychopathology and its treatment to be a more complete explanation than that of structural conflict. This position represented a theoretical advance in which the self, with its line of development separate from that of object love, accounted for many clinical disturbances. Kohut continued to develop his ideas still further in *How Does Analysis Cure?* written to convey his final thoughts and published posthumously in 1984. In this book, he stated that self psychology represented more than an incremental theoretical advance in psychoanalysis.

Kohut did not believe it necessary to devalue classical drive theory by identifying the gaps in what it could explain. He once said: "If you always want to lock horns with Freud, all that you do is deprive yourself of all his greatness" (Kohut, 1996, p. 67). Surely lacking the "imperialistic, all-embracing ambitions" (Eagle, 1984, p. 41) that have been attributed to him, Kohut became increasingly convinced that the perspective of self psychology was greater than he had previously believed. Not without some regret, he came to regard the central conceptual position of self psychology as superseding the structural theory. This position extended beyond narcissistic disorders to incorporate the majority of analyzable psychological disorders, including structural neuroses. Kohut's views also stimulated reconceptualizing unanalyzable conditions as well, such as the psychoses (Galatzer-Levy, 1988; Malin, 1988).

From this perspective, Kohut's theoretical positions rightly appear as the description of a psychology of the self rather than as a theory of narcissism or narcissistic disorders. Several major psychoanalysts took issue with Kohut's position (Curtis, 1986; Loewald, 1980; Wallerstein, 1986/1995), both conceptually as well as clinically. Concurrent developments in psychoanalysis also led to a general shift from a conflict model toward various deficit models of psychopathology. Most of these approaches included treatment views representing varying degrees of departure from standard psychoanalytic techniques.

One important development in contemporary psychoanalysis has been the tendency to treat people with a greater severity of disturbance than had commonly been the practice during previous generations. Thus, conceptualizing deficit states or preoedipal psychopathology has stimulated greater interest in recent years than have issues surrounding conflict, ego function, and defense. Overlapping views about psychological deficit have inevitably produced confusion about various theoretical positions, and questions of mutual influence among theories have inevitably arisen.

For example, in reference to self psychology, it can be argued that Kohut's views are very close to those of Jacobson (1964), Mahler (1968), and Winnicott (1953). These similarities can make it difficult to describe the uniqueness of any one theorist's contribution. Certain aspects of what has been called the interpersonal school, although substantially different from Kohut's psychology of the self in many fundamental ways, nevertheless lead to some confusion about their similarities and differences. Often, this confusion has been based on a misunderstanding of crucial concepts of self psychology. The same consideration applies to intersubjectivity theory, an outgrowth of self psychology championed by analysts such as Stolorow, Brandchaft, and Atwood (1987). Self psychologists such as Bacal (1985) and Basch (1984) have taken positions that also represent departures from Kohut's views, although they are still predominantly anchored within self psychology.

A critical comparison of theoretical systems is well beyond the scope of this book. There are excellent sources for comparisons of theories (Bacal & Newman, 1990; Eagle, 1984; Pine, 1988; Summers, 1994), and their primary contribution lies in point-by-point critical analyses of the many changes in the field of psychoanalysis in recent decades.

In this chapter and the two that follow, I confine the scope of the description of self psychology to Kohut's views. My purpose in taking what some may consider a narrow view is influenced by carefully considering the unique application of Kohut's particular contributions in psychoanalysis to the field of psychodiagnostic testing. The field of projective assessment has also undergone critical developments paralleling the appearance of new currents in psychoanalytic theory during the 4 decades since ego psychology achieved its prominence. Thus, absorbing a large body of analytic theory into the diagnostic testing and assessment literature pioneered by Rapaport and Schafer posed a difficult challenge. Kissen (1986), Kwawer, Lerner, Lerner, and Sugarman (1980), P. M. Lerner (1991), H. D. Lerner & P. M. Lerner (1988), and Schachtel (1966) have made major contributions to this effort. To add to this body of work, the central focus of the present book remains centered on the singular influence of Kohut's psychology of the self.

Another reason for emphasizing the work of Kohut alone is that the concepts he introduced are sufficiently difficult to grasp accurately so that the main principles of self psychology are frequently superficially understood. Thus, I strive for an accurate, in-depth understanding of self psychology to arrive at a sophisticated integration of psychoanalytic self psychology and psychodiagnostic assessment of projective tests.

2   Self Psychology: Major Concepts

In the previous chapter, I introduced many of the central concepts of psychoanalytic self psychology. In framing my discussion around the development of Kohut's thinking, I emphasized that the psychology of the self evolved beyond its theoretical foundations in drive theory and ego psychology into a conceptual system in its own right. In this chapter, I discuss the major concepts of self psychology in greater detail.

A problematic aspect of self psychology has always been formulating accurate and understandable definitions of its concepts. This problem is similar to that of defining metapsychological concepts such as ego or drive. For major concepts such as the self, selfobject functions, and empathy, however, the available literature on meanings and clinical manifestations is less extensive than that available for concepts like ego and drive.

Here I describe several central concepts of self psychology, including the definition of the self and its properties, empathy, compensatory structure, and transmuting internalization. I also discuss several self psychological concepts that differ from classical drive theory, as outlined in chapter 1, such as the self state dream and the self psychological understanding of oedipal dynamics. I quote liberally from Kohut's major writings, particularly the tape-recorded lectures that he gave over a 4-year period between 1972 and 1976 to candidates at the Chicago Institute for Psychoanalysis. These lectures were compiled and edited by P. Tolpin and M. Tolpin (Kohut, 1996) and were published in a book whose contents enhance the clarity of Kohut's ideas by taking advantage of his evocative manner of speaking. Therefore, his examples and clarifications of ideas come across more vividly than in his formal writings.

I devote chapter 3 entirely to an in-depth description of one of the most important contributions of the psychology of the self, selfobject functions. I reserve chapter 3 for a discussion of selfobject functions because this concept is particularly significant for a self psychological approach to projective test content.

CONCEPT OF THE SELF

As a term, the *self* has multiple reference points, not only in the body of psychoanalytic theory, but also in clinical, social, and developmental psychology. Even popularized views about self-image or self-esteem in clinical psychology and the lay press include a concept of the self. The problem of defining the self psychological view of the self is compounded by Kohut's preference for terms such as *cohesive, vigorous,* and *harmonious* (described next) to refer to properties or characteristics of the self.

Kohut's (1984) clearest statement about the self was that it represented a mental content. Earlier, he had stated that he could not give an exact definition because the self is a generalization itself derived from other (experience-near) data. Kohut thought of the self as a mental content or configuration, and he preferred not to regard it as a mental structure at the same level of abstraction as the tripartite structures of id, ego, and superego. Kohut considered the concept of the self to be reducible no further than to the idea of a mental content.

Although he was hesitant to consider the self as a psychic structure parallel to the ego, Kohut did think that the properties of the self could be described. He distinguished between what he referred to as *constituents* and *attributes.* The constituent parts were originally *mirroring* and *idealization;* he later added *twinship,* which was differentiated from the mirroring pole or sector.

Attributes of the self are its particular qualities of *cohesion, vigor* (vitality), and *harmony* (Kohut, 1984). Cohesiveness refers to experience as whole and enduring, ranging from healthy intactness to varying states of fragmentation. To avoid any potential confusion of terms, I should stress that Kohut's reference to wholeness as a feature of the cohesive self is not the same as Melanie Klein's (1930) differentiation between whole and part objects, a central concept of the British object relations school. For Kohut, self-cohesion referred to a sustained, enduring experience of the self as together or intact (in that sense, whole). The attribute of the self that Kohut described as its vigor or vitality entails how people experience themselves as invigorated rather than enfeebled, devitalized, and unable to hold up their heads to face the world. Feeling invigorated is thus a different dimension from the sense of being unable to hold oneself together, a sense that has

more to do with self-cohesion. Finally, inner harmony of the self is represented by the feeling of calmness or being soothed. The absence of this
sense of balance gives rise to the internal experience of chaotic turmoil in
which a person senses that the world does not work as it should or that the
bottom has dropped out. This feeling leads to experiences in which things
and events are seriously out of kilter, in which people cannot rely on orderly
expectations about reality to provide an ongoing sense of a dependable
world. Such experiences, which may occur in both psychotic and nonpsychotic states, are reminiscent of the children's story of Chicken Little, who
fears that the sky is falling. It matters little whether the metaphor of the
bottom dropping out or the metaphor of the sky falling down is invoked.
The crucial experience is that of one's sense of equilibrium or predict-
ability becoming destabilized as a result of a self that has faltered such that
the person can no longer feel sufficiently grounded (to continue my metaphor) by the calm provided by the presence of a comforting selfobject.

Kohut distinguished the self from the concept of identity. He considered
that identity represented a superficial, conscious experience; it was the way
that people describe themselves outwardly with regard to the social environment. This clarification is necessary to differentiate the psychological
connotation of the self in depth from the social or sociocultural environment. Social reality is separate and distinct from intrapsychic life or the
depth psychological frame of reference.

There is thus little doubt that the frequent equation of self and identity is
misguided and usually incorrect. Kohut never intended the term *identity* to
be synonymous with or equivalent to the concept of the *self*. My main reason
for emphasizing this point is that clinicians, particularly those who are
unfamiliar with the language of depth psychology or metapsychology, have
frequently suggested that the sense of self is similar to identity, notably
when they are pressed to give a clear definition of the self. These two
concepts are by no means similar or equivalent, and their relation is not
especially strong or even important from the standpoint of psychoanalytic
self psychology.

In *How Does Analysis Cure?* Kohut (1984) discussed his view of the
concept of the self in relation to other major constructs in psychoanalysis.
He wrote this book close to the anticipated end of his life, largely in response
to criticisms by both friendly colleagues and critics who had urged him to
address concepts that he had left unclarified since *The Restoration of the
Self* (Kohut, 1977). This lack of clarity may well have impeded understanding Kohut's use and meaning of the concept of the self, as a complex

mental system whose clinical relevance has had greater appeal than has its metapsychological precision (Gedo & Goldberg, 1973).

EMPATHIC UNDERSTANDING OF SELF STATES

Definitional (Conceptual) Considerations

Although Kohut (1959) introduced his thinking on empathy early, he continually expanded his view of its clinical significance. Empathy became increasingly important in his work, even as recently as an address entitled "On Empathy" delivered in the week before his death (Ornstein, 1990). Although empathy represents one of Kohut's most far-reaching contributions, it is also probably the most poorly understood of all concepts associated with self psychology. It is important to fully describe this concept, including its evolution and the misunderstandings that have developed around it. Empathy is also a focal point for reconceptualizing psychodiagnostic testing content as informed by self psychology.

Empathic understanding, as it characterizes therapeutic actions, has nothing to do with being or acting pleasant, friendly, or warm. Kohut (1984) eschewed an overly friendly, warm, or sympathetic disposition or therapeutic attitude and noted that such overt responses are neither indicated nor therapeutic in any real sense. Wolf (1988) commented:

> To be empathic does not mean to be doing something good for the patient. Indeed, the knowledge gained by being empathic can be used for or against the patient's benefit ... .The essence of a certain kind of salesmanship (or advertising) is exactly the salesman's empathic "in tuneness" with the customer's needs and wishes. (p. 132)

On a similar note, Basch (1983) observed:

> [S]ome of the world's greatest scoundrels have been exquisitely and unerringly attuned to grasping the significance of the unconscious or unspoken affective communications of others and have used that knowledge to achieve base aims. Is this too empathy? Yes it is. (pp. 119–120).

Although Kohut did not see a therapeutic need for undue warmth, feigned interest, or sympathy, he did not intend treating therapists to act coldly. Indeed, few clinicians disagree that people in treatment do not improve in a cold, distant atmosphere with a therapist who practices with uninvolved listening or understanding. He commented:

[O]n the whole, self psychologists tend to work in a more relaxed fashion, are more easygoing with their patients, have fewer misgivings about making themselves emotionally available to their patients if the need arises, and generally behave in a (comparatively speaking) less reserved manner than the majority of analysts. (Kohut, 1984, p. 81)

Kohut understood that patients also improve when therapists use techniques that do *not* emphasize empathic listening or understanding. Empathy, as described by Kohut and his colleagues, simply refers to therapists' listening to the communications of patients in a particular way. Empathy is a way of introspectively gathering data from which therapists attempt to explain to patients what a therapist understands about crucial aspects of a patient's life. Empathy is the way that analysts comprehend the impact of crucial figures on others' development.

This idea is not a radical departure from major principles of analytic treatment, at least for the predominant psychodynamic therapies. The critical differences materialize in the way that therapists understand, conceptualize, and interpret patients' communications. Empathic listening refers to the way that analysts become sustainedly immersed in what patients say. Analysts or psychotherapists reconstruct what they hear, not in an "experience-distant" manner (from the vantage point of a higher order abstract theory about mental processes), but in an "experience-near" manner (remaining close to the patient's phenomenological experience).

Kohut compared this mode of listening to the basic psychological bond that allows people to grasp one another's intentions or motives and to make them intelligible. He saw empathy as "the capacity to think and feel oneself into the inner life of another person. It is our lifelong ability to experience what another person experiences" (Kohut, 1984, p. 82). Kohut stated that empathy is present at all levels of development as early as a mother's accurate, empathic grasp of her infant's states of satisfaction and distress. Empathy includes a mother's psychological capacity to respond adequately and thus to provide the substrate for the nuclear or emerging self of infancy. Freud (1921/1955) considered empathy to be the mechanism through which individuals can assume any attitude at all about another person.

Kohut (1996) provided a good example of empathy serving as a basis for calming, when it is accurately attuned, or for exacerbating an already distressed self state. A person who is upset by something turns to another person for supportive understanding. Kohut compared this empathic failure to merging with faulty maternal empathic responsiveness. He (1996) wrote:

> The mother picks the child up. What does the friend do? The friend puts an arm around the other's shoulder and imitates the picking up. Although he may feel like a small baby, you put your arm around him and say "I know how you must feel. ... Feeling your calmness while you are united with the other person allows this person now to merge with you ... . A mother who says, "Oh, for goodness sake, don't cry, there's nothing to be anxious about," does not allow this particular kind of merger and does not help the child. She rejects and pushes the child away. A mother who goes to pieces over the child's anxieties also doesn't encourage the merger. Why? Because why do you want to merge into something that is as anxious as you yourself are, or even more so? A mother who misunderstands the child and thinks that he's anxious when he's in pain or in pain when he's anxious is also no good. (p. 7)

As noted previously, Kohut also considered empathy as a method of inquiry, a means of data gathering. Empathy, in this view, is not something actively done or effected. It is the way that a clinician listens to, and later on understands, a patient's communications in treatment or on projective test responses. Clinicians attempt to vicariously understand what the communication conveys about a patient's existence or experiences of the self and of the world. As a therapeutic technique, empathy is a requisite condition for therapeutic interpretation or clarification. It is not by itself the therapeutic intervention. Thus, Basch (1983) wrote:

> Empathic understanding is not curative in the psychoanalytic sense; cure is the function of interpretation. By the same token, empathic understanding is not a substitute for interpretation; rather, it lays the groundwork that makes interpretation appropriate and effective. (pp. 123–124)

As Kohut came to believe with increasing certainty, "experience-near" reconstructions about a patient's life or psychological world provided the optimal understanding of self states. This level of understanding, obtained through sustained empathic immersion, yielded the greatest therapeutic efficacy.

Clinical (Technical) Considerations

Despite these attempts to define empathy, its intended meaning has still confused both traditional psychoanalysts and other psychodynamic clinicians. Even the term itself is unfortunate, because of its surplus meanings. Kohut frequently struggled with others' misunderstanding of his meaning of empathy as a primary tool of investigation. In an effort to clarify empathic understanding, Kohut (1984) wrote:

> My answer is that the greater relaxation of the self psychologist, his greater freedom to respond with deeply reverberating understanding and resonant emotionality, and the generally calmer and friendlier atmosphere of self psychological treatment—these developments do not rest on the self psychologist's increased use of empathy, on the fact that he is "more empathic" than his non-self psychological colleagues. They rest instead on the expanded scope of empathy that is the product of the self psychologist's expanded theoretical understanding. (p. 82)

Although he addressed the way that empathy produces mutative change, he found it necessary to differentiate empathic listening as a technical tool from its casual or familiar connotation. Kohut (1984) noted:

> Clearly, it is not enough for the analyst to be "nice" to his patients, to be "understanding," warmhearted, endowed with the human touch ... all the evidence now available indicates that being nice, friendly, understanding, warmhearted, and in possession of the human touch cures neither the classical neuroses nor the analyzable disturbances of the self. (p. 95)

Thus, acting or appearing "nice" is trivial or irrelevant to the nature of empathic listening. Like the earlier example of the artifacts that may result from exaggerated reserve, he differentiated this quality of acting "nice" for its own sake from acting in a more or less normal or expectable way.

According to Kohut, empathic understanding as a technical approach provides a means for recognizing psychological dynamics that might otherwise be unnoticed. This technique is particularly helpful in distinguishing between object-libidinal and selfobject needs. It fosters the therapeutic action of transference interpretations if remobilized selfobject needs can be recognized and examined to gain understanding. This approach contrasts with the drive theory view in which transference phenomena are considered intrusions that stand in the way of unearthing archaic needs and wishes. Drive theory leads to a position of therapeutic action characterized by defense interpretations of unwelcome intrusions that encumber the real goal of treatment. Defenses, therefore, are viewed as stubborn resistances that obstruct therapeutic progress, and most work during treatment revolves around the interpretation of defenses, resistance, and their transference manifestations.

Kohut thought that interpreting defenses as interferences meant overlooking their emotional value to patients. By dismissively viewing defenses as something to be got rid of, the very selfobject failures that patients had experienced in early development were repeated. In some instances, patients were re-exposed to narcissistic injury and received no help to repair these injuries of their undermined selves. Because defenses in Kohut's view were attempts to hold onto, if not strengthen, vulnerable self-cohesion, patients often experienced defense interpretations as humiliations or assaults, particularly if therapists insistently repeated the interpretations in the belief that it is advantageous to remove stubborn resistances.

One criticism of self psychology has been that empathic understanding provides little more than a corrective emotional experience. This criticism is, however, a misinterpretation of Kohut's use of empathy and is based on misunderstanding empathy as providing warmth or comfort to an injured patient. The reference to corrective emotional experience derives from Franz Alexander's (Alexander & French, 1946) method of brief psychoanalysis. In much the same way that some viewed Alexander's much-maligned corrective emotional experience as an approach to treatment that was distinctively *not* psychoanalysis, critics questioned the use of empathy as an analytic tool.

P. Tolpin (1983) emphasized that the selfobject transference is corrective in that patients' unresponded-to needs of early development are understood and responded to differently. By empathically apprehending the clinical material as arising from faulty selfobject responsiveness rather than from conflict surrounding drive regulation, therapists can establish the corrective, cohesion-building, transmuting internalizations that are crucial in treatment. Kohut, in regard to the misperception of empathy as corrective emotional experience, wrote:

I am not an advocate of the corrective emotional experience. I don't think one needs to give the patient a commendation. But what needs to be made clear to the patient is that you *recognize* what he wants at this particular moment. It is not therapeutically correct to say, "This is a resistance, so let's go back to your drives and defenses." By doing that you slap him down just as he is moving forward, and you misunderstand what is really going on in the patient and in the analysis at that particular moment. (Kohut, 1996, pp. 220–221)

Critics have further charged that empathy constitutes gratification of archaic wishes, that it bypasses genuine clinical understanding leading to the correct interpretation of resistances and defenses in the transference. Although this misunderstanding of Kohut's use of empathy is by now rarely heard, some clinicians nevertheless regard empathic-introspective understanding as too far removed from the central treatment objective of interpretation. This misunderstanding fails to take note of Kohut's consistent stress on the two-part analytic effort of empathic understanding followed by clarification of dynamics together with their genetic roots.

In a forceful statement on this issue, Kohut wrote:

> Let me remind you that you don't have to mirror the patient to be effective as his analyst. That is really a total mistake. The meaning of mirroring, the essence of that concept, is not that you have to play-act with your patient and praise him and respond to him and say that he is wonderful. No such nonsense. But you do have to show the patient over and over again how he defensively retreats because he expects that he will not get what he wants and that he doesn't dare to let himself know what he wants. (Kohut, 1996, p. 373)

In Goldberg's (1978, pp. 447–448) view:

> The analyst does not actively soothe; he interprets the analysand's yearning to be soothed. The analyst does not actively mirror; he interprets the need for confirming responses. The analyst does not actively admire or approve grandiose expectations; he explains their role in the psychic economy. The analyst does not fall into passive silence; he explains why his interventions are felt to be intrusive. Of course, the analyst's mere presence, or the fact that he understands, all have soothing and self-confirming effects on the patient, *and they are so interpreted*. Thus, the analytic ambience that makes analytic work possible becomes itself an object for analytic interpretation. The whole analytic process in this way blocks exploitation for mere gratification.

Goldberg addressed here the erroneous implication that self psychological treatment is psychotherapy, and supportive rather than interpretive therapy at that (Levine, 1979; Wallerstein, 1986/1995). Kohut and his colleagues always maintained that a self psychologically informed treatment fulfilled all the criteria for analysis. The self is reconstructed to permit a newly revitalized self to unfold (Goldberg, 1990). Empathy is a technique for introspectively gathering data, from which the resulting understandings are used to frame interpretations. Empathic understanding is not warmth or support. Support may sometimes be indicated therapeutically, but it is not itself intensive psychotherapy or psychoanalysis.

Despite self psychologists' clear admonitions about confusing empathy with gratification, Kohut knew that therapists sometimes had to do exactly that. Even when such a response was indicated (and virtually all psychotherapists and analysts are familiar with the need for such responses in different degrees), judicious care about what is done and why it is being done must remain in the forefront of therapeutic activity. Kohut stated in a lecture:

> What one does for the patient is really not giving him what he has missed. As a matter of fact, most patients are very sensitive about that and dislike it intensely. If you do that they feel patronized; they feel treated like children, as though you have given to them as to a beggar. I think it is much more sophisticated, and much more a real gift, when one recognizes the need and explains it from one adult to another ... . He [the patient] can occasionally say, "Yes, I know that, but really I do need something." Then maybe from time to time one can, recognizing an enormous need, give something that one knows is, for the time being, necessary. I have a nice phrase for it: I call it the "reluctant compliance with the childhood wish." (Elson, 1987, p. 39)

Kohut also realized that the traditional stance of analytic neutrality produced a serious and sometimes detrimental problem in treatment. The analyst's neutrality that intends to stimulate regression as well as to avoid contaminating the transference produces an artifact that Kohut described in the following way:

> [T]here is an old confusion ... between analytic neutrality, considered as a sterile field in which one must work antiseptically, as a kind of physical or emotional zero point, and the average friendliness and empathic behavior that a patient has the right to expect from a person who has devoted his life to empathically merging with them. That expectably empathic behavior is the true zero or base line in analytic work. It is not some peculiarly remote, emotionally dessicated behavior ... That kind of behavior does not bring out any psychologically important realities in patients, but it does produce peculiar artifacts that may then be misunderstood and interpreted as basic pathology. Of course, it isn't essential pathology, but a reaction to mistreatment ... it is in essence an iatrogenic disease. (Kohut, 1996, p. 325)

Even more forcefully, Kohut stated:

If the patient gets ... silent, oddly unanswering treatment, he will really have been misled and betrayed, and he will, of course, be deeply disappointed and enraged. This is not the expression of repressed or otherwise neurotically defended-against or characterologically determined rage, which now, because of the skillful therapeutic mobilization of his central conflicts, erupts to reveal his true enraged self and the consequent guilt ... That is all utterly spurious; they are all artifacts. (Kohut, 1996, pp. 250–251)

TRANSMUTING INTERNALIZATION

If empathic understanding is the way that therapists identify patients' concerns or injuries, the primary therapeutic technique for conveying these insights remains interpretation. The therapeutic objective is to repair the self disorder by interpretations emphasizing momentary disruptions of empathic attunement and its destabilizing effects. Through the gradual internalization of these insights, patients rebuild or fortify the injured or devitalized self. Kohut proposed the term *transmuting internalization* to refer to this process.

Interpretive work is rarely based on resolving intrapsychic conflict. Patients establish a selfobject transference that inevitably becomes disrupted in the normal course of treatment by the empathic unavailability of the analyst or psychotherapist. Patients experience this unavailability as an injury to self-esteem. Therapists attempt to convey what they understand to have taken place, including the genetic origins of the patient's reaction. Frustration produced by selfobject failure is inevitable in the treatment relationship. It reveals the pre-existing state of self-cohesion before undertaking treatment and may lead to regression based on a patient's specific form of psychopathology.

In the invariable frustrations experienced in treatment, patients are re-exposed in the transference to empathic failures of childhood. This experience particularly revives early failures or traumatic disappointments of parental empathic attunement or responsiveness to the selfobject needs of the young child. The many ways in which these early injuries are remobilized by the momentary empathic misattunements or poorly timed interpretations are part and parcel of analytic or psychotherapeutic treatment.

That these remobilizations are inevitable misunderstandings or missteps of therapists or analysts is to be expected. Misunderstandings occur when therapists attempt to grapple with patients' unconscious dynamics, particularly early in treatment. That patients experience these misunderstandings as injuries or frustrations is not important. What is important is that they are understood and interpreted to patients as revivals in treatment of early injuries to self-cohesion. When they are understood in this way and consistently interpreted as such, the process of working through builds a new, revitalized self. This process and the newly acquired solidification of self-cohesion are the transmuting internalizations. Gradually, as this process unfolds, self-esteem is fortified.

The transmuting internalizations become the basis for seeing, in the transference, the various ways in which patients attempt to protect themselves. When misunderstood, patients momentarily experience a threat to a self struggling to maintain viability or vigor. When therapists recognize that a disruption of the self state has occurred, pointing this out to a patient becomes the reparative or mutative agent in treatment. In time, as a therapist or analyst comes to understand the genetic roots in early development, this material is also included in the interpretation. With repeated interpretations, the process of transmuting internalization gradually strengthens the devitalized self. In a broad sense, transmuting internalizations are the way that treatment enables an enfeebled self to survive and flourish. Through transmuting internalizations, the self is strengthened to remain buoyant and psychologically alive.

Kohut (1984) eschewed the term *resistance* because of its pejorative implication as something unwanted that interferes with treatment and that must be eradicated. He believed that this view is usually incompatible with promoting transmuting internalizations. When therapists view defenses as resistances, they sometimes react to them as stubborn, unyielding aspects of the patient to be fought and overcome. There is a difference between a patient's being told that he or she is resisting and a patient's being told that he or she acts in a certain way for self-protection or self-cohesion. In the second situation, the interpretation is empathically attuned to the patient's need. The first comment makes the patient feel undermined or bad; whatever its therapeutic function, it does not foster self-cohesion. Interpretations about resistances, therefore, do not lead to transmuting internalizations that repair a self disorder. Referring to an interpretation of a dream of his well-known patient, Mr. Z., Kohut (1984) wrote:

> An intruding father loaded with identificatory gifts is psychologically different from an available idealizable father. Our confusion of the two situations is an outgrowth of mechanistic, non-psychological thinking. "Intrusion" is unresponsive to the child's needs; it is not guided by empathy with the child. "Availability," in the psychological sense in which I use the term here, is responsiveness; it is guided by empathy. (p. 149)

Defenses are self-protective in the face of a selfobject milieu that is unresponsive to what the self requires to sustain vitalization. Self psychologists consider defenses to represent the best attempts that a patient can manage to keep a weakened self psychologically afloat. Like the example of Kohut's patient Mr. Z., the patient's need is for an available selfobject. Defenses are not stubborn intrusions that counteract a therapist's efforts at removing encumberances to uncovering conflict.

Through repeated interpretations of selfobject needs, transmuting internalizations are built up. Patients in a self psychologically informed treatment do not generally understand that they are struggling against aspects of their inner life, aspects that must be overcome or purged. Interpretation remains the primary therapeutic technique, but the content of what is interpreted is different. The self psychological approach interprets interruptions that have interfered with ongoing psychological development. This process fosters the continuation of arrested development in an empathically responsive environment, promotes the repair of injuries to the self, and thus fosters optimal self-esteem. Ultimately, through this process of transmuting internalization, the idealizing transference becomes transformed into an idealization of the superego, and the successful working through of the grandiose-exhibitionistic transference results in the strengthening of reasonable ambitions and goals.

The transmuting internalizations that lead to bolstering of self-cohesion represent another essential difference between classical analysis and self psychologically informed treatment. Drive theory stresses the importance of interpreting conflicts and the resistances (defenses) that have developed around these conflicts and their genetic origins. Self psychology favors interpretation of selfobject needs, the way that these have been misunderstood or unresponded to, and the genetic origins of this form of disturbance. The cure is the transmuting internalizations that patients acquire as the self disorder is gradually repaired. With self disorders, this process represents the basis of therapeutic action. For this reason, the psychology of the self has been viewed as a deficit model of psychopathology, in contrast to the conflict model of classical psychoanalytic theory.

COMPENSATORY STRUCTURES

The concept of compensatory structures is less familiar than other concepts in self psychology. Clinicians and theorists whose primary acquaintance with self psychology came from writings before and including *The Analysis of the Self* (Kohut, 1971) may not be very aware of this concept, which may also hold particular interest for those concerned with diagnostic psychological assessment. Many clinical examples that I present in chapters 4 through 8 illustrate that successful and unsuccessful attempts to develop compensatory structures can be identified by using diagnostic testing methods. Psychodiagnostic tests can demonstrate the relative balance among primary, defensive, and compensatory structures.

Kohut first described the concept of compensatory structures in *The Restoration of the Self* (1977). The concept centers on attempting to secure another route to achieve a firmed-up sense of self when the primary pole or sector of the self has been injured in early development. Thus, it is possible to repair self-cohesion if another sector of the self can provide the selfobject responsiveness of the original primary structure that was deficient. Typically, the compromised primary structure is the grandiose-exhibitionistic pole and its associated mirroring selfobject function. The idealized parent imago pole can also be the defective primary structure, although this situation is less frequent. In either circumstance, Kohut believed that children tried to repair the deficit in the impaired primary structure, if the injury was not too extensive, by seeking an alternative route to strengthening the self. Compensatory structure represents a second chance to restore self-cohesion and usually appears as idealization in an attempt to compensate for derailed or chronically interrupted mirroring.

In contrast, defenses operate in much the same way as in ego psychological theory. That is, defensive operations function to protect an injured or devitalized self that has been limited in acquiring compensatory structures. Defenses, therefore, do not provide the possibility of a self-reparative mechanism: the appearance of defenses signifies the failure of compensatory structures.

Defensive structures interfere with self-cohesion by limiting the potential to promote a consolidation of the self. In contrast, compensatory structures represent the possibility of reinvigorated self-cohesion and thus permit development to move forward. Attaining compensatory structures allows self-cohesion to become strengthened and produces a functional rehabilitation of the self. If a compensatory structure does not succeed, then defenses are the best compromise solutions possible.

Kohut (1977) suggested that the work of treatment is to create compensatory structures from defenses, if self-cohesion has not been traumatically damaged by failures of selfobject responsiveness in the weakened sector of the self. Failure to acquire compensatory structures predisposes people to the familiar defensive operations, but defenses may be converted to compensatory structures through treatment.

Kohut was also careful to distinguish compensatory structures from sublimation. He was impressed by some productive and creative individuals' high degree of achievement which, he believed, came about through a preponderance of compensatory structures despite histories of childhood traumatization and selfobject failure. The resilience lay in these productive individuals' capacity to acquire new structures in precisely this way. M. Tolpin's (1993) reinterpretation of certain clinical features of Anna O., Freud and Breuer's well-known patient, is a good example of this phenomenon.

The idealized parent imago pole of the self is usually mobilized to compensate for a mirroring defect of the grandiose-exhibitionistic pole or sector. Thus, idealizing responsiveness from selfobjects may remedy deficiencies of mirroring. Similarly, a twinship selfobject function may buttress self-esteem when a need for mirroring or affirming has gone unrecognized. Twinship may also develop as a compensatory structure if selfobject needs for idealization were not met. Mirroring selfobject needs sometimes compensate for unresponsive or unavailable idealization or twinship when patients seek these selfobject functions, but this pattern is clinically less frequent.

Goldberg (1995) noted that for a structure to be truly compensatory rather than defensive, the compensatory structure had to operate like neutralization of a libidinal or aggressive drive. That is, a compensatory structure should be relatively free of pathological regression and therefore conflict free. Otherwise, the structure might represent a "temporary respite" (Goldberg, 1995) rather than an effective solution to repair self-esteem.

Kohut considered that the self consisted of a combination of primary, defensive, and compensatory structures. Kohut (1984) also believed that healthy people are characterized by a combination of primary and compensatory structures in varying degrees. In these relative states of psychological health, primary structures predominate, although some compensatory structures coexist, and some defensive structures may also be present. Psychopathology, in contrast, is based largely on defensive structures, although well-integrated patients show some compensatory structures and very few intact primary structures (Ornstein, 1990). This picture is one viewpoint of the meaning of cure: transforming defensive structures into compensatory structures leads to a rehabilitation of the self.

Kohut thought that partially successful compensatory structures led to narcissistic personality disorders. The absence of compensatory structures often produced features associated with narcissistic behavior disorders, such as acted-out sexualizations, perversions, and prominent or severe somatization phenomena. Goldberg (1995) considered most forms of perversions as indications of failed development of compensatory structures. In his view, homosexuality was either a perversion or a product of a compensatory structure, depending on the clinical determination about whether the homosexual adaptation represented a well-developed compensatory structure or whether it functioned at the level of most sexual perversions.

Kohut also considered treatment implications of the relations among primary, compensatory, and defensive structures. He recognized that although some selfobject needs were not empathically or vigorously responded to in childhood, neither were these completely thwarted in most treatable self disorders. When people acquire compensatory structures, they have another opportunity to secure formerly unresponded-to selfobject needs. These compensatory structures therefore represent admixtures of partially frustrated needs, together with the more securely firmed-up primary structures of another pole or sector of the self. As long as the frustrated selfobject functions did not become inflexible defensive structures or entrenched behavior disorders such as perversions or somatization reactions, Kohut believed that these selfobject needs could be remobilized in treatment and transformed into workable compensatory structures.

Many patients, however, experience the revival of frustrated aspects of self development with fearfulness and anticipate further disappointment in their treatment. When a therapist interprets a patient's selfobject needs as able to be remobilized rather than making simplistic statements of good will masquerading as empathic understanding, the injured self can proceed from its previously arrested point in development to acquire firmness or cohesion.

If the self has attained sufficient firmness to permit further strengthening through treatment-derived transmuting internalizations, patients can probably acquire compensatory structures. Effective treatment consists of further strengthening these sectors of the self to enable them to "grow with special vigor" (Kohut, 1984, p. 205). Patients can then seek accurately attuned selfobject responsiveness when available from the people in their lives. Kohut compared the process of acquiring compensatory structures to a biological adaptation to unfavorable environmental events:

> Just as a tree will, within certain limits, be able to grow around an obstacle so that it can ultimately expose its leaves to the life-sustaining rays of the sun, so will the self in its developmental search abandon the effort to

continue in one particular direction and try to move forward in another. (Kohut, 1984, p. 205)

Although vestiges of the damaged pole or sector of the self do not disappear, the compensatory structures of the other sectors can take over the selfobject functions of the disabled sector. Eventually, as these compensatory structures mature, their strengthening leads to the unfolding of ambitions, talents, and ideals. The damaged sector does not usually become cured, however, although it may sometimes be revivable after compensatory structures in the other sectors become strengthened.

Kohut regarded the self as seriously damaged when an attempt to acquire compensatory structures leads again to selfobject failure or unresponsiveness. In this circumstance, treatment efforts are uncertain or require special modifications. In terms of Kohut's metaphor of a tree sprouting new roots, a tree with no viable means of rerouting its course fails to thrive when more or less permanently deprived of what it needs for survival. Circumstances may effectively block the enfeebled self from obtaining the "psychological oxygen" needed to survive life demands with sufficient resilience. (Kohut often used the phrase *psychological oxygen* in his writings on self psychology.)

Usually, compensatory structures are reconstructed from a history of turning away from the mother and toward the father with admiration. These compensations typically follow chronic or traumatic disappointment in or unresponsiveness from the mother. Turning to the father in the hope of finding an adequate idealizing selfobject may help stave off the deleterious effects of faulty maternal mirroring. Thus, the father may be approached psychologically to serve selfobject functions of both mirroring and idealization, but Kohut regarded the failure of both selfobject functions to lead to the eventual development of a self disorder.

Children may sometimes turn back to the parent, usually the mother, who originally provided faulty mirroring selfobject needs in an attempt to buttress selfobject failure if the father has been unable to serve a suitable selfobject function for idealization. This form of repeated selfobject failure usually leads to a self disorder as well. An exception may occur in a situation in which the mother's early selfobject failures were attributable to depression but the disorder later remitted. If the father is unable to successfully fulfill an idealizing selfobject function, a return to the mother for mirroring may succeed if the mother recovers from depression.

Kohut regarded compensatory structures as important for regulating drives. In the view of self psychology, drives are not inborn; they appear in the form of breakdown or disintegration products, such as perversions or rage attacks:

> [D]rives in adults are generally disintegration products ... [T]he baby cries, and then the baby cries *angrily* when whatever needs to be done is not done immediately. But there is no original need to destroy; the original need is to establish an equilibrium. (Kohut, 1996, p. 199)

Kohut believed that archaic drive states in the form of disintegration products make their appearance following either traumatic or prolonged empathic failures of an expectable environment or selfobject milieu. Thus, drives are the diffuse, unneutralized reactions to an appreciable interference with the optimal functioning of the self-selfobject unit.

As a result, drive states as disintegration products are prolonged or intensified in the face of failure to establish compensatory structures. Because disintegration products are drive or tension discharges, they cannot provide sufficient self-sustaining responsiveness. The self is thus experienced as devalued or depleted and lacking in psychological oxygen or zest. The initial failure of a primary structure, along with the failure of successfully restorative compensatory structures, exposes patients to a selfobject environment that they cannot experience as alive. Rather than patients' feeling energetic, proud, and invigorated:

> They become fixated on drives because their budding selves were overlooked, were not responded to. They turned to drive-gratification (and later remained fixated on it) because they tried to relieve their depression—they tried to escape the horrible feeling that nobody was responding to them. Such people may have had mothers who satisfied their drives continuously, yet failed to respond to the whole child who expected mirroring responses; they failed to respond with pride and pleasure to the child's increasingly independent self. (Kohut, 1996, pp. 208–209)

THE SELF PSYCHOLOGICAL VIEW
OF THE OEDIPAL PHASE
AND THE INTERPRETATION OF DREAMS

The Oedipus complex is a major explanatory concept of classical psychoanalytic theory so that Kohut's de-emphasis of the oedipal phase's central significance is an important departure from classical psychoanalysis. Although Kohut initially considered his reconceptualization of oedipal dynamics as an expanded version of psychoanalytic theory, he ultimately became convinced that Freud's view of the oedipal situation was uncompelling.

In *The Restoration of the Self*, Kohut (1977) first stated his reservations about the adequacy of Freud's explanation, not the analytically derived data. Kohut initially believed that the self psychological view of the oedipal situation could coexist with the classical view. Thus, patients with primary self disorders could be differentiated from those with predominantly structural neuroses. Yet Kohut regarded structural theory as inadequate to explain self disorders: "[D]rive theory and its developments explain Guilty Man, but they do not explain Tragic Man" (1977, pp. 224).

Kohut regarded the urges or longings expressed at this stage of development as a playful desire for affectionate intimacy or sensual closeness. For children, the psychological issue was not that of sexual stirrings. For the oedipal boy, measuring his strength or importance alongside that of the father is an issue of self-esteem, not competitive or destructive wishes. Such wishes Kohut considered misinterpretations of the crucial dynamics. With regard to the self, the pathological interference takes the form of unattuned empathic failures such as rejection or repudiation from the oedipal child's parents. This rejection produces an injury to a buoyant self in hope of recognition or acceptance. The consequent self-depreciation or propensity to feelings of disappointment or inadequacy represents, therefore, a byproduct of disturbed self-cohesion occurring when a healthy welcoming of this developmental step is rebuffed.

Kohut did not consider the oedipal situation as a fulcrum of psychological development. Rather, he viewed it as yet another opportunity to solidify self-esteem:

Think of a child who is marginally responded to or only occasionally responded to, sometimes lonesome, sometimes feeling unaccepted, exposed to a cold mother who is not able to tune in empathically with the child or is only minimally able to do so. Such a child has a father to whom he can turn for some confirmation and organization of his self by identifying with him, by merging into him as a strong male ideal .... The Oedipus complex, then, is not the rock the psychic self hits and on which it is broken apart. It is, in fact, the other way around. In this instance, the intense onrush of Oedipal feelings becomes the organizing center around which an otherwise fragile self can become coherent again ...

[T]hese individuals repeat their Oedipal conflicts in order to continue the excitement of that stimulating experience, an experience that protects them against underlying or parallel fears of being unstimulated, of being lonesome, depressed, and about to fragment ... It would be the last childhood state in which strong infantile or childhood drives help the self to stay together. (Kohut, 1996, pp. 262–263)

Thus, it was not the emergence of libidinal and aggressive drives that produced conflict in an oedipal child. Rather, the unresponded-to or empathically unattuned response to the emerging self represented the primary threat. Conflict, the cornerstone of psychopathology according to the structural theory, was secondary to impaired self-cohesion. This position is a main reason that many psychoanalytic clinicians have considered the psychology of the self to have a "misplaced (and largely incorrect) emphasis" (Wallerstein, 1986/1995).

From the standpoint of the psychology of the self, a pathogenic oedipal phase is not an inevitable, necessary, or universal part of normal development. Such a phase may appear when there has been appreciable empathic failure at this stage of relatively normal development. Kohut reserved the term *Oedipus complex* for pathological disturbances arising from the parents' unattuned or unempathic reactions to children's needs for selfobject responsiveness at this stage of development.

Kohut did not consider pathological sexualizations as misplaced or frustrated libidinal urges or view assertiveness as derived from an aggressive drive. He thought that many traditional analysts overestimated fear of the parents as a neurotic manifestation of castration anxiety. Kohut believed that attempts to treat oedipal-phase injuries to the self as structural disorders would fail. As an example, Kohut provided the illustration of the jealous erotized material of "pseudohysterics":

The more you interpret the Oedipal period, the worse they get because they are afraid those ideas will be taken away from them. Why? Because it is the continuous activity in the romantic conflict sphere of the Oedipal background that gives them the sense of being alive. Now, side by side, you see indications of deeper pathology ... You must undercut the supposed Oedipal issues by telling the patient you think that all this romantic falling in love probably covers a great sense of neediness ... that he really wants something much more basic from you ... And then the patient will feel understood, and there will be a toning down of all the romantic and jealous and suicide threatening fireworks, and one can perhaps begin to go to work on the depressive sense of the self. (Kohut, 1996, pp. 116–117)

To Kohut, it was not inevitable that "seeming Oedipal material" (Kohut, 1996, p. 346) had to be analyzed, particularly when this material began to emerge toward the end of treatment. Although he did not trivialize oedipal dynamics, his primary interest was clearly in those aspects of the oedipal phase promoting self-cohesion:

> It is nothing else but the final paragraph of the long book of a successful analysis. It need not be analyzed. If it is analyzed, then fine, it won't do any harm. It will be a little lapse, but if you have understood a person for so many years then one final misunderstanding won't destroy him and all the work you've done. The patient will feel rebuffed because now he really can love or really can hate you; now he is strong enough to do that. And the fact that he can do that now is what you should recognize and congratulate him about." (Kohut, 1996, pp. 346–347)

Another instance of Kohut's technical and conceptual departure from traditional psychoanalytic theory and practice is his approach to the analysis of dreams. He distinguished two types of dreams, one of which expressed *conflict-based* themes that could be understood in the customary way. The second type represented the mobilization of unmanageable tension states, arising from fear of overstimulation or dissolution of the self. This second type of dream, which Kohut called *self-state dreams* (Kohut, 1977), occurs less frequently than the first (P. Tolpin, 1983) and should not be approached in the same way as the first kind, by eliciting associations.

Ornstein (1987) did not believe that the distinction between these two types of dreams was critical; he regarded all dreams as representing the self state. Self-state dreams do not typically lead to the emergence of material that is consistent with or interpretible in the framework of drive theory. The associative content characteristically generates only further material pertaining to the state of the self and the self-selfobject environment, particularly about its vulnerability to injury or fragmentation.

Kohut considered one of the salient features of the self-state dream to be its significance for understanding the experience of the self reacting to an empathic failure or momentary fluctuation in attunement. Frequently, self-state dreams are reactions to rebuffs or misunderstandings, including those occurring in a patient's selfobject transference during treatment. In Kohut's (1977, 1984) view, interpretations are best framed by remaining close to the manifest content. This approach demonstrates to patients that dreams reflect something about their current life, something that threatens a viable self organization or stable self experience (Gabel, 1994; P. Tolpin, 1983). Fosshage (1989) contributed the idea that the self-state dream may point to a glimmer or budding of reintegration of the self, an emergence that consolidated important current experiences with structural changes of the self.

To those interested in personality assessment, it is not surprising that the relevance of the self-state dream, with its meaning contained in the manifest content, frequently parallels the relevance of similar material in projective test content. Reconstructing meaning about the self state from content is a central point to which I devote the major portion of the second half of this book.

3 The Central Role of Selfobject Functions

In the first two chapters of this book, I showed that Kohut viewed narcissistic personality disorders as nonresponsive to the conventional interpretations of conflict and defense derived from drive theory and ego psychology. He discovered that patients with these disorders, when correctly understood, nevertheless formed stable and recognizable transferences, which permitted psychoanalytic treatment to proceed without a need for technical modifications. Kohut originally identified two basic transference patterns of mirroring and idealization, which represented the bipolar self, and first referred to these as narcissistic transferences. His original emphasis on narcissistic pathology and narcissistic transferences evolved into a broad concept of the self and the self's requirements for responsiveness, the self-selfobject environment. Thus, he came to see mirroring and idealization (and later, twinship) as selfobject functions that sustain and invigorate self-esteem. The mobilization of these functions in treatment takes the form of a selfobject transference.

"[T]hat dimension of our experience of another person relates to this person's functions in shoring up our self" (Kohut, 1984, pp. 49–50). This perception led Kohut to develop the concept of selfobject function, which describes a psychological state that is experienced in depth, the innermost experience of a self that is either buoyant and firm or injured and devitalized. The actual relationship between one person and another is secondary and frequently irrelevant.

The selfobject is necessary to sustain optimal self-cohesion or self-esteem. Although Kohut considered selfobject functions to be necessary for healthy self-esteem throughout life, he recognized their particular importance when the self is injured or undermined. At these moments, the primary function of the selfobject is to repair an enfeebled or devitalized self. Through the attempt to revive or rebuild a diminished or depreciated self state, selfobject functions are most evident clinically.

In this chapter, I describe in detail the unique importance of selfobject functions in the psychology of the self and continue the theoretical discussion of the major concepts of self psychology. The material in this chapter has three parts: First, concepts of what a selfobject is and is not; second, clinical consideration of how selfobject functions are apprehended or identified in treatment; third, the three selfobject functions of mirroring, idealization, and twinship. These selfobject functions are not only central to Kohut's work; they are also crucial for a self psychological reconceptualization of psychodiagnostic testing content.

SELFOBJECT FUNCTIONS: CONCEPTUAL DEFINITION

When selfobject needs are mobilized in a patient's relationship with another person, that person is not experienced or reacted to primarily as an individual with needs and wishes (that is, with a center of initiative). Rather, the person exists largely to provide a needed function for the patient. The patient does not "use" the other in the common sense of the word but relates to the person as though his or her raison d'être is as an extension to the patient. The process is not a form of boundary disturbance or a cognitive failure in which a person providing a selfobject function has lost his or her independent existence. Instead, the psychological essence of how the person is experienced predominates in the individual's sense of the other person. In effect, other people become what they are needed to be or to provide.

A selfobject function represents a transference that is an internal mental representation of need states. Such functions are crucial for maintaining a cohesive self or stable self-esteem. They appear clinically and in interpersonal relationships as ways of relating to others on the basis of perceived properties of individuals for satisfying particular needs.

Selfobjects, therefore, are crucial functions for sustaining or strengthening the self, in health as well as in psychopathology. Their mobilization is signaled through affirming, accurately attuned, and optimal responsiveness so that selfobjects serve to bolster the self. Selfobject functions are the needs for mirroring, idealization, or twinship, needs that patients seek to satisfy by engaging with the analyst as a transference object. Understanding selfobject needs provides a basis for talking to patients about what they lack (that is, what selfobject functions they seek) in the transference and ultimately in life. Kohut regarded mirroring, idealization, and twinship as selfobject functions that revive the need for a viable presence when the self lacks sufficient resilience for sustaining itself.

How is a selfobject best defined? What is and is not a selfobject? It is simpler to say what a selfobject is not: It is not another person. A selfobject is a purpose or function that another person serves; it *is* the psychological function. It is both correct and incorrect to think of selfobject functions as simply experiences of need states that other persons satisfy or provide for and that the self is unable to carry out independently in the absence of such assistance. Another person may sometimes function in this manner, but interpersonal relationships constitute only a simplistic view of a person's in-depth intrapsychic states.

Thus, to say that a selfobject is another person is correct but only to a point. It is more accurate to consider the selfobject phenomenologically as a function that a person needs as a substitute for a missing, defective, or deficient aspect of the self. In this respect, the selfobject function is reparative or restorative. A misplaced emphasis on the nature or quality of interpersonal relationships for understanding selfobject functions (such as cooperative, paternal, or malevolent) serves only to direct attention from the central issue. De-emphasizing the interpersonal context promotes an appreciation that self-cohesion is primarily an internal experience of feeling invigorated and whole.

In reference to defining a selfobject, Basch (1994, p. 2) wrote:

> What exactly is a selfobject? A selfobject is not a person. A selfobject is an intrapsychic event, an experience. So, for example, when the analyst assists a patient to cope with the anxiety generated by heretofore unsuspected feelings, the analyst is not a selfobject; rather, he or she functions to promote the patient's selfobject experience.

Perhaps this phenomenon is best conveyed through the often-reported experiences of analysts and psychotherapists who have felt that they are not "in the room" or are not even noticed by a patient. Therapists first recognize these experiences psychologically when a patient becomes angry or disappointed by the therapist's failure to function as an extension of the patient's self. This narcissistic breach is only compounded when the analyst or therapist does not recognize what is occurring and misinterprets the selfobject failure incorrectly as a displaced drive or wish, usually as destructive rage.

This phenomenon initially led Kohut (1971) to discover the mirroring selfobject function during his analysis of a patient, Miss F. This patient urgently demanded that the analyst only restate her own opinions about events in her life and not offer any interpretations of his own. Rather than insisting that this transference reaction represented a reactivation of libidinal conflict and interpreting her anger and feelings of being undermined from that viewpoint, Kohut pursued an approach based on the fact that the patient relegated him to little more than an impersonal function. In his attempt to understand the meaning of this experience for Miss F., Kohut ultimately discovered the phenomenon he came to describe as mirror transference.

A selfobject is not characterized by self-preoccupation or selfishness. Turning to others to provide a selfobject need is not the same as being selfish, self-absorbed, or even self-aggrandizing. Although these features may sometimes be present, selfishness is not equivalent to selfobject need. Selfobject needs may exist side by side with the capacity to appreciate another person's separate existence or needs (including selfobject needs).

Selfobject needs are not always experienced with reference to another person. They may be realized through other means, including satisfactions derived from literature, the arts, or abstract ideas. Selfobject functions may even take the form of gratifications or states of relief provided by a drug or erotized object such as a fetish, and in such cases, they are no less psychologically compelling.

Other self psychologists have subsequently proposed different meanings of the term selfobject. Some of these definitions are based on the way that people experience having selfobject functions (Stolorow, Brandschaft, & Atwood, 1987) or relationships (Bacal, 1994; Rowe, 1994). In Basch's (1994) view, however, the crucial characteristic of a selfobject function is the way that another person responds affectively, acts, or otherwise fosters an experience for the individual so as to promote a firmed-up, invigorated sense of self. In this way, the self becomes a cohesive and enduring mental structure.

Whatever the similarity between a selfobject and an interpersonal relationship, the selfobject clearly does not assume a relational meaning. Clinicians associated with psychoanalytic self psychology have at times casually mentioned selfobject transferences as if they were describing a relationship. Self psychologically informed practitioners or theoreticians, however, do not consider a selfobject to be a person (Wolf, 1988). However tempting it is to think of selfobject functions as an interpersonal quality or relationship, selfobject functions are still fundamentally stable psychic structures formed as a result of optimal frustration in early development. If the normal, ongoing internalizations of selfobject functions are interfered with in early development, the stable, internalized structures of self-cohesion fail to develop in a sufficiently robust or reliable manner.

CLINICAL AND DEVELOPMENTAL CONSIDERATIONS

In normal development, selfobject failures occur regularly but briefly as part of the "ups and downs of self-esteem" of a cohesive self that strives to "straighten it out again" (Kohut, 1996, p. 73). These failures are easily repaired in a selfobject environment capable of providing empathically corrective responses in a timely manner. More out-of-step empathic ruptures may also occur, and these predispose people to temporary fragmentation states. Empathic failures are reversible under circumstances in which some degree of self structure has already been established.

Sometimes, however, fragmentation-prone self states remain as unintegrated self structures that are isolated or affectively walled off. A fall in self-esteem or a diminished capacity to experience pleasure in major life activities frequently accompanies such states. Deficiencies of the idealized parent imago sector may produce disturbances of drive regulation and insufficient development of the ego ideal. These disturbances give rise to a sense of inadequacy of values or guiding principles and ultimately lead to impoverished capacities for empathy, humor, and wisdom. Deficiencies of the grandiose-exhibitionistic pole may interfere with, if not cripple, realization of ambitions, strivings, or goals.

An enfeebled self attempts to preserve whatever selfobject responsiveness can be salvaged from the experience of an unrewarding or hurtful environment. This attempt often takes the form of grossly misaligned behaviors, prominent among which are various addictions, perversions, certain forms of sociopathy, and vague cravings for mystical unions with omnipotent figures or images. These self-destructive and ultimately unresourceful attempts to repair a self threatened by fragmentation have their roots in childhood experiences of parental selfobject failures. Such addictive or antisocial behaviors occur with some regularity or frequency, and represent desperate attempts to buoy self-esteem. An addiction or fetish, for example, substitutes for a self-regulating psychic structure. Such adaptive failures, which Kohut referred to as disintegration products, constitute an emerging but thwarted self, not yet capable of performing self-sustaining functions on its own (M. Tolpin, 1978).

Other disintegration products in adulthood are remnants of children's insufficient attempts at calming themselves in the face of threatened self-cohesion. These can include compulsivity, ritualistic activities, and the pathological breakdown of normal assertion into chronic narcissistic rage. Attempts to substitute for missing structure may take the form of sexualizations such as lonely masturbatory stimulation (with or without associated fantasy), promiscuity (with or without depressive voyeuristic and exhibitionistic acts or related sexualizations), or both (Goldberg, 1995). Morrison (1984) expanded on Kohut's (1977) view that narcissistic rage was closely linked to affect states associated with shame: Narcissistic rage arises as a final disintegration or breakdown product in the face of some aspect of the shame reaction, which is itself the result of a sense of helplessness stemming from selfobject unavailability or failure.

M. Tolpin (1978) has described depletion depression, a phenomenon characterized by emptiness and having its roots in similar childhood states that were unrelieved through faulty parental responsiveness. M. Tolpin and Kohut (1980) later described experiences of children whose parents as selfobjects have "psychologically vanished" so that feelings of energetic buoyancy and self-confidence are replaced by emptiness and devitalization:

> They [such children] feel unreal, shadowy, ghost-like, empty; their human surroundings, their possessions, their world, become dead, devoid of substantiality; they suffer a drop and loss in self-esteem (they feel "smaller," "ordinary," instead of proud of themselves and what they can do); they are depleted and depressed ("underpowered") ... the healthily proud and jaunty aspects of the patient's childhood self, their body-mind-self no longer works right. (p. 430)

Kohut observed that some patients with narcissistic pathology have a disturbed capacity to regulate skin temperature, are unable to feel or keep warm, and are unusually sensitive to low temperatures such as drafts and susceptible to simple upper respiratory infections. Indeed, other morbid hypochondriacal fears and somatic concerns may also indicate a disturbed self state, particularly if these concerns are excessive and are associated with fantasies of falling into groundless (psychological) space, of coming apart, or of feeling "unglued."

In a more severe form, exclusive of psychotic presentations, clinical psychopathology may appear as symptomatic narcissistic disturbances or chronic, ingrained characterologic states. These can include a notable propensity for any of a variety of addictive behaviors or sexualizations in the form of perversions, promiscuity, or hypo- or hyperarousal or both. Hypo-chondriacal or somatization reactions, frequently associated with fantasies of falling apart, fears of disintegration, or boundary disturbances, can occur. These phenomena are best understood as failures of regulating self-cohesiveness. Reactions characterized by rage (understood as narcissistic rage) and related disintegration products (including depletion depression or anxiety) may also be seen as clinical manifestations of narcissistic pathology.

A related phenomenon concerns the ways that others rebuff or depreciate a person's efforts to turn with pride in anticipation of mirroring. In treatment as well as in early development and in virtually all areas of life, patients (and students, and children) expect with pride or healthy assertion about their accomplishments a mirroring selfobject response from another person who should understand the person's need. When these hopeful strivings are mobilized, people anticipate an appropriate self-affirming reaction rather than misunderstandings or responses that diminish self-esteem. Failure to react in keeping with legitimate selfobject needs sets in motion propensities for shame, rage, disintegration products, or related fragmentation phenomena.

Psychotherapists may unwittingly revive childhood precursors of devaluation when they do not understand patients' needs. Such revivals often occur because of incorrect (but not inexact [Glover, 1955]) interpretations and empathic errors, particularly early in treatment, when therapists attempt to understand a patient's central dynamics. Patients may experience such interpretive errors as hurtful reminders of feeling misunderstood, especially when a therapist is adamant about being correct because the patient's reaction of feeling depreciated revives the therapist's own feeling of injury. In such instances, patients frequently reject an interpretation. Once this phenomenon is correctly identified, however, the therapeutic action should be one of repairing self-cohesion through interpretation of the injury to the self.

It is unfortunate for treatment when this situation cannot be rectified, as in situations in which treatment is regularly characterized by chronic failures to correctly understand a patient's developmental need or self state. In these circumstances, symptoms can intensify, iatrogenic regressions can occur, and ultimately treatment failure or disappointing treatment results. On this point, Kohut (1984) wrote:

> If there is one lesson that I have learned during my life as an analyst, it is the lesson that what my patients tell me is likely to be true—that many times when I believed that I was right and my patients were wrong, it

turned out, though often only after a prolonged search, that my rightness was superficial whereas their rightness was profound. (p. 94)

Kohut clearly recognized that, in life, selfobject attunement and responsiveness are by no means infallible or perfectly consistent. The occasional lapse in responsiveness creates the very conditions for optimal frustration, an occurrence that is customary and usual, if not actually necessary in the course of normal development. In this way, such experiences of optimal frustration give rise to transmuting internalizations if the frustrations brought about by lapses in attunement, empathy, or phase-appropriate selfobject responsiveness are not too prolonged or frequent.

The firming up of a sense of self is ensured in gradual increments through accurate and timely responsiveness from selfobjects. This bit-by-bit process is what Kohut meant by transmuting internalization. As described in chapter 2, under optimal circumstances, transmuting internalizations result from the favorable circumstances of a relatively healthy development in which primary caregivers as selfobjects provided sufficient empathic attunement and responsiveness to a growing child. This situation assures an environment (or selfobject milieu, as Kohut sometimes phrased it) that recognizes phase-appropriate needs for mirroring and idealization and provides these reliably and with in-step timeliness.

The vitality of affect surrounding the selfobject milieu is crucial (Lichtenberg, 1991), whether this environment, in infancy, takes the form of a feeding that satisfies, a hand that plays pat-a-cake, or a mobile that commands attention (Beebe & Lachmann, 1988; Stern, 1985). In treatment, this environment emerges through the affective engagement necessary to solidify the experience of feeling understood (P. Tolpin, 1988). Psychotherapists, by interpreting the selfobject deficit, affectively promote salient transmuting internalizations. These empathically grasped insights about what went wrong in a patient's development become an essential ingredient in treatment. Therapists do not rectify the selfobject deficit by their actions or affective involvements with the patient. Instead, they empathically grasp the difficulty and find a way to revive the affective quality of the experience in framing interpretations about how and why normal selfobject needs went awry.

Kohut emphasized that the self requires selfobject responsiveness for its maintenance throughout all phases of life. This aspect of mental life, once formed, does not necessarily remain stable and unchanging. Kohut's view was that it is normal to expect selfobjects to respond throughout life with welcoming admiration to important aspects of life. Selfobject responsiveness should be accurately attuned to a person's needs for enlivening engagement. At different times, the self requires its selfobjects to serve as sources of idealized strength and calmness or to provide a mirroring or twinship companionate function, which is also a normal or legitimate expectation.

One outcome of a successful self psychologically informed treatment is that patients are able to extract the needed degree of selfobject responsiveness from the people in their lives, or to establish an alternative satisfying selfobject environment. In the latter case, this favorably responsive environment may come about through relationships (such as a healthy spouse capable of responding in this way) or through rewarding activities (such as developing a career or interests that provide fulfillment).

Thus, the emphasis on a lifelong need for selfobject responsiveness represents yet another aspect of the difference between the psychology of the self and traditional psychoanalytic theory and practice. Whereas in the classical view the renunciation of archaic needs and wishes, including their embodiment in the transference, is the goal of successful treatment; in the self psychological view a favorable outcome implies that the self does not become independent of its selfobjects but uses them more efficaciously than before treatment.

To clarify this distinction between traditional and self psychological views, consider Menninger's (1958) comments on the successful termination of a patient in analytic treatment:

> By the end of his analysis, he had learned that most of the things he hoped for he failed to get. Most of his expectations were never realized. Instead he only learned that one shouldn't expect to get certain things and then cry one's eyes out in disappointment or scratch out other people's eyes in rage ... No one ever gets as much love as he wants, no one gives as much love as he might. Choices can be made but choice involves the assumption of responsibility and the necessity for renunciation ... Self-improvement will continue, autonomously, but the treatment, as such, is ended. The parties part company. The contract has been fulfilled. (pp. 178–179)

In contrast, Lichtenberg (1991) called attention to Kohut's emphasis on "the self's ability to use selfobjects for its own sustenance, including an increased freedom in choosing selfobjects" (Kohut, 1984, p. 77). For Kohut, an essential criterion for cure was a lifelong, ongoing selfobject presence and confirmation (psychological oxygen, as it were) rather than renunciation. In a letter to a critic questioning his treatment approach, Kohut wrote:

Throughout his life a person will experience himself as a cohesive harmonious firm unit in time and space, connected with his past and pointing meaningfully into a creative-productive future, [but] only as long as, at each stage in his life, he experiences certain representatives of his human surroundings as joyfully responding to him, as available to him as sources of idealized strength and calmness, as being silently present but in essence like him, and, at any rate, able to grasp his inner life more or less accurately so that their responses are attuned to his needs and allow him to grasp their inner life when his is in need of such sustenance. (Kohut, 1984, p. 52)

PREDOMINANT TRANSFERENCE CONFIGURATIONS

I now describe the three major selfobject functions that incorporate Kohut's (1984) final considerations on the subject. Kohut recognized that self psychology was not a static theory; accordingly, he acknowledged that additional selfobject functions beyond the three he described might eventually be identified. Kohut actually discussed the mirroring and idealizing selfobject functions as the two major forms of selfobject transferences as early as 1966, when he noted that subtypes or variants of these functions could be identified. Not until 1984 did he differentiate the twinship or alter-ego selfobject function from mirroring; previously, he had considered twinship as a subtype of the broad group of mirror transferences. Nearly 20 years later, Kohut (1984) came to view twinship as having a status independent of mirroring. Kohut and Wolf (1978) and Wolf (1988) also described several other possibilities of this sort, although at present the status of selfobject functions remains largely confined to the three major forms (mirroring, idealization, and twinship) described next.

Mirroring

Kohut (1971, 1977) was impressed by the importance of young children's wishes to experience prideful satisfaction surrounding their accomplishments. He was particularly aware of children's desires to have these budding steps recognized and admired. Thus, this mirroring or echoing response ("the gleam in the mother's eye") serves as the prototype for the mirroring selfobject function, arising from the grandiose-exhibitionistic pole of the self.

Admittedly, grandiosity is an unfortunate phrase in view of the pejorative connotation of the term narcissism. The term, however, stems from the perspective of normal young children's inability to grasp their limitations and their tendency, therefore, to overestimate their abilities (M. Tolpin & Kohut, 1980). Kohut (1971) originally conceptualized this idea in the framework of narcissism because he wanted to expand on this aspect of psychological experience while remaining closely allied with structural theory. Kohut (1977, 1984) increasingly departed from certain classical psychoanalytic formulations, and it remains a matter of conjecture whether he would have retained the term grandiose-exhibitionistic self.

Kohut stressed the importance of children's needs to have their achievements affirmed, in a phase-appropriate and timely manner, originally by the mother, but throughout life as well. In this way, the responsiveness of the adequately mirroring selfobject leads to the internalization of stable and enduring feelings of self-esteem, which serves as the basis for sustained feelings of worthwhileness, buoyancy, and vitality. Ultimately, mirroring gives rise to a person's ambitions, goals, and strivings, as these develop and crystallize in adulthood.

The self is particularly prone to fragmentation in the face of injury or assault. Its viability can be compromised by chronically occurring selfobject failures. Clinicians see this fragmentation when they understand how empathic failures of mirroring selfobject responsiveness occurred. Selfobject failures predispose people to develop pathological forms of narcissistic personality or behavior disorders when the failures are severe. These disorders are frequently characterized by symptomatic phenomena of empty depression and a failure to achieve genuine enjoyment from work or pleasurable activities. There is a characteristic lack of zest expressed as prolonged experiences of boredom or ennui, accompanied by chronic dissatisfaction or disappointment. Impoverished initiative or ambition is notable and leads to a failure to achieve goals commensurate with native talents or skills. This phenomenon is the horizontal split (Kohut, 1971), representing the repression barrier, in which feelings of emptiness, boredom, and hypochondria are clinical manifestations of the split between experience of the self (self state) and the self's relation to reality.

Patients with narcissistic personality and behavior disorders for whom the central selfobject disturbance centers on defective mirroring are particularly hypersensitive to criticism. Such patients react strongly to even minor slights and show a limited capacity to recover easily. Their clinical picture is dominated by symptomatic manifestations of experiences of shame or rage on exposure of their shortcomings. Kohut considered shame to be a reaction that occurred when selfobjects failed to respond admiringly to a child's joyful enthusiasm. This view of shame differs from the familiar object libidinal interpretation of shame as a response triggered by failure to sufficiently satisfy the demands of the ego ideal.

Similarly, Kohut viewed narcissistic rage as an understandable reaction to selfobject failure. His position contrasts with the predominant drive theory interpretation of rage as derived from an inborn aggressive drive. For some patients, narcissistic rage reactions assume primitive forms of discharge, such as the disintegration products of fragmenting self-cohesion. Thus, aggression not based on healthy assertion is thought of as a breakdown into isolated fragments of previously structuralized aspects of the self.

The characterologic description of many patients with defects of the grandiose-exhibitionistic self includes prominent features of coldness, sometimes accompanied by arrogance. These manifestations of arrogance or self-aggrandizement defensively conceal feelings of shame and depreciation. Often, however, self-depreciation emerges quickly and sometimes surprisingly early in treatment, even when a patient is otherwise relatively asymptomatic. This phenomenon is the vertical split that was Kohut's (1971) way of describing how the experience of grandiosity is walled off from the experience of reality.

Kohut's view differs from Kernberg's (1975) interpretation of grandiosity as a defensive reaction to conceal feelings of rage, envy, or dependency. Kohut's (1977, 1984) subsequent expanded view of mirroring went beyond its clinical description in psychopathology. In its broadened scope, he emphasized the importance of in-step confirming, echoing, or affirming responses that are crucial to mirroring. He understood these mirroring responses to be normal, expectable, and legitimate needs, setting the stage for realizing goals in keeping with a person's talents and skills. Rather than falling prey to atrophy or derailment through neglect or unattuned responsiveness, these more or less normal needs should give rise to a firm and vigorous sense of the self.

This normal development of the self, strengthened by the availability of suitably responsive mirroring selfobjects, leads to the capacity to turn to the world with assurance that one's efforts are noticed and responded to empathically. From such a position people derive satisfaction from their abilities and interests. This reaction is accompanied by confidence and sufficient vitality or enthusiasm to strive to reach life goals. The need for mirroring extends from normal appreciation of one's basic abilities in health to pathological forms dominated by a profound sense of devitalization of self-esteem, propensity for sexualization and addictions, and chronic empty depression. This selfobject function of the mirroring, echoing, or confirming presence is sought in both pathology and health.

In Kohut's (1971) early description of the mirror transferences, the most primitive or archaic form, which predominated in severe narcissistic disorders, was merger transference. Merger is characterized by the greatest regressive disturbance with the least degree of differentiation between self and object. A second subtype of mirroring was twinship or alter-ego transference (discussed in detail in a subsequent section because Kohut [1984] later distinguished twinship as a distinct selfobject transference). The twinship transference preserved a greater differentiation between self and object than did merger transference, although the selfobject had to be a faithful replica of the self.

The third and least archaic mirroring selfobject function is mirroring proper, or mirror transference in the narrow sense as Kohut (1971) originally referred to this phenomenon. This transference is developmentally more advanced with respect to the degree of differentiation between self and object as independent centers of initiative. Together with a greater capacity to distinguish self from other, this mirror transference is a less regressive form of self-selfobject differentiation than are the other two forms. The need for the selfobject is still, however, primarily that of providing admiration. The affirming or echoing presence remains central to sustaining self-cohesion.

Idealization

With idealization, the idealized parent imago, which is Kohut's term for this pole or sector of the self, emerges alongside the grandiose-exhibitionistic pole and becomes another means of strengthening self-esteem.

Although idealization can take the form of holding others in awe, sometimes even putting them on a pedestal, this aspect of its clinical appearance is not invariably present. Much more common are the relatively silent idealizations that are more subtle and less overt. This circumstance frequently requires close examination over time before it can be defined as genuine idealization. For this reason, psychodiagnostic testing may be useful to detect its presence. Idealized selfobjects can be experienced as omnipotent; when this reaction occurs in the transference, the analyst or therapist is often revered as powerful and all-knowing. More often, idealization is mobilized when the need for a calming but strong presence is predominant. Thus, a young child's need for both calm strength and limitless power is expressed through this selfobject function. A person who is looked up to in this way becomes a presence with whom the child can merge and thereby turn to for restoring equilibrium when the self is experienced as weakened or injured.

The selfobject responsiveness that is needed requires the presence of the selfobject to supply a calming feeling without withdrawing from the idealizing need. Otherwise, feelings of abandonment or disappointment can arise. The idealized selfobject function becomes embodied in those persons who steady the course when the going gets rough. Ideals or abstract representations can also provide an idealizing selfobject function, in the form of religion or related forms of spirituality or of sources of inspiration such as music, literature, or ideas. Seeing an ideal, such as a beloved art or musical style or a cherished scientific or philosophical principle, undermined or attacked can produce a feeling of being let down or abandoned, if a patient is inclined to experience idealizing selfobject needs in the form of ideas or art forms rather than of personal relationships.

Mirroring selfobject functions do not disappear with and are not necessarily replaced by idealization. Rather, all selfobject needs continue to be present and exist side by side throughout life. At various times, one or another predominates or becomes pressing. Some therapists have erroneously considered Kohut's view of idealization to represent a transformation of needs for selfobject responsiveness more highly developed than that of mirroring. Although idealization often appears as a route to self-cohesion in normal development, Kohut did not believe that it replaced mirroring or that it represented a more developmentally advanced selfobject function.

For some people, idealization appears alongside the mirroring needs of the grandiose-exhibitionistic pole of the self. This phase of selfobject experience may emerge as a favorable developmental step. Although mirroring needs are not renounced, they may be transformed into idealizing selfobject needs. In this way, children welcome the availability of figures who can be idealized, who offer an opportunity to revive needs for power and greatness through "feeling linked to the admired other: the self, in effect, walking proudly in the shadow of his admired object" (Bacal & Newman, 1990, p. 232).

Idealization becomes important for any hope of repairing the injuries to the self when mirroring needs have met with selfobject failure. To forestall the ensuing devitalization of self-esteem, the possibility for a second chance at buttressing a weakened or vulnerable self presents another opportunity to attempt repair of the self. This process is the basis for the concept of compensatory structure that I discussed in chapter 2, as Kohut came to see the complementary roles of these two sectors or poles of the self. The possibility of turning elsewhere to repair self-cohesion through idealization may be crucial if the grandiose-exhibitionistic sector is no longer sufficiently robust to sustain invigorating self-esteem.

Another way in which idealizing selfobject needs become mobilized is through young children's gradual realization that they lack the omnipotence associated with the grandiose-exhibitionistic sector of the self. Normally, this recognition is nontraumatic if sufficient mirroring has enabled children to feel that they have assets and capabilities.gradually relinquishing the need for greatness or omnipotence does not become devastating but provides the inevitable optimal frustration in normal development promoting the internalizations Kohut (1971, 1977) regarded as strengthening for the self. Presumably, the dosing and timing of selfobject disappointment are not inordinately out of step with a child's needs so that omnipotent longings diminish and can be transformed into admiring or idealizing the strength outside oneself.

Idealization is potentially fraught with land mines. It requires, first, adequately empathic responsiveness from an idealized selfobject. People hope for welcoming responses to their idealizing attempts; it can be devastating if instead these needs are repeatedly met with rebuffs. For example, a parent whom a young child hopes to admire for the parent's abilities or strengths may be too narcissistically vulnerable or depressed to provide this selfobject function. The parent may fail to understand empathically what the child needs. One result of this selfobject failure is the depletion depression of a narcissistic personality disorder or the acting-out addictions or perversions of a narcissistic behavior disorder.

Another result of thwarted idealizing selfobject needs is a continual clinging to a vaguely sensed ideal of perfection built up in an effort to maintain an ongoing connection with the idealized object. This process represents an attempt to create an illusion of stabilization of the self, albeit an unreliable and transitory perception of equilibrium. This temporary state remains fragile and does not lead to self-cohesion; instead, it predisposes to vaguely experienced feelings of emptiness (depletion) or powerlessness. Intensely held childhood fantasies of parental greatness are typical examples, along with an adamant refusal to abandon beliefs about a powerful parent in the face of adversity or loss.

Thus, a young child may fervently refuse to acknowledge the death or separation of an idealized parent, sometimes with near-delusional intensity.

The child attempts to preserve self-esteem by holding onto the idealized object for dear life despite all external evidence that the selfobject is psychologically absent or unavailable. A well-known literary illustration is the character of Sally Bowles in the musical *Cabaret* (adapted from Isherwood's [1935] *Berlin Stories*), who vigorously holds onto the belief that her busy, world-traveling father whom she adores and admires will eventually visit her. Despite years of disappointing cancellations, she refuses to entertain the idea that he has psychologically abandoned her.

The selfobject failure of rebuffed or empathically misunderstood needs for idealization also prevents children from acquiring a capacity to soothe or comfort themselves when narcissistically injured. This failure does not protect a child from experiencing withdrawal or rage when equilibrium is disturbed, however temporary or fragile this state may have been in the first place. Deficiencies or disappointments in parents, or other potentially idealizable figures, may produce a disinclination to turn with sufficient eagerness to such figures for a calming presence or idealization. In addition, swings or alternations between idealization and mirroring needs, often precipitated by disappointment in an idealized object, can occur. Thus, several selfobject needs may coexist in an unstable way, and these need not be mutually exclusive. Typically, however, one or another need forms the basis for the central selfobject transference.

The clinical manifestations of disturbances of the idealizing selfobject function are identical to those of the grandiose-exhibitionistic sector of the self. Thus, self disorders arising from selfobject failures of idealization resemble those associated with defective mirroring and can include prolonged periods of an empty, depleted quality of depressive affect or fragmentation phenomena associated with intense tension states that are not easily dispelled. Affect states often expressed as feeling adrift, unanchored, or "unglued" may also form part of the character pathology of self disorders, particularly in mild or subclinical varieties. These conditions are the narcissistic personality disorders as Kohut (1971) first described them. Disintegration products, such as the narcissistic behavior disorders in Kohut's (1971) original typology, may also occur. Prominent among these are sexualizations of painful affect states, addictions, or intense outbursts of helpless anger (narcissistic rage).

In its healthy forms, the idealized parent imago pole of the self is the basis for the ego ideal (idealization of the superego) that solidifies standards, values, and goals and leads to the capacity for creativity, humor, empathy, and wisdom. Naturally, the maturation of such qualities depends on the adequacy of responsiveness of idealizing selfobjects. The development of the ego ideal and its mature, adaptive transformations such as humor and wisdom occur in parallel with internalizations that are crucial to firmed-up self-cohesion (Kohut, 1966). Thus, young children optimally undergo gradual disappointments in the idealized object: They gradually acquire a realistic picture of the true-to-life limitations of the idealized figure. If these disappointments are indeed gradual and not traumatic in extent, children can give up unrealistic and excessive idealizations and remain capable of admiring a person's virtues and attributes, which are internalized as part of the child's system of values.

If the idealized object is experienced as faltering or disillusioning in a too severe, sudden, or phase-inappropriate manner, children do not acquire the internalizations necessary for developing optimal self-esteem. In its place, there remains a chronic dependence on idealizable figures, which Kohut (1971) referred to as an intense form of object hunger. He argued that this dependence on idealized objects assumes the desperate quality of a search for substitutes to compensate for missing parts of vital self structure.

Kohut compared the compelling quality of this dependence on idealized selfobjects or "object hunger" to the urgency of an addict's craving for a soothing drug. In this comparison, the addict needs the drug as a replacement for a defect of self structure. The compelling quality of the drug is its soothing or calming property of buoying up a self that is too deficient in cohesiveness to recover from an injury without the substance. For patients with such dependence, other people as potential idealizing selfobjects are too unavailable, disappointing, or fearful to become internalized despite the intensity of the need. Withdrawal from such selfobject needs of others leaves patients who experience their self disorders in this way with little recourse other than injurious narcissistic behavior disorders that often take the form of destructive sexualizations or addictions.

When capable of becoming engaged in treatment, a driven, unrelenting, idealized selfobject transference sometimes appears in the therapeutic reactivation of the search for the omnipotent object. This process can become, in effect, an addiction to the treatment process itself. In unfavorable treatment environments, related attempts to internalize an idealizing selfobject function can take the form of perpetual reliance on self-help structures or organizations, such as the popular 12-step programs. Patients in need of such efforts usually remain chronically dependent on these equivalents of institutional transferences because structural change (that is, transmuting internalizations) rarely occur. Counseling or supportive psychotherapy situations of this type do not usually bring about the most optimal internaliza-tions; counselors, therapists, or therapeutic milieus like this are, in effect, "swallowed whole." As with hunger, satiation of archaic selfobject needs requires perpetual nourishment.

Kohut (1971) identified three forms of the idealized parent imago. In the most archaic type, a merger with the omnipotently perceived selfobject protects the self from traumatic overstimulation leading to diffuse narcis-sistic disorganization. In a less archaic form, associated with a greater degree of differentiation between self and selfobject, the idealized selfob-ject serves a function of strengthening the enfeebled self in the control or neutralization of drives. Kohut described a still less archaic form of the idealizing selfobject transference during the oedipal period of development, associated with maximal differentiation between self and selfobject; here, the power and perfection of the selfobject is needed for approval and for providing guiding ideals and values.

Twinship

Kohut's (1971) earlier work referred to the "mirroring transference in the broad sense" and the "mirroring transference in the narrow sense." He intended the broad designation to refer to the generalized need for mirroring in all its various forms: merger, twinship (alter ego), and mirroring in the narrow sense. Kohut (1984) regarded the twinship selfobject function as sufficiently important in its own right to be differentiated from mirroring. Thus, twinship is equivalent to mirroring and idealization as an independent selfobject function. The analysis of one particular patient initially suggested the twinship function, and clinical observation in several other analyses further demonstrated it.

The selfobject can be somebody (sometimes a thing or object) with whom a person can talk or keep company; it can also exist as a silent presence to evoke when needed. Twinship selfobject needs arise to combat self states of depletion, loneliness, or related experiences of devitalization of the self. Kohut considered the twinship function as a person's experience of being one among others and deriving a deeply felt sense of security from this realization. Its central purpose is to represent the need for a selfobject to operate as a twin or faithful replica of the self. Thus, a person as selfobject acts like oneself but does not merge with one's sense of self.

Twinship is a basis for feeling a sense of belonging or psychological connection. LaFemina (1996) described it thus:

Twinship maintains or assists the cohesion and viability of the self. Twinship does not refer to an actual relationship between two people, nor to the fantasies of a relationship designed to maintain defensive purposes. A twinship relationship is established to provide specific narcissistic functions.

An important feature of the twinship selfobject function is that the "twin" is experienced as a part of the self, specifically a part that is sensed as just like oneself. This alter-ego feature provides people with the feeling of not being alone with their sense of injury or devitalization. The twinship selfobject offers a sense of calming in that it can be evoked as a silent presence when a person's self-esteem is undermined or vulnerable. The twinship need emerges to reinstate a feeling of companionship, based on similarity of need or empathic understanding.

Kohut's (1984) example is that of a person who responds to another so that the two feel a source of joy or pleasure in each other. Ultimately, the internal experience is one of feeling invigorated or enlivened. People seek a selfobject experience to create the feeling that another person is just like them, a faithful replica. They need another person to share their experiences. The selfobject is experienced as a "soulmate" in whose presence a person can feel calmed or soothed. This reaction may occur when the one who fulfills this selfobject function replicates the person's self state and need for empathic responsiveness. Thus, the "soulmate" is experienced as injured or as a source of greatness or strength, just as the person experiences himself or herself.

The companionate function may take several forms, and Kohut's phenomenologic description is particularly evocative:

Someone will gradually appear in the patient's memories from childhood who, differing from the hypochondriacal, anxious, nonsustaining member of the family, was, or at least had once been, strong and idealizable ... a person for whom the patient's early existence and actions were a source of genuine joy ... as an alter ego or twin next to whom the child felt alive (the little girl doing chores in the kitchen next to her mother or grandmother; the little boy working in the basement next to his father or grandfather) will gradually become clear. (Kohut, 1984, p. 204)

Kohut also recognized that twinship functions can be mistakenly deduced from the similarity of external resemblances. He emphasized that "identity of significance, similarity of function" (Kohut, 1984, p. 198) should be considered the predominant psychological factor. Thus, comparisons to twins and people who resemble one another are superficial. It is the core of the experience that gives the twinship selfobject its urgency or importance for a person's self-cohesion. A child who talks to a beloved toy or comforting companion, such as a teddy bear, as if the object were experiencing the feelings that the child experiences, comes closer to the spirit of twinship. The selfobject may be a person, object, or even an abstract idea; its form is secondary because the essential function is the companion-ate or faithful replica quality.

Kohut considered the problem of distinguishing twinship from the other selfobject functions. In the example of a friend who placed a comforting hand on a person's shoulder when the person is troubled or hurt, Kohut observed that this gesture might represent a twinship selfobject function if the friend understood exactly how injured the person felt. He dismissed this possibility, however, by comparing the weakened or injured self that experienced the invigorating gesture of the hand on the shoulder to an unhappy baby picked up by the mother. Here, the mother's ministration permitted the baby to merge with her calmness and omnipotence. This interpretation emphasizes that lifting the baby represents a remobilization of a mirroring selfobject need, as does the arm around the shoulder. Kohut noted, however, that the gesture of the hand on the back might connote a twinship function in particular clinical circumstances.

An illustration of healthy twinship is the intense creative relationship between the playwright Jon Robin Baitz and the actor Ron Rifkin. The depth of intuitive understanding between them has enhanced the work of both such that the playwright regards the actor as "my Lear" and the actor says of the playwright: "Robbie is part of me. You know, we finish sentences for each other. Certainly he understands something about me that I don't" (A. Klein, 1996). Their collaborative relationship was described in a *New York Times* article as: "a rare and empathic alliance between playwright and actor, as if a singular esthetic identity arose out of collaboration" (A. Klein, 1996).

M. Tolpin (1995) gave an illustration of a related but more subtle twinship dynamic—the lengthy friendship between Anna Freud and Dorothy Burlingham. Tolpin regarded Dorothy Burlingham as essential to ensuring the lifesaving self-cohesion of Freud's daughter. Tolpin considered their twinship bond as crucial to consolidating what Anna Freud referred to as her "circle of health." In this circle, she could hold onto the unwavering, unconditional, self-affirming regard of Dorothy Burlingham as a firmly established internalized psychological structure. Thus, through the twinship with Burlingham, Anna Freud was able to revitalize a profoundly injured self state. Freud could free herself from unsuccessful attempts at mirroring and insufficiently sustaining idealizations to allow her to pursue work that was productive and satisfying, work that she accomplished together with Burlingham. This productive "we-self," as M. Tolpin (1995) put it, led to their achieving mutually productive studies of war-traumatized children and pioneering contributions to child psychoanalysis.

If twinship selfobject needs are massively or chronically interfered with in the course of normal development, failures to secure these needs can produce states of acute disconnectedness from people or groups that define a person's work or existence. Such failures lead to a feeling of being distanced from humanity. For some people, these failures can take the form of feeling alienated from cherished values.

As with mirroring and idealization, but more subtly so, twinship often goes unnoticed until it is disrupted. For example, a smoothly proceeding psychotherapy may suddenly appear to break down if a therapist or analyst is, for the moment, no longer experienced as thinking just like the patient or having the same values or views as the patient. This disruption, with its symptomatic appearance in depression, agitation, or anger, is the marker of the patient's selfobject need that has become perturbed. If the analyst or psychotherapist thought that the patient was predominantly displaying a mirror transference, he or she would be surprised if the patient were to react strongly with depression or rage at the analyst's slight or misunderstanding.

Suddenly, so it appears, the patient reacts with eruptions of affect or disorganization as though a critical function has been interrupted. An empathic failure is now experienced around the twinship need. This reaction may occur alongside other selfobject functions, and in fact mirroring and twinship needs frequently occur simultaneously. As an example, a patient becomes anxious when he or she feels that the analyst no longer exists as an alter ego who is exactly like the patient. If the analyst or therapist is now perceived to have an independent existence beyond the patient's selfobject need for an exact replica, this perception may provoke a fear of loss and feelings of disconnectedness or isolation.

Part II
Selfobject Functions:
Psychodiagnostic Indications

4 Content Analysis of Psychodiagnostic Testing: A Pathway to Understanding Self States

In previous chapters, I presented the general principles of psychoanalytic self psychology. Here I propose a framework for conceptualizing these phenomena by using psychodiagnostic tests. I describe the links that bridge key concepts of self psychology with psychological testing findings, in the hope of specifying how self psychological concepts, particularly selfobject functions, can be evaluated in the test material. It is my intention to emphasize a way of viewing the material generated by a battery of projective psychological tests. Thus, unfolding content, associations, fantasy productions, and manner of engagement with the examiner may produce a systematic way of understanding this material from the viewpoint of self psychology. Although I stress conceptual guidelines to the interpretation of test content derived from Kohut's ideas, neither specific criteria nor formal test scores or indices should be expected to emerge from this attempt.

Empirically derived formal scores, algorithms, or combinations of scores producing decision strategies may eventually be derived; a score-based interpretive strategy necessarily lags behind a precise articulation of the theoretical foundation of Kohut's crucial concepts. The general approaches to interpreting psychological testing that I present are those described by Rapaport, Gill, and Schafer (1945, 1968), Schachtel (1966), Allison, Blatt, and Zimet (1968), and Lerner and Lerner (H. D. Lerner & P. M. Lerner, 1988; P. M. Lerner, 1991).

I do not attempt to restore a former tradition or to argue for one conceptual approach over another. Rather, my intent is to provide a theoretical structure that makes use of a content-derived interpretive strategy for examining and understanding self disorders. I begin by reconsidering indications for diagnostic testing in light of contemporary theoretical formulations of clinical psychopathology. I then review several customary approaches to the clinical interpretation of psychodiagnostic testing, including those of the Menninger school and the clinical contributions of Ernest Schachtel to Rorschach psychology, the Lerners, and Exner's (1991, 1993) Comprehensive System for the Rorschach test. I also include the contributions of Aronow, Reznikoff, and Moreland (1994) to content analysis as well as important interpretive approaches to the TAT and figure drawings.

One major section of this chapter concentrates on the inferential strategies of psychodiagnostic testing or assessment of personality. The focus is on broad principles of inferential thinking rather than on differences in conceptual frameworks. I discuss the integration of findings across tests in a battery and devote special emphasis to synthesizing test findings pertinent to differentiating conflict from deficit states as these were described in chapters 1 and 2. After establishing this basic foundation, I then state the case for incorporating a self psychological approach into the armamentarium when using psychological tests to understand self-esteem regulation, self states or self disorders, and selfobject functions.

DEVELOPMENTS IN PSYCHODIAGNOSTIC TESTING

My approach to the clinical examples in Part II has been influenced by the contributions of Roy Schafer (1954, 1967). Written more than 40 years ago, Schafer's work, building on the pioneering efforts of David Rapaport at the Menninger Clinic, has been a major influence on clinical thinking about diagnostic testing. My proposed conceptual formulations differ in several respects from the theoretical propositions of Schafer and his colleagues, but the inferential approach that they refined serves as my model. Largely in respect to their tradition, I use the terms *psychodiagnostic* and *psychological testing* throughout, instead of the more current terms *psychological assessment* or *personality assessment*. My usage not only acknowledges a tradition no longer so prevalent in clinical writing and practice, but it also differentiates my content-based approach from empirical approaches to studying personality.

As in many fields, not only in psychology but also throughout science and applied technology, practitioners of psychodiagnostic testing have become increasingly concerned with reliability and validity of measurement. More and more attention has been paid to sophisticated statistical and psychometric methods necessary to establish the empirical basis for psychological tests of personality. Few can fault this development. Admittedly, advances sometimes have a price, in this case, a diminishing appreciation of the content behind the verbalizations, the very factor that makes the familiar projective tests truly *projective* in the first place.

One reason for the revival of interest in the Rorschach test is that it is scorable, and it has been subject to the renewed scrutiny that contemporary psychometric theory and methods can offer and in fact demand. Other instruments with a strong empirical foundation, such as the Minnesota Multiphasic Personality Inventory (MMPI-2) and the Millon inventories, have attracted attention for the same reason. Consequently, tests like the TAT, figure drawings, and Sentence Completion Test, which never benefited from well-studied empirical foundations, have been relatively neglected, perhaps because the scoring basis for these instruments has been too inconstant. Their use has declined somewhat, and there has been some disinclination to examine their potential utility.

The relatively diminished interest in the TAT and related projective tests contrasts with the resurgence of interest in empirical Rorschach scores and indexes since the introduction of the Comprehensive System (Exner, 1993). Furthermore, young clinicians are unfamiliar with many projective measures, which are no longer widely or routinely taught in clinical psychology programs. The same is true for content and sequence analysis on the Rorschach test, despite Lerner (1991) and the recent publication of a second edition of one of the few volumes on the subject (Aronow et al., 1994).

Bellak's volume on the TAT survives and has undergone numerous revisions (Bellak & Abrams, 1997), and Handler's (1996) review of figure drawings methods has been a valuable contribution. Other books chronicling tests such as the TAT and projective drawings (Goodenough, 1926; Harrower, 1965; Holt, 1978; Machover, 1949), although considered classics by many, are nevertheless either out of print or difficult to obtain. Some of these rest in dusty libraries rather than on the shelves of working clinicians. Arguably, this fate may be well deserved.

In addition to these problems, several major test instruments have undergone revisions, such as the Wechsler Adult Intelligence Scale (WAIS), which has been revised three times after the Wechsler–Bellevue scale in use in the 1940s and early 1950s and studied by Rapaport and Schafer. The MMPI-2 and Millon Clinical Multiaxial Inventory (MCMI-III) are the current versions of these instruments, both of which represent revisions in the past decade.

Certainly, the Comprehensive System for the Rorschach is substantially different from the Menninger scoring and administration procedures. Rapaport had wide-ranging interests in the psychoanalytic implications of cognitive and perceptual functions. He was particularly interested in reconciling ego psychological views of higher mental processes with the findings from experimental psychology laboratories. This interest disposed him to view memory as a particularly important psychological process and influenced his decision that the Rorschach inquiry should be conducted after each card during the association phase, to minimize potential distortions arising from memory factors between the two stages of the Rorschach administration.

The enhanced psychometric advances that invariably come with test revisions have included improved normative reference groups and careful attention to contemporary statistical analytic procedures. These interests have outpaced attention to the in-depth understanding of test instruments for interpreting psychological phenomena such as conflict, defense, and self-esteem. One can be more confident of the MCMI-based or Comprehensive System-based decision rules for the diagnosis (using current nomenclature and criteria such as that of *DSM-IV*) of various psychiatric disorders than of the pre-*Diagnostic and Statistical Manual of Mental Disorders* (*DSM-I*)-influenced diagnostic views available to Rapaport and his colleagues. It is by no means clear, however, that the understanding of the use of these instruments for assessing ego functions, conflict–defense configurations, quality and nature of object relations, and self-esteem regulation is thorough or of sufficient depth.

The issue remains a matter of emphasis, which for Rapaport et al. (1945, 1968), rested on the overarching rationale of the projective hypothesis:

> [E]very reaction of a subject is a reflection, or projection, of his private world. This approach to testing contrasts sharply with that usually characterized as "psychometric." The main aim was not to attribute to a person a percentile rank in the population or any other numerical measure allegedly representative of him. The aim was rather to understand him: to give him a chance to express himself in a sufficient number and variety of controlled situations, the nature of which has been well enough explored to enable the psychologist to infer, out of the subject's reactions, the gross outlines of his personality make-up. (Rapaport et al., 1968, p. 52)

Psychometric enhancements clearly are crucial, as are the more sophisticated statistical methods of measurement diagnostics, such as sensitivity, specificity, and power. As Rapaport's quotation indicates, however, even newer methods of measurement do not settle the issue decisively. The scientific basis of psychodiagnostics requires, as it should, careful attention to sophisticated psychometric properties of the test instruments. Nevertheless, there remains a lag in understanding the meaning of the content of well-constructed tests with reliable scores. This lag may have contributed to a neglect of the very psychological principles that the Menninger group developed to such a high clinical standard. Although it is a mistake to dismiss this approach as simply an art form, those in the field of personality assessment are probably best advised to pay attention to re-examining the art to try to do it justice as a science, insofar as the concepts and limits of understanding permit.

THE CHANGING LANDSCAPE
OF PSYCHOLOGICAL TESTING

Clinical Indications for Assessment

Therapists have generally recognized the clinical interview as the chief method for understanding a patient's symptom picture and adaptational problems. The interview or anamnesis remains the primary reference point for gathering clinical information to understand specific recent or acute events (precipitants) superimposed on habitual patterns of reacting to life events and relating to others (clinical history). Several comprehensive, in-depth diagnostic interviews are usually necessary to conceptualize a person's problem and to devise a treatment approach.

Psychological testing is generally not indicated for this purpose if a referring clinician is well trained, informed, and accustomed to disciplined clinical thinking. The routine use of psychological tests is usually atypical, except possibly for children and adolescent patients. The standard has generally been, and will probably continue to be ever more so, one of requesting psychological tests for consultative purposes when clinical interviews are inconclusive or when differential diagnostic questions remain unresolved. This situation includes the majority of symptom-focused or behavioral disorder complaints requiring either acute treatment or emergency intervention as well as chronic, characterologically based personality features or syndromes that affect treatment outcome.

Sound clinical indications for psychological testing consultation include the need to distinguish psychotic symptoms of patients with affective or cognitive disturbances, to determine the predominant features of those with mixed depressive–manic–anxiety syndromes, and to augment a complete diagnostic study of treatment-refractory patients. Diagnostic testing can sometimes be informative, even under suboptimal conditions, for patients who are uncooperative or noncompliant, including those with acute psychosis and confusional states, and for patients with alcoholism, substance abuse, and related toxicities that preclude a reliable diagnostic interview.

I have chosen to emphasize the use of psychological testing in the context of the best-informed contemporary understanding of nosologic and descriptive symptom–syndrome clinical presentations. It is easy, however, to think of other examples of acute treatment or forensic intervention decisions such as removing a child from a home, involuntary hospitalization, or documenting a conservatorship need. Furthermore, identifying the nature and pattern of disturbances of higher cortical processes in distinguishing between psychiatric and neurological illnesses has recently come to occupy a central place in psychodiagnostic testing. The use of personality tests may be valuable when the psychiatric aspects must be examined as comprehensively as are the neuropsychological components. The assessment of personality and psychopathology is indicated when the psychiatric component is a prominent part of a neurological condition, particularly when the premorbid personality is important to consider, as in cases of traumatic head injury.

Another category of diagnostic testing consultations that does not necessarily occur in a specific diagnostic or clinical disposition context is that of evaluating chronic maladaptive difficulties in living, for which people occasionally refer themselves for long-term intensive psychotherapy or psychoanalysis. This psychodiagnostic testing consultation presents some of the best opportunities for capitalizing on the greatest strengths of tests, particularly the projective instruments. Few clinicians with sufficient training and experience to perform this type of in-depth analysis of personality dynamics of characterologic conditions may now be available. Notwithstanding this possibility, many people with characterologic states and Axis II personality disorders continue to seek treatment.

Some of these patients can also be treated to good advantage with knowledgeably applied pharmacotherapy. For many, pharmacotherapy is an adjunctive rather than a first-line treatment strategy. For some, behavioral methods may not have offered sufficient symptomatic amelioration.

For these people, it may be important to use projective tests to carefully evaluate subtle but stubborn features that can complicate treatment and are not otherwise readily detected, regardless of the eventual treatment of choice. These features include both Axis I disorders and the comorbidities between Axis I and Axis II conditions. Much of the improved understanding of the biological and genetic relations among such disorders has come about through the efficacy of pharmacotherapy.

Major advances in nosology and biological psychiatry have had little bearing on developments in psychological testing. These advances neither spelled the decline of testing and assessment nor suggested a widening schism in the uneasy interface between psychology and psychiatry. The considerable advances in the knowledge of the nature of psychiatric disorders and their somatic treatments have, however, helped to target areas for psychological testing. Answers to diagnostic questions are now more feasible with the awareness of and sensitivity to contemporary diagnostic criteria and symptom complexes. The Comprehensive System, the MMPI-2, and the MCMI-III have benefited from this refined diagnostic nosology.

At the same time, the failure to keep pace with sophisticated developments in the fields of both biological psychiatry and psychometric test development has worked to the disadvantage of instruments such as the TAT and figure drawings, which are useful for identifying character pathology. Clinicians have always understood that personality and characterologic features persist, whether they are secondary to or independent of pharmacologically targeted syndromes. These personality characteristics can be better understood, if not actually better treated, once complete and enduring remission of the Axis I syndromes is achieved.

As mentioned earlier, chronic personality disturbances may also influence the clinical outcome of Axis I disorders. These personality features are sometimes present as distinct personality disorder syndromes or as premorbid ingrained personality deficiencies. In the latter case, such personality defects may be subsyndromal but are nevertheless usually persistent and contributory to the clinical picture. When the waters are muddied as they often are with acute syndromal features and contributing or aggravating personality features hopelessly entangled, it is extremely difficult for a treating clinician to understand the role of characterologic factors in the total clinical picture.

Although it was once hoped that psychological testing would help to unravel these complexities, there has always been a limit to understanding the meanings of test scores and findings, just as there are limits to construing sometimes confusing and discrepant clinical interview findings. Testing may help unravel inconsistencies and subtle influences but can also add to the confusion. As clinical sophistication expands, powerful, targeted treatments of demonstrated efficacy achieve their therapeutic benefit more rapidly than was once the case, and clinical indications for psychodiagnostic testing under the worst "battle conditions" diminish. Psychological testing can achieve its most beneficial result when tests are not taxed beyond their diagnostic capabilities. Thus one need not expect tests to solve problems for which empirical evidence has often been dubious, particularly the TAT and figure drawings. Some psychologists such as Schafer, Schachtel, Lerner, Holt, and Harrower, have always believed that the greatest usefulness of psychological tests lies in their descriptions of the depths of human experience and the specification of the dynamics of conflict, deficit, psychological structure, defenses, and object relations.

THE EXPANDED VIEW OF SELF DISORDERS AND PSYCHODIAGNOSTIC ASSESSMENT

Some patients with acute Axis I conditions also have subclinical but still maladaptive personality disorders that aggravate the Axis I disorder. Such patients include those with disturbances of self-esteem regulation that may or may not be recognized as contributing factors to the overall clinical picture. As for other personality disturbances, disruptions of self-esteem or prominent selfobject failure are important precipitants for some Axis I illnesses, including mood disorders, addictions, and sexual perversions. Therefore, the identification of self disorders is often important.

Some self disorders can exist independently, of course, as the primary condition, that is, as an Axis II disorder. Self disorders can also underlie or precipitate many conditions not usually considered to be narcissistic disorders or related disturbances of self-esteem regulation. These conditions may be secondary to an acute Axis I disorder, such as psychotic episodes, severe episodes of affective illnesses (including manic and hypomanic disorders), anxiety syndromes, and subsyndromal conditions such as dysthymia, with or without a history of comorbid major depression (so-called double depression) or mania (Akiskal, 1980).

Such self state disturbances often require special diagnostic challenges to detect them. Careful interviewing with an eye to the clinical problem frequently helps to identify an underlying self disorder, but psychodiagnostic testing is sometimes needed to elicit the self state disturbance. Difficulty in diagnosis can arise because the primary treating clinician does not recognize the nature of the pathology or because the acute illness is prominent or urgent enough to disguise a comorbid self disorder.

Indeed, the main purpose of this book is to specify the theoretical links between the principal concepts of self psychology and their corresponding psychological test indications. To provide a coherent conceptual approach for bridging these two areas, I make inferences informed by self psychology about test indicators and content. This task is the entire focus of Part II.

The clinical inferential process to be discussed here should *not* be construed as an effort to describe narcissism or narcissistic personality disorder. In light of the evolution of psychoanalytic self psychology that I described in detail in chapters 1, 2, and 3, the view of the self examined here is derived from a major reformulation of several principles of classical psychoanalytic theory. I have reconceptualized some psychoanalytic concepts as secondary to repairing or preserving self-esteem and self-cohesion, such as the drives and the oedipal conflict. This reconceptualization is the broadened psychoanalytic psychology of the self; it is not a theory of narcissistic pathology.

In chapter 1, I have already discussed at length how self psychology has advanced beyond a clinical theory of narcissistic personality disorders. These conceptual viewpoints influence the interpretation of projective test findings in ways departing in content, although not in spirit, from those generated by Schafer (1954), Schachtel (1966), and P. M. Lerner (1991). I approach the psychology of the self not as an *expanded* version of drive theory or of narcissism, but as an appreciably *modified* version of psychoanalytic theory. The psychodiagnostic testing examples and vignettes in chapters 5 and 6 illustrate that responses usually conceptualized from drive theory and ego psychological perspectives can be understood in the alternative psychodynamic framework of self psychology.

CONCEPTUAL APPROACHES
TO PSYCHODIAGNOSTIC TESTING:
GENERAL PRINCIPLES

Psychological assessment of mental functions has a history over 100 years old. Major early achievements were the instruments measuring intelligence, notably the Binet and Wechsler scales. The development of tests for the measurement of personality followed not long thereafter. At that period, testing centered on identifying traits or temperaments as dimensions of normal personality, including aberrant forms of these personality features. Symptomatic illnesses such as obsessions or compulsions, psychotic disorders, and mood disorders received attention later.

Still later, the asymptomatic character neuroses became a subject for study by using projective tests, primarily under the influence of psychoanalytic theory. The framework for using psychological tests was influenced by the conceptual anchor of Freud's (1926/1959) second theory of anxiety, which crystallized in his structural theory and the evolving ego psychology that followed. In other theoretical frameworks, such as social learning theory, the interest in psychological tests to examine conflict–defense configurations was generally minimized in favor of identifying trait or state personality characteristics more than psychodynamic mechanisms.

During this period, David Rapaport wrote extensively about psychoanalytic metapsychology. He gave considerable attention to the theoretical rationale and clinical interpretive importance of projective tests of personality. Rapaport was also interested in nonprojective tests of cognitive functions as well, particularly their significance for evaluating the apparatuses of ego autonomy or conflict-free ego spheres. Hermann Rorschach's (1921/1981) inkblot technique was known to Rapaport, as was the monograph outlining Rorschach's preliminary but still tentative formulations about personality. Together with Henry Murray's (1938, 1943) Thematic Apperception Test, these instruments formed the basis for the first systematic investigation of psychological tests for in-depth personality analysis, tests informed by psychoanalytic theory at that point in time (Rapaport, Gill, & Schafer, 1945, 1968).

Rapaport and his colleagues studied these projective tests together with several other instruments, some nonprojective in nature, like the Babcock-Levy Story Recall Test, Wechsler-Bellevue scale, and Hanfman and Kasanin's Object Sorting Test. Rapaport et al. (1945, 1968) developed an interpretive framework to use these instruments for the diagnosis of specific pathologies. Equally important, they described how to use these techniques to identify predominant conflicts, defense operations, and levels of adaptation. Although Rapaport was perhaps best known and respected as a brilliant psychoanalytic theoretician, it was principally Roy Schafer (1948, 1954, 1967) who developed the clinical utilization of the Rorschach and TAT to its fullest. Important contributions by Mayman (1967, 1970), Schachtel (1966), and Holt (1978), were notable additions to this early work.

A distinguished contributor to psychoanalytic theory in recent years, Schafer's early contributions in the area of diagnostic psychological testing articulated the major principles of projective test interpretation identified with the Menninger tradition. Other schools of thought have also influenced diagnostic psychological testing, notably those based on preoedipal disturbances of object relations. Kwawer, Lerner, Lerner, and Sugarman (1980) have applied this viewpoint to psychodiagnostic testing in the past 2 decades. Exner's (1993) Comprehensive System represents the most systematic and empirically sound overhaul of scoring necessary for reliable and valid interpretation of Rorschach signs and indicators.

The interpretive approach of Rapaport, Schafer, and their colleagues has had a continuing and far-reaching influence even beyond its applications to ego psychology. The Rapaport–Schafer system influenced object relations–based approaches to projective testing as well as some aspects of the Comprehensive System. It is this specific tradition that I emphasize in the following description of strategies for interpreting psychodiagnostic tests, as enhanced by contributions from Schachtel (1966) and P. M. Lerner (1991). Although this selective emphasis does not ignore different approaches, it emphasizes the Rapaport–Schafer approach to the clinical interpretation of content. This approach serves as the basis for incorporating Kohut's self psychology with the psychoanalytic concepts influencing diagnostic psychological testing.

One focal point of the Menninger method is the use of a battery of tests; this method eschews relying on one or two tests as the basis for deriving the principal findings. Rapaport considered several reasons for this decision, including the view that all tests are subject to error. Thus, relying too strongly on one or two instruments maximizes the possibility that error variance from fluctuating mental states and uncontrolled influences of premorbid or attitudinal factors contributes to atypical or confounded clinical findings. This consideration is partially psychometric and affects both reliability of measurement and validity. Another reason for Rapaport's preference for the test battery approach is that psychopathology is selective in its effects on psychological functioning. Thus, in view of the operation of conflict-free ego spheres and the differential sensitivity of various projective tests to particular areas of personality functioning, multiple tests are necessary to minimize diagnostic error resulting from false negatives.

CONCEPTUAL APPROACHES
TO PSYCHODIAGNOSTIC TESTING:
SPECIFIC PRINCIPLES

Regardless of whether content, supplementary verbalizations, or examiner–patient interactions are emphasized in a diagnostic study, all approaches to test interpretation and analysis begin with consideration of formal test scores. The customary approach starts with the summary of principal scores, indexes, or percentages based on test protocols like the Rorschach structural summary, WAIS-III subtest profile or index score patterns, MMPI-2 clinical scale profiles or two-point configurations, or some other psychometric pattern. Certain measures are isolated for special consideration, such as particularly revealing Rorschach responses or unusual dimensions of the response. For example, responses in which statistically infrequent determinants, such as vista or texture, occur might be singled out for particular attention. Inferences are made on the basis of patterns that conform to empirically derived interpretive conclusions. Varying levels of importance are attached to interpretive decisions that can sometimes be considered hierarchically.

For example, a greater importance is attached to a positive Comprehensive System Schizophrenia Index than to any of the findings contributing to the index, such as thought disorder variables or $X\text{-}\%>Xu\%$. Thus, analysis of empirically supported global indexes, ratios, or specific scores provides the anchor for hierarchical clinical interpretation. Consideration of the components of the major indexes (second-order indexes or scores) generates other psychopathology variables that may be important to add to the total clinical picture. A level of analysis using only the Schizophrenia Index on the Rorschach or relying exclusively on an elevated 6–8 MMPI-2 configuration to consider the applicability of a schizophrenia diagnosis does not usually contain sufficient information to determine clinical phenomenology, such as paranoid, schizoid or withdrawn, positive or negative syndrome type, or chronic versus acute course.

Few psychodiagnosticians disagree with such an approach. Its crucial value is as a starting point in the clinical workup. The nature and subsequent levels of analysis are the basis of the controversies in the field about how far and on which forms of evidence should deeper investigation proceed. How far to probe and what data to use depend on the theoretical frameworks of various diagnostic testing specialists.

Deeper levels of analysis of psychological test material may include content, sequence analysis of responses, and test behavior and verbalizations. These areas of inquiry are typically not anchored in an empirically based foundation beyond theoretical conviction or accumulated clinical wisdom or experience. Consequently, such inferential strategies as content analysis are speculative. They require caution and judicious application to prevent reaching conclusions that may be "fascinating, deep and brilliantly explanatory, but they may have little or nothing to do with the specific patient" (Schafer, 1954, p. 141).

Psychological testing is not unlike the clinical thinking that informs most areas of insight psychotherapy, yet it rarely has the benefit of the self-corrective steps that psychotherapists can accumulate from experience with patients that is built up over time. Every clinician's theoretical persuasion dictates the level of depth of analysis that is relevant to conceptualizing personality. Some clinicians do not consider findings that are not empirically well grounded. Others regard constructs like object relations, defenses, central conflicts, self-cohesion, or adaptational resiliences as clinically important and most likely prefer to understand projective test indicators of these depth psychological characteristics. They also attempt to make peace with the fact that they are delving into uncharted territory with test findings that are less firmly grounded than are the higher order variables that the examiner started with. However, while stepping with care, and if so disposed, this need not be like walking in quicksand.

ROY SCHAFER: THE MENNINGER TRADITION

Schafer's comments on clinical evidence for interpretation are just as important today as over 40 years ago when he first wrote on the subject. The reason for its importance is different, however: The psychometric sophistication that is now de rigueur barely existed in the 1940s. Then, content analysis was considered crucial to interpretation because empirical scores were thought to be insufficient by themselves. Although understanding content was necessary for Rapaport and Schafer, it is possible today to dispense with this approach entirely, just as students learned basic arithmetic calculations before calculators became available. Understanding what content analysis may offer is analogous to understanding the fundamental concepts of numerical operations as compared to pushing buttons on a calculator.

Holt, in his 1968 revision of *Diagnostic Psychological Testing* (Rapaport et al., 1945, 1968), commented frankly on the psychometric criticisms of the original work, criticisms so stinging that they overpowered many of the work's rich clinical insights. In 1945 (and even in 1968), rigorous approaches to item analysis, power, diagnostic efficiency statistics (such as sensitivity and specificity), and multivariate designs were not understood very well. The issue of the day was determining the optimal balance between using test scores and content analysis to arrive at a conceptually disciplined but in-depth clinical analysis of personality. The method eschewed surface trait-like characteristics in favor of plumbing every response to its very depths, in search of sound inferences that were theoretically coherent, internally consistent, and rich in meaning.

The issue that prompted Schafer to consider criteria for inferential thinking was the way to determine an appropriate degree of depth that was logically and clinically supportable from psychological tests. Interpretation corresponded to the predominant psychoanalytic nosology of the time, preceding even *DSM-I*. Thus, the conflict neuroses, such as hysteria and obsessive-compulsive neurosis, were characteristically emphasized. Contemporary clinicians familiar with post-ego psychological psychoanalytic theory and the substantially reformulated post-*DSM-II* nomenclature would recognize few of the classifications highlighted by Rapaport and Schafer in the same way that the Menninger group understood them.

Consequently, depth of interpretation meant something different before the influences of *DSM-III* and its revisions. Clinicians nowadays need not be overly concerned about what may seem like an archaic terminology to them. They should be concerned, however, with the main reason that criteria for depth of interpretation were important in the first place; at the time that Schafer proposed these criteria, just as now, psychometric approaches went only so far.

As a result, thematic analysis was necessary to reach the level of sophisticated understanding sought by Rapaport and Schafer. In contrast, contemporary psychometric advances make it possible to rely on empirical scores for clinical test interpretation, supported by a sophisticated reliability and validity literature. Particularly among nonpsychoanalytic clinicians, there are a growing number of diagnostic testing specialists who subscribe to the view that psychometrically based findings are sufficient, and that content analysis has too little empirical support to be clinically valid.

The issue is not resolved and is partly a matter of clinical temperament. Apart from the question of whether content analysis is a valid or credible method for understanding projective test findings, the issue can benefit from rethinking to optimize the contributions of psychometric advances while remaining embedded in psychoanalytic theory. For many clinicians favorably disposed to psychodynamic formulations, Schafer's concern about the proper approach to interpretive criteria cannot, therefore, be dismissed as misplaced or outdated. Instead, his criteria can be applied regardless of the psychoanalytic views that have influenced psychodiagnostic testing, whether these be ego psychology, object relations, self psychology, the French school of Lacan (1978), interpersonal approaches (Greenberg & Mitchell, 1983), or intersubjectivist schools that include offshoots of self psychology (Stolorow, Brandchaft, & Atwood, 1987).

Schafer (1954) asked: "How are we to decide whether our explorations have led us home or astray, whether we have glittering gold in hand or just glitter: And how are we to distinguish between thoroughness and recklessness?" (p. 141). He offered a solution in the form of criteria for judging the adequacy of interpretations. These criteria provide a useful basis for the analysis of content and the observation of patients' test behavior and associated verbalizations. They are best thought of as reasonable guides for arriving at diagnostic decisions rather than definitive, empirically grounded rules. Schafer's criteria, therefore, offer discipline to the investigation of projective test findings based on content analysis. Written well over 40 years ago, his work provides a cogent, compelling statement of a systematic, logical strategy for approaching these potentially murky areas of subjective analysis. These criteria also serve as an excellent foundation for conceptualizing self psychological concepts through psychodiagnostic tests.

Sufficient Evidence

Foremost among the criteria for judging the adequacy of clinical interpretation is the issue of sufficient evidence to substantiate an inference. This criterion is usually satisfied by considering converging lines of evidence, sometimes based on several recurrences of a particular theme, but at other times derived from associations to particular test responses. These responses characteristically serve to clarify or fine-tune the specific connotation underlying a motivation or drive state. Schafer (1954) wrote that "patients usually help us out by giving not one but a number of images, score patterns and attitude expressions that confirm, modify, offset or de-emphasize the interpretive leads provided by one response" (p. 141).

To extend Schafer's metaphor of "not flying blind" (p. 146), the strategy resembles navigating an airplane; the pilot steers the plane by consulting instrument panels, his co-pilot, and his navigator, who in turn rely on data and feedback from a control tower or other devices. More to the point, the strategy resembles a patient in psychotherapy responding to an interpretation by recalling a memory, having a dream, or producing an association that further amplifies or corrects the interpretation to steer it in a more precise direction.

How does this criterion appear specifically when performing diagnostic testing? An image or verbalization, presented in a nonspecific manner, may strike a hypothesis-generating chord in an examiner's associative process but still not yield a decisively formed interpretation. (What I referred to as striking a chord is the psychodiagnostic testing equivalent of empathic understanding in treatment, as Kohut would probably have noted.) A response may be unusual in the sense of being statistically infrequent, or it may be unusual in the sense of being suggestive of something more than it appears. It may also be unusual in the way that the response is perceived or described, regardless of whether it is familiar or idiosyncratic.

For example, on Rorschach Card I, a patient might report the familiar and popular bat or an airplane, a rare but not necessarily odd, idiosyncratic, or striking image by itself. Alternatively, the patient might report a tree in the same area, an infrequent response although it still falls in a range of normal tolerance. The patient might also note that the bat is falling, faltering, or injured, the airplane is heading for a fall, or the tree's leaves are falling. Fortunately, most scoring systems capture the irregularity of the elaboration of these percepts, and the irregularity appears as a distinctive pattern or elevation of scores of special concern. A number of such irregularities rather than one response in isolation are necessary for the formal scores to accurately reflect appreciable departure from normative values. Alternatively, the distinctive anomaly flags the response for the examiner's attention, such as an $M-$ code, a moderately notable or serious special score, a color-shading blend, or a determinant of special significance combined with an FQu or $FQ-$ form quality rating.

Precision of formal scores is well and good as far as it goes, but it probably does not go far enough to fully capture the dynamic significance of percepts like a falling airplane, a tree with its leaves falling, or an injured bat. The diffuse quality of some anomaly (such as a special score of *morbid*) might be detected for several of these responses, but the phenomenologic significance of responses such as these could be overlooked or minimized as idiosyncratic. How responses are noted, recorded, or captured in the form of a score or code, or by inferring some meaning in addition to a formal score, is an issue directly related to Schafer's criterion of the nature of the evidence.

The critical test centers on how distinctive or psychologically evocative a particular response appears, in terms of statistical frequency of occurrence or unusualness, to substantiate an inference of deterioration or diminished vitality. The persistence of the theme in other responses or tests needs to be considered as well. Thus, other percepts of trees without leaves, a similar manifestation of trees in an unhealthy state, or percepts of other images with similar evocative meaning can be examined to determine whether these, too, provide evidence consistent with the working hypothesis. This approach also extends to higher order interpretive inferences such as concern about intactness or experiencing oneself as firmed up and securely anchored.

It can be difficult to determine the precise meaning of the evocative qualities in the way that a patient voices a projective test response or in the nuances of a response. For example, Schafer (1954) described the different shades of interpreting aggressive imagery ranging from explosive to hostile, or engulfing to piercing. He alerted examiners to the caution required when judging the affective connotations provoked by such adjectives. He also called attention to the importance of remaining alert to shifts in intensity of affects both in and across stimulus cards. This type of variability can be a potentially rich source for revealing subtle vulnerabilities undermining the adequacy of defenses, for example.

Another example of a problem in making interpretive inferences concerns genetic reconstructions based on test responses. This type of inference is even more speculative and uncertain than is estimating the intensity of an affect state such as the difference between an angry and a vicious animal percept. With a genetic reconstruction, great caution is needed. An examiner should be circumspect before extrapolating from a response such as a towering monster figure to a statement about the patient's perception of the father. This line of speculation is not necessarily incorrect and should not be dismissed entirely, however. It should be considered, albeit at a lower degree of certainty or confidence relative to other lines of evidence.

Schafer (1954) allowed for another type of genetic reconstruction about which clinicians can be potentially more assured. This type concerns specifying the character pathology derived from a conceptual understanding of regression to a particular level of psychological development.

If there is evidence indicating that the personality structure is predominantly paranoid or compulsive, for example, an examiner can presume or infer the kinds of defenses and conflicts to be expected. This approach can enable an understanding of the resulting central conflict as well as the type and maturity (that is, developmental level) of defenses. It also permits a reconstruction of the family constellation and the way that this sets in motion the conflicts associated with particular stages of development.

Although it sounds like a fairly straightforward formulation specific to classical drive or ego psychological theory, this form of genetic reconstruction can easily be extended to other theoretical systems, such as object relations theory or self psychology. It need not be limited to a conceptualization based on the classical developmental trajectory of psychosexual stages. In any case, Schafer (1954) regarded this level of genetic understanding as more reliable than that based on preconceived ideas about particular responses (such as the towering monster example) in relation to the family constellation and personality dynamics.

The process of listening to projective test responses requires examiners to keep the range of clinical inferences broad rather than narrow. To prevent a hypothesis-generation process from becoming prematurely closed off, preconceived ideas based on a theoretical framework should guide the workup but should not too quickly or narrowly foreclose the direction of inferential thinking. Nevertheless, early tentative hunches are not necessarily undisciplined. The clinical attitude is analogous to Freud's concept of evenly suspended attention (Freud, 1923/1961). Examiners listen to the material, entertain pertinent associations, and screen them for their clinical relevance. This process is one of empathic understanding as Kohut meant it to be. While letting the imagination roam over possible meanings, the examiner simultaneously operates at another level of ego functioning by informally attaching a marker of inferential certainty to the various possibilities under consideration.

Although making a different point, Goldberg (1990) posed a related question about how many hairs make a beard or how frayed must a fabric be to appear threadbare. His answer in both cases was when it is seen as such. Scores and ratios, like hair counts, help determine an interpretation, but disciplined impressions about content add something useful. Just as the perception of a beard is more than the sum of a number of facial hairs, projective test inferences are more than scores alone, but only when these inferences are logically and cautiously considered.

Holt (Rapaport et al., 1968) wrote about Rapaport's attempts to understand test responses empathically and analytically. This process was not unlike that of psychotherapeutic listening. In treatment, although clinicians often do not know the specific meaning of a verbalization, they have more opportunities for clarifying associations over time than does a diagnostic testing examiner. In projective testing, by contrast, opportunities for clarification may mean little more than the number of Rorschach responses or TAT stories remaining to evaluate. Thus, the therapeutic and diagnostic situations are not equivalent in this respect.

Some Rorschach images are symbolic in that universal meanings or compelling connotations can often be agreed on. Schafer (1954) considered symbolic referents to have an independent confirmatory basis, for which he relied on evidence obtained from dreams, parapraxes, free associations in psychoanalytic treatment, and certain types of symptoms to provide necessary confirmatory support. He regarded the symbolic references in thematic material from projective tests to be sufficiently persuasive to indicate that "we are not flying blind" (Schafer, 1954, p. 146), and his examples included imagery pertaining to churches, guns, madonna figures, devils, lambs, puppets, and the like.

Not flying blind does not mean that there is a one-to-one correspondence or absolute connection between imagery and meaning. The same idea extends to omitting mention of images with common symbolic connotations, such as the rifle on TAT Card 8BM. The problems associated with the mechanistic application of rules of symbol interpretation are well known. Especially with genetic reconstructions, inferences based on symbolic connotations must be conveyed with full recognition of the limitations of their credibility, unless there is good corroborating evidence. Otherwise, inferences of this type should be foregone entirely. As Schafer (1954) said: "The Rorschach record can neither support nor refute the interpretation. The interpretation in effect does no more than remind the therapist to whom the report is submitted what Freud, Fenichel et al. have said about overwhelming father-figures" (p. 144).

Dreams provide a good example of how to think about this problem. The usual ego psychological approach is to elicit associations to understand precipitants, rather than to build interpretations that rely heavily on the meanings of symbolic imagery. There is a difference between interpreting primary process content such as a dream about a menacing snake as a symbolic phallus and interpreting a broad psychodynamic pattern. For example, the snake might be interpreted as an indication that something dangerous or disturbing is being experienced, not necessarily as a symbol with phallic-sexual content. The same way of approaching dreams also occurs in self psychology. Thus, Kohut (1996) stated in a lecture:

I think that you probably have a reasonably good batting average in some very clearcut instances when the symptomatology is of chronic depression and the parental personalities are described in a way to indicate there was no responsiveness, or where there was the withdrawal of the father, a depressive mother, something on that order. If long periods of loneliness are already beginning to be described in the diagnostic interview, if there is dream material about abandonment, if there are lonely landscapes or snowy landscapes, that kind of thing—I mean there are certain things that make the diagnosis iron clad. (p. 121)

Kohut (1996) added:

Dreams of machines and of disturbed machinery are quite frequent, and they usually give you a pretty good idea that the patient is experiencing himself as not human, as not alive, but as a set of functions that are being disturbed. In that sense, the dream shows you something quite specific about particular propensities that he already had as a child, when he felt unsupported and unresponded to, and began to feel less than alive and less than human about himself. (p. 164)

In this framework, dreams as well as Rorschach responses can be viewed as indications of a general state of disequilibrium. Whether this state is represented by dysfunctional machinery, snowy landscapes, or wilting leaves on a Rorschach blot, the connotation is not that of a specific conflict or feature of the personality as much as of a disruption taking place. The disturbance is viewed in different ways according to various theories. As with dreams, examiners are of different temperaments about how specific an interpretation should be.

The test of sufficient evidence also implies that the most salient personality dynamics should appear broadly on projective tests. Genuine motivational states characteristically reappear across tests, although each test may show selective sensitivity to various psychodynamic features. For instance, defense–conflict mechanisms may be expected to emerge more clearly on the Rorschach, interpersonal dynamics and object relations may be more apparent on the TAT, and self-image or self-esteem can sometimes be ascertained from figure drawing procedures. Integrating these components or aspects of psychological patterns becomes an examiner's synthetic ego function. There is perhaps no better example of the faltering appreciation of the test battery than this very situation, and Schafer (1954) made the point: "Of course, other tests are indispensable in the search for secure interpretations that are at the same time specific and penetrating. Also, there are larger order convergences and complementary emphases to establish *among* tests" (p. 143).

It is frequently difficult to know whether Rorschach images such as injured animals or destroyed objects are intended to represent patients' experiences of themselves as damaged or of their hostile or malevolent impulses. A similar dilemma can occur with TAT or human figure drawing responses. The matter is not always clarified sufficiently, even with multiple percepts or responses of a similar nature. When there are many similar percepts, not that rare an event, an examiner has little recourse but to indicate what the psychological dynamic appears to be, although certain crucial aspects of the response may remain of uncertain clinical significance. This tactic is one way of indicating that certain forms of evidence are inconclusive or insufficient. A definitive result invariably requires a search for confirmatory evidence, usually across tests, in the psychodiagnostic protocol.

Depth of Interpretation and Manifest Content

The question of how deeply clinical inferences should extend is complex. Schafer regarded it as legitimate to understand a percept of a mouth as an indication of orality if the overall Rorschach protocol contained other frequent percepts of food, teeth, or devouring creatures. An example such as a mouth percept as an indication of orality is of limited value in isolation from a broader base of related confirmatory responses. Schafer added the important but frequently overlooked proviso that examiners must also consider major regulatory functions, such as intensity of the drive and the defensive operations associated with its expression or inhibition. The mere mention of a response, like the example of a mouth, is far less important than how it is seen (for instance, opened in anticipation of being fed, closed, or drooping).

Schafer also discussed different levels of confidence about clinical inferences. The Rorschach percept of a mouth is probably a relatively clear manifestation of oral wishes, at least from the standpoint of drive theory, but responses such as Santa Claus or hands raised in prayer may not be as compelling as indications of passivity or a receptive position. Although responses like these could be considered suggestive, Schafer still viewed them as nonspecific. Such responses are intermediate between a clearly direct indication suggested by the mouth of the previous example and other percepts that are even less specific. Examples of nonspecific inferences are interpreting oral-dependent wishes derived from responses such as waiting for something or resting while listening to music, in the absence of additional substantive elaboration. In such cases, Schafer advised caution about interpretations that reach too far.

He argued that examiners should state that a defense is operating and reserve inferences about the intensity or the underlying conflict only for clear indications of its presence, if only the defense is "seen," not the archaic impulse or drive. Schafer recommended a conservative approach to interpreting vague responses with weak or uncertain specification about underlying psychodynamic features. For example, commenting about constriction as a general defensive posture is preferable to denoting a specific defense operation, unless it is clearly indicated. Schafer's general point is that it is advisable to be conservative about depth of interpretations that might overextend their reach.

I have already noted Schafer's cautionary recommendation about avoiding too specific genetic reconstructions particularly when these are derived from fixed symbolic meanings. Most interpretations of this type are gratuitous and thus "arbitrary, presumptuous efforts to deepen interpretation *in spite of the patient*" (1954, p. 150). This caveat applies to projective tests such as the TAT, sentence completions, and figure drawings and to the Rorschach. I restate the point here because none of these other projective instruments has a clearly accepted formal scoring system with built-in safeguards and normative reference points like the Rorschach. Tests other than the Rorschach present even greater problems in generating interpretive findings on the basis of the depth or level of understanding of content-based material.

A formal scoring system with norm-based "protective" features still does not entirely eliminate the problem of depth of interpretation because overreliance on scores and ratios runs the risk of closing off examination of indications of greater depth. The problem of depth still arises, although in a different way when considering test scores such as those derived from the Rorschach. These scores are typically based on the formal aspects of responses, such as quality of thinking, perceptual accuracy, and organization.

For example, on Rorschach Card III, a patient might report two people circling each other, but omit the area conventionally representing the legs from the location. The scores reflect the inaccuracy of goodness of fit of the specific area indicated for a human percept, but the movement score does not capture the specific quality of circling each other as distinct from an activity such as looking at each other. It is also not considered to represent an activity meriting a separate code for aggressive movement, at least when stated this way.

Similarly, to a Sentence Completion Test stem "A mother ... ," a patient might respond "is sometimes there when you need her." A story might be given to TAT Card 1 in which the violin is misidentified as a guitar or on Card 8BM the story might ignore the rifle. The defensive aspect of these features might be considered for its interpretive value, but just as often the interpretation does not proceed beyond noting the perceptual inaccuracy. This case is no different from using only the formal scores on the Rorschach example and not assigning interpretive significance to the people circling one another.

The problem that Schafer described as depth or level of interpretation is no greater in the analysis of projective tests without formal scoring systems than of tests with reliable scoring systems. The crux of the issue concerns how to interpret responses such as people circling each other or a failure to incorporate the large figure of the rifle into a TAT story. A scoring system does not alleviate the problem by itself. Should circling each other, for example, be confined to the incongruity between this response and the failure to specify the leg area, or should it be taken to represent hostile or predatory impulses? Should the addition of the word "sometimes" in the Sentence Completion Test example cited be left uninterpreted, or should an inference be entertained about a complaint of maternal neglect or indifference?

Schafer's discussion of the depth or level of interpretation applied to just these situations. As with the criterion for adequate evidence, he favored the view that "the interpretation should not push below the level of defense" (1954, p. 150). Many of Schafer's clinical examples clearly indicated his willingness to attempt interpretations of drives or conflict when sufficient evidence appeared to substantiate that level of analysis. In this respect, the criteria of depth and adequacy of evidence are closely linked. The level of an interpretation is influenced by the sufficiency and quality of the evidence permitting an interpretation to extend beyond the level of defense analysis.

Schafer did not leave the issue here; his next criterion for judging the adequacy of an interpretation, the use of manifest content, continued from the point that defense analysis left off. I have combined the two criteria in this discussion because they are interrelated. When one identifies the conflict that underlies defenses, one deepens the level of the interpretation. The manifest content is now considered as a basis to speculate about its meaning. With appropriate cautions, Schafer argued that there are more than enough times when the evidence supports at least some *consideration* of an interpretation of the manifest content. He wrote: "There are in fact good reasons to support the inclusion of this criterion, particularly if we modify it so: *'Whenever possible,* the manifest form of the interpreted tendency should be specified'" (Schafer, 1954, p. 151).

Schafer acknowledged that it is generally easier to understand defensive and adaptive manifestations than drive manifestations (manifest content). Examiners can more easily attempt interpretations about drives or conflicts, however, when they consider the analysis of manifest content. To be sure, the argument is strengthened when formal scores, clinical validation by history, repetitive patterns of scores or responses, and a battery of tests can also be relied on to buttress an interpretation under consideration. Initially, it is preferable to consider interpretations that are based on content. The decision to proceed beyond the level of a defense interpretation depends on other evidence that either supports or renders uncertain a deeper level of clinical interpretation.

Intensity and Hierarchic Position of Specific Features in the Overall Personality Structure

In this section, I discuss Schafer's criterion about interpreting the intensity of personality dynamics such as conflicts and defenses. I combine this topic with his view that intensity should determine the relative importance of each dynamic in the total personality structure. Although distinct, these two points, intensity and hierarchic position, are so conceptually linked that it makes good sense to combine them for the purpose of discussing their individual importance as well as their interdependence.

Providing an indication of the intensity of a feature from the clinical protocol means denoting its strength or persistence in projective test response content. Therefore, to say that a patient has hostile wishes is not so remarkable by itself; no one is without hostile wishes. To single out this feature among other clinical characteristics, or to refer to a strongly evident or even overwhelming hostile wish, however, calls attention to a trait's special prominence in the overall personality structure. Personality is composed of trait-like characteristics, defenses, and conflicts, as well as degrees of self-cohesion or vulnerability to self-esteem failure. What is important is the relative balance of drives, the wishes opposing these drives, and the degree to which various defensive operations are deployed.

As for the criterion of intensity, Schafer emphasized that personality features should be specified in respect to their relative importance for a patient's central problem. For some people, defenses and their failure may be critical to overall psychopathology; for others, the pressing or salient problem may center on drive regulation, guilt, or self-cohesion. From the standpoint of psychoanalytic self psychology, clinicians should try, when possible, to specify the differential prominence of selfobject functions or transferences, such as mirroring, idealization, and twinship, in the management of self-esteem regulation. With regard to the question of how to specify intensity, Schafer acknowledged that quantitative delimiters such as marked, extreme, or strongly evident are not precise and convey no greater accuracy than do their counterparts based on the clinical interview (such as mild, moderate, and severe).

Schafer (1954) realized that the links between intensity or pervasiveness demand a thorough understanding of a cohesive body of personality theory. This level of theoretical conceptualization goes beyond grasping terms or concepts in isolation; it requires a clear understanding of the relations among concepts. Thus, he wrote: "The point is to avoid chain-like interpretation in which each trend is simply juxtaposed to other trends, and no hierarchy of importance, generality, stimulus and response, push and restraint is established" (Schafer, 1954, p. 154).

Schafer's reasoning presumed that the working theory in which the projective test findings are anchored provides a basis for hierarchical ordering of psychodynamic processes. He also stated a strong case for requiring understanding of the hierarchical possibilities inherent in certain aspects of psychoanalytic theory. This approach requires disciplined understanding of theory to avoid the "psychological nonsense" sometimes appearing in reports of psychological testing. For example, in structural theory, conflict precedes defenses, and failure of defenses leads to symptom formation. It makes no sense to speak of symptoms producing defenses or defenses producing conflicts. As Schafer (1954) noted, hierarchic integration should proceed from a systematic theoretical system that specifies hierarchical links or cause–effect relations "and not on ad hoc, test-centered and sign-centered improvising" (p. 157). Exner (1993) advocated a similar preference for following a systematic chain of dimensional links, the cluster strategy, which is based on key variables for interpreting Rorschach findings.

Finally, Schafer recognized that it is rare for any single test to produce an accurate hierarchical position and that examiners must use a test battery. Otherwise, the understanding of the workings of the personality as a whole becomes simplistic and is compromised. Schafer observed: "A battery of tests is invaluable in organizing hierarchic test pictures; on the basis of the Rorschach test alone one cannot do a thorough job in this respect" (Schafer, 1954, p. 154).

Specifying Adaptive and Pathological Tendencies

Schafer's (1954) thinking was influenced by the prevailing ego psychological viewpoint when he proposed his criteria for diagnostic testing evidence. Thus, it should come as little surprise that one of these criteria concerned the adaptive aspects of personality dimensions. Although symptomatic complaints reflect the relative success or failure of defenses for containing anxiety, personality traits (some of which may stem from ingrained characterologic formations) can nevertheless have adaptive aspects. Rigid reaction formation against hostility may dispose people to helpfulness or generosity toward others, or schizoid withdrawal may lead to an overdeveloped cultivation of people's artistic interests, despite the constricting or otherwise debilitating consequences of these defenses. Many people with chronic dysthymic disorders or characterological depressions (Akiskal, 1980) may be masochistically selfless, duty bound, and all too willing to sacrifice personal needs for the good of others. Although sometimes seen as the pillars of the community despite their profound sense of despair, self-depreciation, and guilt, such people characteristically confine their experiences of distress to quiet, selfless suffering.

Kohut (1971, 1977), in his contributions to self psychology, noted that well-developed transformations of normal narcissism lead to mature goals and ambitions as well as to expanded capacities for humor and wisdom. He also showed that some pathological manifestations of mirroring and idealization may have adaptive consequences, for example, the sense of loyalty and devotion to causes stemming primarily from an idealizing selfobject need. Similarly, many patients with a self disorder display an exquisite sensitivity to nuances of others' reactions or comments, a sensitivity arising from hyperalertness to the possibility of injury or of being slighted when mirroring selfobject functions are undermined. They may appear to have a heightened capacity for empathy, for sensitive understanding of others. (This use of the term *empathy* does not necessarily correspond to Kohut's use of the term in its technical sense.)

Adaptive aspects of projective test material are usually the last elements that students appreciate, and sometimes even seasoned practitioners need to be reminded of their possible presence. Adaptive aspects are among the least likely aspects of projective test analysis to be taught, and students readily overlook these characteristics in their often single-minded pursuit of pathological features. Not infrequently, in an effort to impress their teachers and supervisors with their capacities for probing the depths of human personality, students may miss adaptive signs, unless their own defenses interfere with appreciating true psychopathology.

Psychodiagnostic examinations are first and foremost a method for identifying psychopathology. Overt disturbance or aberrant personality emerges most clearly and forcefully and detecting this may sometimes overshadow an examiner's balanced attention to test indicators of adaptation. Although psychotherapists sometimes have difficulty recognizing adaptive or relatively healthy aspects of thinking or behavior, diagnosticians can have still more difficulty grasping these features because their contact with patients is usually limited. Despite efforts to minimize the tendency to view patients as specimens, the brief and pointed clinical contacts of examiners direct their attention to narrow and focused areas because of the nature of this clinical activity.

Schafer was most concerned about the topographic and structural points of view of psychoanalytic metapsychology, but he also considered Erikson's (1950) concept of ego identity to be one of promise for the psychodiagnostic assessment of adaptive characteristics. Schafer did not discuss diagnostic testing indicators in this area as thoroughly as he did his other criteria, perhaps because the Eriksonian view was still too new and not yet sufficiently understood. His main recommendation was to consider the opposing wishes of drives. Also relevant for recognizing the potential for adaptation were expressions of ambivalence, wishes and counterwishes, and alternating ego-dystonic or ego-syntonic aspects of the same basic instinctual urge.

Incorporating Erikson's contributions, Schafer wrote of alternating identity states, such as good or wished-for imagery coming forward or receding in prominence against bad or rejected aspects of a patient's sense of identity. Nevertheless, he still observed: "It is a major weak point in the interpretation of test results that we are often so much better at identifying pathological potentialities and weighing pathological trends than we are at identifying and weighing healthy, self-integrative 'normal' trends" (Schafer, 1954, p. 159). Over 40 years later, this statement is still true. Although Erikson's work was an early attempt to understand the self, his emphasis on identity formation arose from a different theoretical position than that of Kohut about 2 decades later. Although Kohut's ideas about maturational or adaptive aspects of personality do not clearly offer greater potential than does Erikson's understanding of identity, Kohut's theories offer another viewoint of healthy aspects of psychological life. Kohut's self psychology also enables diagnostic testing examiners to derive insights about self states and the self's strivings for vitality and cohesion through analysis of projective test imagery. Several clinical examples in the following chapters demonstrate these points, particularly the self psychologically informed reinterpretations (suggested in chaps. 5 and 6) of many of Schafer's clinical examples.

THEMATIC CONTENT ANALYSIS: OTHER VIEWS

Aronow, Reznikoff, and Moreland

Users of the Rorschach test have often emphasized quantitative scores. Indeed, most of the disputatious history of diagnostic psychological testing has centered on debates about the relative merits of particular measures or ways of computing scores. Diagnosticians have used the content of Rorschach responses far less as a primary basis for interpretation, although one hallmark of the Rapaport–Schafer tradition was its attempt to combine the scoring and content analysis methods. Nevertheless, there is a small literature on content analysis, some of which is thought provoking and sensible but largely unsubstantiated. A thorough familiarity with content analysis rarely extends beyond the experience or opinions of a diminishing number of senior clinicians.

Aside from the sometimes ad hominem history of scientific debate on the issue of quantitative and content analysis approaches, most psychodiagnostic clinicians consider both forms of evidence and favor one or the other because of temperament or the requirements of a given case. Clinicians have characteristically understood content as they understood interview material. As a result, clinical historical facts may sometimes be less crucial than are fantasy and related introspective material, such as dreams, early memories, associations about parents, and selective distorted recollections of childhood events and motivations of the people in patients' lives. This approach is similar to using projective content as a type of interview, much as Zubin, Eron, and Schumer (1965) recommended, although they were dismissive of the scientific credibility or merit in attempting to use projective tests in any other way.

The work of Aronow and Reznikoff (1983), and their revision (Aronow et al., 1994), represents a clearly presented, balanced view of how content analysis may augment clinical interpretation, although only for the Rorschach. Aronow et al. (1994) arrived at their principles for clinical interpretation, partially influenced by the approach of the Menninger school, in the spirit of combining content analysis and formal scoring. They described their work as a content-idiographic approach and stated their case as follows:

> We view it as a fundamental mistake to try to "regiment" this clinically sensitive procedure into some sort of inkblot version of an MMPI. Too much is lost in the process, and too little gained as a result. Psychological assessment of personality should include both nomothetic and idiographic—objective and projective—approaches in combination. This brings the unique strengths of each to bear. If one wants an objective test, there are many more suitable instruments available, with time demands on the psychologist far more modest. Why sacrifice the clinically sensitive and versatile Rorschach technique in such a quest? (p. 16)

Although the specific context for this statement is a discussion of their view of certain limitations of the Comprehensive System (Exner, 1993), the broad context is not obscured by singling out any particular system or scoring approach. The historical animosity sometimes generated by conceptual debates has no place in a clinical-scientific argument about guiding principles in clinical interpretation. Thus, Smith's (1992, p. 5) comment that "the Americans were frequently dismissed as obsessed with numbers and conceptually bankrupt" is best seen as overpersonalized.

Aronow et al. (1994) described three types or levels of inference, the first of which they designated as *informational*, consisting of declarative statements or remarks of a low level of inferential depth. More important, their second level of understanding thematic information is concerned with *symbolic associations* that are amenable to psychodynamic understanding, similar to Schafer's criteria for judging clinical indications of response content. Aronow et al. (1994) proposed a third type, *complex idiographic images*, resulting from specific probes for idiographic associations. This level is represented by questions designed to elicit how a patient feels about a Rorschach percept or what the percept evokes or suggests.

Although this form of inquiry is anathema in several Rorschach administration systems, it is necessary for Aronow et al.'s (1994) third level of idiographic imagery. Should this administration style be adopted, inquiry must be conducted judiciously and in a nonleading fashion to minimize bias that can potentially influence subsequent inquiry. This type of inquiry may be nearly impossible if the necessary safeguards are severely or rigidly enforced, so that the resolution of the issue rests with balancing the potential richness of the clinical yield against the problem of contaminating the response process.

A probing if not leading inquiry of this sort is frequently employed on the TAT, where the rules for inquiry are less constrained and the influence on the response process is also more poorly understood. Some diagnosticians have utilized a form of inquiry for figure drawings designed to elicit fantasy material, self representations, and other internal states suggested by the drawing of human figures of both sexes. Such inquiries can be specific, pointed, and geared toward eliciting simplistic trait-like descriptions, or provocative in the sense of probing for depth or complexity of motivations and phenomenologic experience. The depth of a patient's psychological experiences that an examiner wishes to understand undoubtedly influences the degree of probing inquiry. A knowledgeable and well-trained clinician carefully observes the boundary between accurate (but still in-depth, probing) and forced motivations.

My point in emphasizing the nature of the probing inquiry process of Aronow et al.'s (1994) third level of clinical interpretation is twofold. First, a probing or provocative inquiry is crucial to detect fantasy material needed for this type of content analysis. Second, in relation to the central focus of this book, an intensive, in-depth inquiry is essential to derive the psychodiagnostic information necessary for understanding selfobject functions.

Aronow et al. (1994) recognized that their typology based on idiographic or content analysis falls far short of customary requirements for rigor. They argued that speeding the process of psychotherapy might be a sufficient justification for idiographic analysis, but their emphasis on speed of treatment rarely produced deepening of treatment. They discussed several guidelines for judging the validity of a clinical interpretation of content, such as cautious inferential thinking, especially for responses of doubtful significance and uncertain referents. Like Schafer, they eschewed the use of fixed meanings or mechanical application of symbolic associations and stressed vigilant attention to examiners' "blind spots."

Aronow et al. (1994) also emphasized the caution necessary to differentiate true projections from commonly reported responses and alerted clinicians to be aware of how far an interpretation should be taken. In the analysis of sequence, they emphasized directing attention to select responses as further associations to, or expanded elaborations of, central aspects of patients' experiences of their internal world. Aronow et al. (1994) regarded sequence analysis as important but advised against an uncritical misapplication of this approach.

Schachtel

The culmination of Ernest Schachtel's work on and thinking about the Rorschach is represented by his 1966 book. In this work, he presented his views about the major determinants and scores, particularly from the standpoint of their experiential basis and the nature of the test situation. Schachtel's approach has its roots in the writings of Rorschach and the Rapaport–Schafer, Beck, and Klopfer traditions. These approaches influenced his synthesis of some of the finest traditions in the history of psychodiagnostic testing.

Schachtel's unique contributions centered on his emphasis on the experiential nature of the Rorschach technique. His viewpoint stemmed from the ego psychology tradition, and he was concerned with the perceptual and cognitive features of the Rorschach in relation to affects and motivational states. In this respect, Schachtel's thinking about the relationship between personality dynamics and perception was influenced by Hartmann's (1939) concept of ego apparatuses of primary and secondary autonomy and Rapaport's (1951) approach to the subject. His ideas about experiential processes should not be confused with contemporary uses of the term, such as those in philosophical phenomenology, the Rogerian or Gestalt psychotherapy schools, or for that matter, empathic understanding as in psychoanalytic self psychology.

Schachtel (1966) distinguished between allocentric and autocentric modes of perception and the influences of each on Rorschach responses. In allocentric perception, the emphasis is on objectification of the perceptual process. An object such as a Rorschach percept is described in terms of what it resembles: a person "figuratively or literally, takes hold of it, tries to 'grasp' it" (p. 79). In contrast, the subject-centered autocentric perceptual mode stresses attending to how the feeling tone of a projective test stimulus impinges on a person. The response creates a fusion between a sensory quality and an affect state, a fusion that Schachtel characterized as essentially pleasure or displeasure.

From this view, which unites perception and affect or motivational state, Schachtel (1966) considered major Rorschach determinants and noted that the scoring features may be either allocentric or autocentric, even in the same person at different times. He addressed the cognitive-perceptual process of forming a Rorschach response to show how a percept can be understood (i.e., how form is perceived influences the decision to produce or withhold a particular response). Thus, Schachtel described a process in which patients initially apprehended an ink blot in some fashion by taking its contours and other form elements into account. The allocentric mode leads to a tentative association with objects that resemble the ink blot. A goodness of fit test, determined largely by an active or critical evaluation of the likeness, is attempted, and finally the patient decides to accept or reject the comparison. Any given response is either produced or leads to a search for a better alternative, in keeping with a patient's reality orientation and capacities for critical analysis and judgment.

Schachtel (1966) noted that the autocentric mode influences the experiential aspect of this form-generating process. For example, affect states like depression and boredom may interfere with perceptual processing of form. Diminished interest constrains the vividness of the range of form likenesses, although the accuracy of perception is usually unaltered.

To this point, Schachtel's (1966) approach to the Rorschach response process provided a conceptual basis for understanding how responses are formulated and how affect or motivational states influence determinants. The final interpretation of the full protocol, however, is another matter. In this area, Schachtel used content analysis as a supplement to formal Rorschach scoring. His thoughts on the subject revealed a use of content-based material narrower than that of Rapaport and Schafer and not unlike Exner's (1991) view. Schachtel's approach to content analysis was based on formal response characteristics such as the use of particular determinants, in contrast with the broad, albeit judicious, use of content in Schafer's and Lerner's approaches. Schachtel's approach is certainly more restrictive than are the "dictionary" approaches that he criticized, as did Schafer (1954) before him.

Schachtel (1966) argued that content based on verbalizations and associations is not suitable for understanding drive states, defenses, and adaptive efforts. He thought it was difficult and "most of the time impossible" (p. 259) to distinguish among these characteristics of the personality by using content. He singled out the tendency to attribute specific meaning to card details for special criticism and advised against interpreting references to parental figures on Cards IV and VII, a caution generally accepted by most Rorschach clinicians. Thus, stripped of unsupportable inferences and associative comments about particular percepts, the essence of Schachtel's (1966) strategy for interpretation is best captured in the following statement:

> The data we study in Rorschach's test are what the testee saw in the blots and how he saw it, in the full concreteness of the percept and with all the emotional overtones and undercurrents that color what he saw, and all the intellectual and emotional effort, its quality, its process, its smoothness, or conflicts which entered into the work of perceiving, associating, and judging the fitness of the percept. From his words we try to reconstruct his experience. The score is merely an abstraction of this experience, and the verbal content of the responses is also an abstraction. (p. 261)

Lerner

P. M. Lerner (1991) and H. D. Lerner and P. M. Lerner (1988), together with Schafer (1954) and Aronow et al. (1994), also emphasized the usefulness of content analysis and the cautionary approach that this form of interpretation requires. The Lerners emphasized the importance of tracing the inference back to the primary response data that are its source by including each step in the process giving rise to an interpretation. P. M. Lerner (1991) emphasized searching carefully for confirmatory evidence from other test findings and considering the internal consistency of a content-based interpretation in the framework of the total personality. The Lerners are champions of an approach to diagnostic testing informed by contemporary theories in psychoanalysis, including Kohut's view of self psychology (Lerner, 1988). In this respect, they considered internalized object relations at least as important as drive–conflict–defense analysis.

P. M. Lerner (1991) also regarded sequence analysis as a crucial aspect of content analysis. He agreed with Schachtel's (1966) phenomenologic view in which sequence contains major clues to understanding a patient's experience or feeling state about the projective test process. Lerner (1991) expanded on Schachtel's (1966) and Klopfer's (Klopfer & Kelley, 1942) emphasis on formal Rorschach scores in sequence analysis with a broad approach compatible with that of Aronow et al. (1994). Lerner (1991) discussed using sequence analysis to identify regressive shifts conceptualized in both the conflict and deficit models in psychoanalysis. He relied especially on the sequence of form level and thought disorder scores in understanding regression and its impact on reality testing.

P. M. Lerner (1991) reaffirmed Schafer's guidelines for valid content analysis, to which he contributed additional clarifications, and stressed remaining close to patients' experience as expressed in the testing situation. Lerner (1991) therefore highlighted the increased clinical validity that results from a sustained focus on features unique to each patient.

Comprehensive System

In the 75-year history of Rorschach psychology, no attempt to bring this instrument to a scientifically and clinically respectable level exceeded that of Exner's (1993) Comprehensive System. Exner's work is anchored in contemporary psychometric theory and benefits from concurrent advances in diagnostic nosology, reliable measurement, and test validation. Not only has the Rorschach achieved a needed revitalization, but the Comprehensive System also serves as a standard of psychological and psychometric sophistication for other projective tests of personality. My discussion centers on the role of content, which Exner referred to as *Verbalizations* and *Sequence of Scores* in his terminology.

Exner did not reject content analysis approaches to interpretation. He considered content analysis to be potentially useful when applied judiciously as a secondary approach following the sequence of Comprehensive System scores and the clusters arising from combinations of major scores. On this subject, Exner (1991) commented:

> Although it is reasonable to expect the structural data to offer the greatest utility in forming interpretive hypotheses, some of those hypotheses can be too general, too narrow, or even misleading. Therefore, it is critically important to review the other data groups intelligently in the context of findings from the structural data. The Sequence of Scores often provides information that clarifies or expands postulates developed from the structural data, and sometimes unusual sequencing effects give rise to new hypotheses. Similarly, although new hypotheses developed from the Verbalizations must be regarded with the utmost caution, the astute interpreter should be able to cull considerable information from the verbal material that can relate to other data in the test. (p. 141)

Exner's Comprehensive System approach did not advocate ignoring content analysis, but argued for its inclusion in a carefully considered manner. Most advocates of content interpretation have made the same argument, namely that analysis of content follows formal scoring and that its cautious application should be based on clear guidelines. Thus, Exner (1991) was not alone when he wrote: "The picture is drawn together by merging nomothetic and idiographic information in a manner that highlights the uniqueness of the subject" (p. 127), and "Postulates generated from verbal material are likely to have the greatest validity when derived from a composite of responses that are homogeneous for content or verbiage" (p. 141).

Clearly, however, the Comprehensive System relies prominently on the formal scores and ratios from the Structural Summary. The main strategy for interpretation starts with and departs rarely from selecting the most appropriate psychometrically derived cluster-search routine suggested by the key variables that represent the starting point in the interpretive workup.

The main approach is twofold: It begins with a systematic examination of findings from each cluster and progresses by weaving together the findings across all clusters to evaluate the total personality. Previously, a data-driven examination began with the evaluation of the core cluster, assessed stressors and adaptive resources, and focused on how these are mediated in consequence of the basic introversive-extratensive configuration. Exner's preference now begins with the cluster-search options that offer a starting point superior to the previous approach that began with the core operational cluster. He identified 10 key variables that determine a priority for searching through various clusters of personality and cognitive variables. This strategy has become predominant for arriving at the eventual clinical interpretation of the protocol.

Like Schachtel, Exner (1993) subscribed to Rorschach's disinclination to view the task of responding to the ink blot series as a test of imagination. He eschewed embellishments to the basic task of producing percepts. Exner thought that the technique essentially requires subjects to "misidentify" the stimulus. The resultant problem-solving exercise requires some violation of reality. This process of misidentification provokes a series of cognitive processing operations, which are influenced by current mental status and level of psychological equilibrium. There are three phases: visual input and preliminary rank ordering of acceptable possibilities, a decision-making process involving discarding and censoring low priority response options, and a final selection of suitable responses reflecting an individual's personality traits or styles.

Exner (1991, 1993) regarded projection as "only a possibility in the Rorschach" (Exner, 1991, p. 109) and as having a minimal role in the primary perceptual-cognitive processing approach. Projection, in this view, emerged typically as a state variable that may color the richness of the verbalization, not as a fundamental feature of the main response process. Virtually all prominent figures in Rorschach psychology have also observed that projection was one of several psychological processes involved in the formulation of responses. Its importance as a primary mechanism varied among the developers of the Rorschach, despite the fact that all of these leading figures acknowledged that projection was induced by the instrument itself.

THEMATIC APPERCEPTION TEST
AND OTHER PROJECTIVE METHODS

As noted earlier, most psychodiagnostic literature on interpretive strategies has been devoted to the Rorschach, probably because formal scoring systems have been developed for its use. The popularity of the Rorschach continues, despite some persisting questions about the merits of particular codes and their meanings. This state of affairs is healthy; heuristic questions that can lead to empirical answers are important for a clinical science such as personality assessment. A reliable Rorschach scoring system makes it possible to continue discovering optimal strategies for combining scores to generate accurate psychological inferences. The matter of content and sequence analysis also continues to stimulate considerable interest, but the lack of an empirical approach to this form of analysis is the same problem that confounds much psychodynamic clinical practice and theory. The question of combining thematic analysis with formal scoring remains another major unsettled area in projective test psychology.

The lack of widely accepted scoring systems is no small part of the reason that projective tests besides the Rorschach are ambivalently valued. Because other projective tests can easily be overlooked or minimized, it is surprising that they continue to be used as much as they are by many clinicians, often in combination with the Rorschach. Certainly, tests like the TAT and figure drawings are considered important and valuable, notwithstanding clinicians' reservations about these instruments' empirical value.

Although several such instruments continue to be used as part of many test batteries, the TAT remains perhaps the most frequently used among this group of tests, and more has been written about its clinical applications despite the absence of an accepted scoring system. Leopold Bellak has for many years been one of the chief advocates of its study. To provide a balanced view on strategies for using diagnostic testing in this chapter, I include Bellak's main views on the TAT (Bellak & Abrams, 1997), together with other approaches to understanding this instrument.

Bellak assumed that patients respond to the figures in the pictures not as real people in real situations, but as determined by inner feelings and need states. Like most psychodiagnostic clinicians who have written about clinical interpretation, Bellak advised that TAT interpretation should be built up from repetitive patterns across several data sources. He regarded the principal elements of TAT analysis to be those denoting the main theme or conflict and identifying the figure with whom a patient appears most closely allied. By examining how feelings, wishes, and conflicts are associated with the various TAT figures, Bellak reconstructed a patient's psychological world, including the important people in the patient's psychological environment. These people may be seen as exploitative, hostile, benevolent, and so forth. Bellak attempted to arrive at a structural description of anxiety, including how it produces defenses and adaptation as these are revealed in the TAT imagery.

Other psychodiagnostic clinicians have also suggested interpretive approaches to the TAT, several of which overlap in many ways. Murray's (1943) traditional categorization of TAT responses stressed internal need states or *press* (to use Murray's preferred term) as these impinge on the patient. Henry (1956) emphasized the distinction between form characteristics of responses (e.g., organizational features, language structure) and content characteristics (affective tone and positive or negative contents). Rotter (1947) emphasized several key principles in TAT analysis, prominent among which are frequency of occurrence or persistence of a theme, degree of unusualness of important aspects of the story (such as atypical plot or misidentification of a figure or object), and delineation of the central identification figure. Rotter proposed interpretive hypotheses emphasizing familial attitudes, social and sexual attitudes, academic-vocational attitudes, personality characteristics, and etiological considerations.

Rapaport et al. (1945, 1968) differentiated formal characteristics of TAT story structure from content in their discussion of this instrument. Story structure represents compliance with the task instructions and includes omissions and distortions, excessive emphasis on the concrete picture rather than the situation it depicts, and introducing figures not present in the picture. The story structure is also evaluated for consistency with the patient's total production. This consistency may be seen in deviations from common themes and variations in these themes across the entire TAT set. Finally, the analysis of story structure also includes noting any idiosyncratic features of verbalizations. For Rapaport et al. (1945, 1968), like Bellak (Bellak & Abrams, 1997), the story content analysis took into account affective tone, identification with story figures, obstacles that may appear in the stories, and strivings represented by the story content.

Most of this literature appeared during the 1940s and 1950s, and there has been relatively little renewed clinical interest in the TAT since that time. There has been little revision or clinical reconceptualization of the TAT since Rapaport et al. (1945, 1968). Many aspects of their approach to the analysis of the TAT can be applied to figure drawings as well. The fact that empirically based interpretive principles for the TAT, figure drawings, and Rorschach content and sequence analysis have not kept pace with the major developments of instruments like the Rorschach and MMPI does not mean that these tests have no value. Their potential usefulness has always needed to be examined better than has been the case to date. Without a refined empirical foundation for the use of these instruments, there exists little more than the traditionally loosely applied approaches.

One can apply Schafer's (1954) sufficient evidence criterion for judging interpretive adequacy of Rorschach responses to interpreting the TAT (Schafer, 1967) and figure drawings. The same characteristic of unusualness or idiosyncracy applies to TAT stories and drawings as it does to Rorschach percepts. A story about a boy who prefers to play with his friends rather than practice the violin is one thing; the familiar story to the same card about a boy compelled to practice under threat of punishment by his parents is another matter. Still another psychological state is suggested when the story takes the form of the boy's parents being unaware of or unconcerned with his wish to play the violin well or to be accepted by his friends. Thus, a departure from the normative story or a related variant may provide clues to a person's psychologically salient concerns.

Projective test content, such as TAT stories like those just cited, may be understood in different ways, under the influence of various theoretical frameworks. Thus, material may be "heard" or listened to by an examiner on the basis of his or her conceptual viewpoint. Indeed, examiners may select questions for inquiry under the influence of theoretical preferences.

This situation becomes a bias only when a response is either ignored or attended to according to the meaning that an examiner hopes to find. It is not a bias when a theoretical orientation influences the way that examiners seek evidence to support or refute a clinical hypothesis, if they conduct the inquiry in a disciplined way and dispassionately consider alternative connotations.

For example, in the response of the boy made to practice the violin, a classically trained diagnostician may choose to elicit more associations about the outcome of not practicing from the standpoint of punitive action, guilt, or outwitting the parents. An object relations theoretical focus may lead an examiner to be particularly curious about punitive action or affects about rage at being ordered about or having initiative stifled. A self psychological orientation may dispose an examiner to inquire about the boy's concerns about not living up to his or his parents' expectations.

The TAT is more likely than the Rorschach to be subject to potential bias of this sort. Ideally, examiners should elicit patients' entire available range of associations without directing attention to any particular aspect of the story. Examiners would then decide which inference comes closest to a patient's phenomenologic experience of the situation represented by the TAT card. Although this approach may sound objective and fair-minded, clinicians do not work in this fashion. Fairness or impartiality, defined in this way, has little to do with clinical thinking. Being impartial or attempting to be unbiased does not necessarily lead to more accurate interpretations than those obtained in the customary way. The main reason that an apparently objective inquiry of this type fails is that theoretical orientations are not decided on the basis of the winner of a race or contest. Examiners cannot help being other than who they are, and their framework for understanding others and their experiences *is* who they are. Consequently, it is not a question of an examiners being more or less correct but of the recognition that they view the clinical material from the vantage point of their preferred conceptual approach.

As in psychotherapy, a patient seeking a cognitive-behavioral treatment is not advised to consult with a psychoanalyst. Analysts and behavior therapists evaluate patients in different ways, as a patient with jaw pain might be evaluated differently by an otolaryngologist and a dentist. Thus, a different theoretical view or method is not synonymous with bias. In regard to understanding personality dynamics from content analysis, such as the above TAT example, all that can reasonably be asked of examiners is that they keep open other theoretical possibilities besides their own. It is not a bias to hold a theoretical preference; a bias arises when a preference excludes other viewpoints.

As for Schafer's interpretive criteria of sufficient evidence, a distinctive feature of a TAT story should persist as a continuing theme across cards. Thus, a recurring theme, conflict, or defensive preference should be detectable on several cards (and probably on other tests as well), although it need not be present to the same degree on each card. This requirement of continuity reflects a convergence of evidence to build a persuasive case for the consistency of salient personality features. Some unique or test-specific interpretive evidence varies in its intensity across tests. Nevertheless, it is crucial that clinicians should examine evidence across tests to bolster their confidence in the accuracy of the final interpretation.

The interpretation of the boy on TAT Card 1 as one who is forced to practice does not *necessarily* mean that the patient perceives his or her parents as dogmatic or authoritarian. Nor does it mean that the girl on Card 2 who remains on the farm instead of pursuing a career in the city is *unequivocally* bound to her parents. An examiner can consider the possibility that the boy on Card 1 feels psychologically abandoned rather than oppressed by his parents and that the girl on Card 2 feels unable to separate from her parents by pathologically idealizing their values rather than by experiencing guilt about leaving them. Interpretations like these assume, naturally, that there is sufficient evidence to support such inferences throughout the test protocol. The same reservation about assigning specific meanings to particular images on the Rorschach applies just as compellingly to the TAT and figure drawings.

Examiners should propose interpretations as tentative or exploratory impressions, which gain credibility when the distinctive quality of the content compels the conclusion. There are no fixed or universal symbolic referents in projective test material. The imagery and associative threads of test responses can remain open to expanded interpretations as theoretical knowledge advances. Thus, the drive theory or ego psychological framework available to Rapaport and Schafer need not foreclose other positions about the meaning of test responses, whether these be informed by psychoanalytic self psychology, object relations theories, or other theories.

Similarly, inferential material from figure drawings need not routinely be bound up in symbolic statements such as the equivalence between hands drawn behind a figure's back and aggressive urges. Although such an interpretation is a possibility, the universality of this and many other types of equivalence has never been firmly established, despite the useful contributions of Machover (1949) and Harrower (1965). The possibility that hands drawn behind the back reflects other dynamic conflicts should not be discounted; an examiner can consider unassertiveness, shame, or even brittle self-esteem, with appropriately converging support from other projective content, for their potential interpretive merit.

A SELF PSYCHOLOGICAL APPROACH
TO PROJECTIVE TEST INTERPRETATION

Schafer's criteria follow straightforwardly from an ego psychology viewpoint. Thus, the analysis of defenses, together with their intensity, pervasiveness, and resilience, is the key factor to consider. A traditional drive theory approach, although not in any fundamental way at odds with the ego psychological approach, is more concerned with the type of intrapsychic conflict and its specific dynamics, in addition to the analysis of defense operations and their vicissitudes.

A shift in emphasis is expected in an object relations conceptualization. One example is a focus on primitive or archaic devouring-aggressive urges as described by Melanie Klein (1935/1975), who referred to them as the paranoid and depressive positions. Another approach is the schizoid withdrawal–avoidance adaptation as described by Guntrip (1969). P. M. Lerner (1991) and several contributors to H. D. Lerner & P. M. Lerner's (1988) book have provided rich illustrations of Winnicott's (1953) concepts of the transitional object and the false self for understanding projective test content. In a similar fashion, therefore, the regulation of self-esteem or self-cohesion and the nature of selfobject functions become the central focus of a self psychological point of view.

When Rapaport's and Schafer's seminal works on diagnostic psychological testing appeared, psychoanalytic self psychology was unknown. The predominant theoretical view in psychoanalysis was that of ego psychology, influenced appreciably by the work of Hartmann, Kris, Loewald, and Loewenstein. Melanie Klein's work was also actively in progress at the time. There were other formulations of preoedipal (deficit) pathology by well-known precursors of contemporary object relations theorists, such as Edith Jacobsen and Margaret Mahler. As Freud's structural theory led naturally to a renewed emphasis on the psychology of the ego, the evolving views of psychoanalysis inevitably placed emphasis on elucidating the defenses, character pathology, and adaptive-synthetic ego functions.

Anna Freud's (1936) pivotal study of defenses served as an important bridge in this effort. The prevailing views of this period of psychoanalytic thinking provided a compatible theoretical focus for Rapaport and his colleagues' effort to discover the complimentarities between clinical psychopathology and cognitive-perceptual functions studied in the experimental psychology laboratory. One result of this effort was the battery of personality and perceptual-cognitive tests that became the foundation of personality assessment, or in Rapaport's term, *diagnostic psychological testing* (Rapaport et al., 1945, 1968).

How, then, can one attempt to incorporate Kohut's theories into projective testing? There is no reason to believe that the same criteria that Schafer proposed for inferences derived from drive theory cannot be applied in just as logically systematic a way for a self psychological formulation. Because empirically based test scores or markers do not exist, the conclusions about self-esteem regulation or self-cohesion must rely almost entirely on content and sequence analysis. Schafer's criteria can be readily extended to investigate self states and self disorders because the method of analysis of the response pattern is not affected. Instead, the theoretical viewpoint guiding the clinical interpretation of test findings has changed or expanded.

For example, consider Schafer's point about commenting interpretively on the unusualness or provocativeness of a response. This point becomes apparent when an incidental feature or an infrequent (and perhaps idiosyncratic) elaboration is mentioned. Thus, a Rorschach response of an airplane that is spontaneously described as falling or leaves that are seen as hanging limply from a tree illustrates the point. Additional recurrences of responses like these add to the interpretive salience of images about falling or not being in good shape, such as a TAT story of faltering health or a deteriorating object. To this point, calling attention to a response or a class of responses for its psychological meaning is not specific to any particular theory.

Thus, in a drive theory interpretation of these examples, a falling object or wilting leaf reflects a relatively mature level of psychosexual development, representing phallic defeat, oedipal failure, or loss of object love. If the developmental level and maturity of defenses based on the total record were judged to indicate a more regressed level, the same imagery could be conceptualized as representing oral or anal stage manifestations of fear of loss of the object itself. Object relations theorists could consider imagery of falling or wilting as a reflection of dissolution of the self or object world, in this sense representing a deficit view of psychopathology rather than one anchored in conflict. From a related but not identical perspective, a self psychological view might also regard a percept of falling or wilting as one that is not rooted in conflict. Such responses indicate a self state conveying the sense that the self is unable to experience itself as sustained or buoyant.

It is customary to attribute specific meaning to an image from a determination of the level of psychological organization and not from the associative content proper, which includes structural conflict or defect, quality and maturity of defenses, and the resulting pathological syndrome or clinical picture. Although formal scoring and empirical decision rules are typically a decisive influence on this clinical determination, content should be consistent with the syndromal or characterologic diagnosis, and the specific meaning of the content should follow from the clinical developmental diagnosis. Thus, a falling object or wilting image follows from a phallic-oedipal interpretation if the diagnosis principally involves structural neurotic conflict. The same response could indicate fear of fragmentation in a transient psychosis or decompensated borderline state, and it would be viewed as a reflection of an enfeebled self if the central disturbance is conceptualized as a self disorder.

In general, Rorschach percepts with imagery having to do with deterioration states are noteworthy, whether these refer to objects (peeling off, coming apart, wilting, faltering, leaking, crumbling, breaking into pieces, decaying, rotting) or to people or animals (faltering, aging, withering, injured, ailing). Related indications of a self disorder or of vulnerable self-cohesion may be expressed in TAT stories having to do with failure, degeneration of varying degrees, or illness. Similarly, figure drawings may denote faltering body parts, clothing in disarray, or details connoting weak supports, such as a broken umbrella, a button or zipper needing repair, or a worn-out purse. A tree with drooping leaves, worn bark eroded by the weather, or a house with a leaking roof or in need of painting also contain related indications of vulnerable self-cohesion.

Probably even more than in the specific images, such as deteriorated body parts or objects, the most distinctive indications of self pathology are revealed in patients' narrative descriptions, on inquiry, about how a figure or TAT story is seen. The self psychological significance contained in these narratives may be particularly pertinent for identifying selfobject functions or needs. Thus, a man standing with a broken umbrella may be described as having resources to seek another means of protection, as being able to repair the umbrella on his own, as becoming helplessly drenched, or as seeking a strong, protective figure to assist him with a function he cannot otherwise perform.

As an illustration of the self psychological approach, a TAT story to Card 1, for example, may refer to the boy as trying to figure out how to play the violin with no mention of parents or teachers in the background to help him. The story might be accompanied by an affect state of despair or helplessness, or it might simply describe finding a solution but with neutral affect. The key, then, is the meaning of the affect state and its expression. Thus, the story denoting the feeling of despair might characterize a self that is devastated to the point of giving up hope of rescue; there is, in effect, no potential selfobject on the horizon. In contrast, a patient who emphasizes feeling helpless may be expressing inability or weakness of the self to sustain itself hardily; therefore, a state of feeling underpowered or vulnerable is suggested. This response also provides an indication of a need for selfobject responsiveness, although the specific type of selfobject function requires additional evidence. A description with no particular affect state other than thoughtful contemplation related to problem solving may represent a sufficiently viable self that does not falter in helplessness or crumble with despair.

In this last example, it might be an error to view the absence of a strong expression of affect as a defensive reaction formation such as isolation or repression. For example, the neutrality of the expressed affect may reflect a patient's joyful pride in relying on his or her own talents. Although Kohut believed that the self is not entirely devoid of any selfobjects, the experience of isolation or solitude as defensive or healthy must be determined from other test indications.

Inquiry about affective qualities is crucial for arriving at these clinical distinctions, particularly for TAT stories and figure drawing images. Obtaining such information, therefore, should not be neglected or minimized; a sensitive but astute examiner can obtain it without sacrificing clinical objectivity or leading the patient off course. Examiners must remember that the purpose of diagnostic testing is to expose and reveal the depth of personality rather than to support or abet a defensive posture. Psychodiagnostic testing is not the lollipop after a feared injection; it is the injection itself! The psychodiagnostic examination should be undertaken with probing incisiveness; it is not a mechanical repetition of routinized administration procedures. The examination usually does not perturb patients; if they are perturbed, this reaction can be used to good advantage, and the patient will recover.

As for the self psychological analysis for interpreting TAT Card 1, a common outcome of this story is that the boy becomes a famous violinist. This outcome is sometimes misunderstood as an indication of grandiosity. Actually, an inference closer to the real spirit of Kohut's view is that the outcome is a statement of pride in one's abilities or accomplishments. In development, it parallels toddlers exploring their world with abandon and pleasure. Although derived from the sector of the self that Kohut called the grandiose-exhibitionistic pole, an interpretation of grandiosity may be incorrect and it may exaggerate the pathology—healthy pride and ambitious assertion may be all that is indicated. To quickly assume that pathological grandiosity is indicated fails to grasp this aspect of a vibrant self; thus, it may miss the boat. Further exploration about this story outcome is best directed toward eliciting how a patient imagines the successful outcome is responded to or mirrored.

The story for Card 1 more typically describes a parent or teacher compelling the boy to practice; through understanding the give and take between the boy and the parent, the nature of the selfobject function can best be understood. Can the parent not see the boy's need? Does the parent fail to size up what the child needs? Is the parent truly absent, in reality or psychologically, so that the boy is left too much on his own? Does the boy seek some degree of responsiveness from the parent, in the form of control, discipline, attention, or affection? Can the parent or teacher manage to fulfill the authority function while still leaving room for the boy to feel that he is listened to or that he has some recourse? These are important questions to try to answer on inquiry; they are crucial to understanding the boy's (that is, the patient's) experience of the self-selfobject milieu.

From this vantage point, the selfobject function as represented in what the parent means to the child is a critical feature that the examiner should be able to empathically understand. Analysts and psychotherapists listen in the same way, but to different material. An examiner can understand what selfobject function is missing or has interfered with a patient's development by attending as much to what the patient fantasizes about the self state of the boy of Card 1 as to what the patient sees. It may also be important to attend to the psychological characteristics of those figures that are unseen but are still important parts of the patient's description of the boy's experience of himself and his need for selfobject responsiveness. Simply reducing the typical story to a relatively brief adjectival description by staying close to the surface of the picture itself does not "cut the mustard," whether one adopts a self psychological approach or any other psychodynamic point of view.

It is possible to infer useful information about a patient's self state from the three examples provided earlier. In the story of the virtually absent or unavailable parent, the lack of empathic understanding hinted at by the feeling of despair describes a parent who sees nothing of the boy's dilemma. The story foreshadows the patient's expectation that he or she is not heard and is the helpless pawn of others' needs. Mirroring and idealization selfobject needs are likely to be unacknowledged. The example of the unaware or absent parent unavailable to attend to the boy's selfobject need is similar to the first in that selfobject functions are probably deficient. But the reason in this second example is different, and there is the hope of restoring a needed selfobject response. The reason is that the boy experiences helplessness rather than despair; the injury to the self might potentially be repaired with adequate empathic responsiveness. The example of thoughtful contemplation conveys a situation in which selfobject functions are likely to be operating relatively normally. There is no implied injury to, or devitalization of, self-cohesion; it might describe an optimally responsive parent who works with the child to allow him what he wants while still insisting on what the parent wants or believes is good for the boy. Although this third story does not specifically describe mirroring or idealization functions, it can be assumed that neither is deficient or unavailable.

These examples demonstrate that self states may be inferred from TAT stories, but they are neutral with respect to specific selfobject functions. How can mirroring and idealization needs be seen on TAT stories? To answer this question, I again describe several directions that various stories for Card 1 can take. One possibility is a story in which the parents insist that the boy practice with no realization or concern for what he wants. Inquiry directed specifically to elicit the parents' motivations or needs reveals that they do not listen to the boy and do not let him do something else, such as play with his friends. This version points to an experience in which the boy's complaint is dominated by feeling unheard or unresponded to. It is an indication of deficient mirroring, seen frequently in stories in which the boy's wish to make his own needs known is ignored. He is left feeling unaffirmed, insignificant, or unable to hold his own or to feel buoyed up. The case would be strengthened were the patient to comment that the boy's efforts to get through to the parents go unheeded and so he feels ineffectual, sad, or undermined.

Indications of faulty idealization characterize a story in which the boy wants to look up to an admired figure but his wish is unnoticed or rejected, so that the boy feels unworthy or ashamed of his wish. The boy may lack enthusiasm to practice because he worries that he cannot live up to a teacher's or parent's expectation or expects that the teacher will reject his admiring overtures. Still another indication of an unresponded-to idealizing need is a reference to the boy's feelings about not having an adequate model for how to play the violin. The boy may be described as too bored or understimulated to sustain the work of practicing in the absence of a parent who listens, eggs him on, or provides some other encouragement or reason to emulate the authority figure. In these instances, one can infer that the idealizing selfobject function is undermined, particularly if accompanied by evidence of an earlier attempt at mirroring needs that were unmet.

Finally, a patient can describe the boy as searching for someone like himself, a twin, to whom he can feel attached, who shares his plight of failed empathic understanding. The story may express predominant feelings of shared misery or hopelessness. Alternatively, the twinship selfobject function can provide just enough vitalization to the self to allow the boy of Card 1 to rise to the occasion. It is important to ascertain whether this self state of vigor and accomplishment requires the continued presence of the selfobject to sustain itself in a sufficiently robust manner.

It usually requires an inquiry more vigorous than is often the case, together with a patient capable of indicating this affect, to be certain about the nature of the selfobject function stimulated by this TAT card or by any projective test stimulus. Patients may fail to elaborate on many TAT stories in sufficient detail, a response suggesting only that a selfobject experience has not been elicited. The inquiry elaboration does not indicate often enough the specific selfobject function that is mobilized. The absence of an empathic response does not necessarily imply deficient empathic understanding, but chronic and ongoing lack of responsivity to need states, seen over and again on several TAT card stories, does suggest some disturbance of selfobject function.

Although Card 1 usually contains material that typically concerns a patient's relationship to authority figures who place demands on the patient, it may not be the most suitable card for eliciting content that best characterizes selfobject functions. These examples suggest that the customary stories provide a general indication of self states. A deeper nature of selfobject needs is usually revealed when accompanied by a richly detailed description, offered either spontaneously or, more typically, only on vigorous inquiry. Other TAT cards can yield better examples of selfobject functions on the basis of their natural or evocative "pull," such as cards that depict more than one figure so that some type of relationship, such as a struggle or intense emotional encounter, is powerfully evoked.

For example, Card 2 frequently contains a story line revealing how the patient has managed the developmental step of separation from the family of origin. The nature of the relationship between daughter and mother may also be captured in the story. In particular, the mother who cannot let go of the daughter raises the specter of a mother who is lonely or fragile if left alone. This response offers useful albeit presumptive information about the daughter's selfobject needs from a mother who is unable to tolerate loss or separation. The mother may be described as though she would lose an important part of her own self, and the daughter may be experienced as a narcissistic extension of the mother. This description provides a hint about what the child of such a mother may be re-exposed to on Card 2. The mother can also feel as if her maternal function is no longer needed and she is therefore unmirrored and empty or depleted. The mother can derive pride and sustenance from the daughter who turns to this mother as an object of idealization. The bond between them can be experienced as so tightly knit, from the point of view of the mother, that the potential interruption of a possible twinship selfobject function represents a specific threat or vulnerability.

A related if not identical pattern can also appear on TAT Card 6BM. The fullest understanding of the psychodynamic meaning of the relationship requires a level of inquiry that proceeds beyond simply eliciting that a separation or rupture has occurred. The fantasied meaning of the separation should be ascertained to understand what it represents for both characters. A close inspection of Card 7GF, frequently seen as an interaction between a girl and her mother, also yields an understanding of the selfobject functions surrounding the intimate nature of this mother–child relationship. At one level of analysis, the girl may be described as looking away or as absorbed in internal fantasy as the mother reads to her. At a more deeply revealing level, the patient may note that the girl who looks away has withdrawn or decathected from the mother. This response is quite different from feeling content in the company of the mother. Only when a patient is pressed does the typical story reveal whether a breach between mother and child has exposed an empathic failure or disruption and how it is remedied. Does the mother realize that the girl is not paying attention and attempt to enter her world to re-engage her, or does the mother persist in reading to the child apparently unaware if not unconcerned that the girl is not psycho-logically present? Examiners need to determine how patients perceive the affective attunement of the mother, and by inference, the intimate figures in their lives. Even a story indicating maternal involvement does not by itself imply empathically attuned responsiveness. A level of responsiveness in which the mother insists that the child listen to her or in which the child listens obediently misses the boat if taken to mean that an optimal self-sel-fobject environment is indicated.

A telling feature of these responses is the child's concern about securing a needed selfobject function. This feature is typically one of seeking admiration or affirmation from a parent who is often unaware of what the child looks for. The story about obedience implies that the patient complies with almost anything to win the mother's responsive mirroring, even if the story outcome suggests that the girl feels subdued or that she quietly tolerates sadness or disappointment over a deficient self-selfobject milieu. Some outcomes to this story convey similar reactions to a self-selfobject unit that is not working optimally. The girl may be left psychologically immobilized with no choice but to listen passively until the mother's "lecture" is over, or the girl's depression may lead her to fantasize that she will be a different kind of mother to the doll she is holding, or the girl may become angry.

The same TAT card may also emphasize the girl's relationship to the doll on her lap. This feature is particularly distinctive for denoting an idealizing or twinship selfobject function. Some common stories take the form of the child's imagining that she becomes as good a mother as her own, that the mother in the picture teaches the girl how to care for her "dolly," or that the girl asks the mother to show her in fantasy how to minister to the doll as an imagined baby. When such story lines do not contain veiled references to maternal disinterest or resentment on the part of the girl, a normal or healthy revival of the idealizing selfobject function may be indicated. Aspects of twinship may also be present, a not unreasonable assumption if the girl emphasizes her role as an exact replica of the mother's attunement or ministration, which the girl then extends by imitation to her doll.

In its most unsatisfying form, and from the standpoint of psychopathol-ogy a serious indication of a potentially untreatable self disorder, the story may describe the mother as unresponsive to the girl's needs, and the girl may not manage to reinvolve the mother or, in fantasy, to work through some way with the doll to achieve a sense of restored self-cohesion. Here, neither mirroring nor idealization is operating properly. This response suggests not only a defective primary structure but the absence of acquiring compensatory structure as another route to attempt to restore an injured self. A repetitive series of outcomes to TAT stories permeated by pessimism or depression is sometimes the expression of hopelessness resulting from a seriously undermined or devitalized sense of self with limited selfobject resources to assist with its repair.

5 Clinical Indications of Selfobject Functions: Mirroring

In this chapter, I consider the mirroring selfobject function as it appears on projective tests. I focus here on mirroring as a selfobject function that results in the sense of vitalization or buoyancy of the self. Mirroring is a way that people experience feeling affirmed or admired, a view that comes close to Kohut's (1977, 1984) final thinking about mirroring. Although mirroring originates in the grandiose-exhibitionistic pole of the self, to use Kohut's (1966, 1971) earlier description, his later writings emphasized affirmation rather than surface grandiosity as the more fundamental self state. I first discuss psychodiagnostic testing indicators of grandiosity, but I emphasize that grandiosity as seen on projective tests should be reconsidered in terms of an expanded view of disturbed or insufficient mirroring.

The remainder of this chapter consists of a large number of clinical examples of mirroring. I illustrate admiration as a normal mirroring selfobject need and disillusionment and devaluation as pathological forms of mirroring selfobject failures. These examples include both Rorschach and TAT responses from Schafer, Lerner, Holt, and Sugarman. In my discussion, I attempt to demonstrate that the self psychological view of mirroring can be applied to projective test responses to provide an alternative view beyond drive theory or object relations frameworks for understanding personality dynamics and psychopathology.

The clinical illustrations to be presented are vignettes of projective testing responses rather than complete cases. (I present two cases in their entirety as the focus of chaps. 7 & 8.) Although the in-depth material of fully integrated cases does not appear until chapters 7 and 8, I am not advocating basing completed clinical interpretations on isolated examples such as those used throughout the present chapter. The following examples are illustrative, but not necessarily decisive.

115

GRANDIOSITY

A long tradition in diagnostic psychological testing has equated grandiosity with narcissism. Kohut expanded that tradition by reconceptualizing grandiosity as not necessarily pathology (although it may, of course, represent that, too) but as the expression of a normal need for accurate, empathic responsiveness or mirroring. Kohut (1966, 1971) first came to understand the importance of the mirror transference as originating from the grandiose-exhibitionistic pole of the self. Therefore, it is probably no accident that his early clinical descriptions used the term *narcissistic disturbances*. Kohut and his colleagues subsequently de-emphasized grandiosity and the term *grandiose-exhibitionistic pole of the self.* This de-emphasis of pathological grandiosity came about as it became increasingly clear that its appearance (as well as its other manifestations colloquially and too casually termed *narcissistic*) is fundamentally a normal developmental need for empathically attuned recognition.

With self disorders considered in this way, grandiosity takes on a different meaning in the psychodiagnostic examination. The easily recognizable indications of grandiosity are readily detected on projective tests. Some common examples include Rorschach percepts that denote exaggerated power, such as "the greatest airplane ever known to man," "the most powerful force to destroy the planet," "a king sitting on his throne and looking over his kingdom," and TAT story outcomes such as "he becomes the best violinist of the century" or "the young man gets the best lawyer in the country to get him off on the speeding ticket." Such test indications pertaining to grandiosity should not automatically be construed as narcissism, but rather as defensive efforts to buoy up a faltering sense of self-cohesion. Examiners should look for those aspects of the protocol that suggest deficient self-esteem rather than exaggerated elevations of self-esteem. Such test indications are frequently subtle rather than immediately evident.

Many of the examples that follow denote the appearance of grandiosity. Some are from records of patients with inflated self-worth or a sense of entitlement diagnosable as narcissistic disorders by most criteria. The majority of the examples, however, imply the diagnosis of a narcissistic disturbance but are too infrequent or too transitory to convincingly sustain this impression. My reason for selecting such examples is to demonstrate that many responses that appear to suggest grandiosity are more usefully considered as defensive bravado overlaying a self disorder. Several examples represent little beyond an essentially normal need for admiration.

Characteristically, the desire for admiration either reveals a deficit of mirroring or provides an indication that an injury to self-esteem has occurred as a result of an empathic failure of mirroring selfobject responsiveness.

Kohut came to view grandiosity as an exaggerated manifestation of normal children's joyful pride in their abilities. Grandiosity becomes pathological as a self disorder only when an expectable response to a person's prideful achievements is chronically unresponded to or still worse, when a person has been made to feel excessive shame about even normal "tooting one's horn." In normal development, Kohut argued, the appropriate response to children's expressions of greatness and omnipotence is joyful acceptance ("the gleam in the mother's eye"), which forms the basis for the internalization of feeling proud that gives rise to normal self-esteem. This quality of self-esteem persists in an exaggerated form as grandiosity only when its normal stirrings have been unrecognized, suppressed, or devalued by others.

With maturation, young children's unbounded omnipotence is less prominent if, as a result of normal development, it becomes transformed into the basis for ambitions and strivings. Maturation continues, despite failures or disappointments and without a fall in self-esteem, but only if selfobject responsiveness has been optimal enough to permit young children, and later on, adults, to tolerate the idea that talents and abilities may sometimes falter. Empathically attuned parents or similar figures convey the feeling that they love the children or regard them with pleasure despite their "warts." Otherwise, children may re-experience the devitalization, depression, or rage characterizing an undervalued or unmirrored self that persists into adolescence and adulthood. Mirroring is thus the normal response to a budding self in need of being recognized, admired, or affirmed. It becomes the substrate from which emerges a stable, internalized basis for feeling confident and energetic about pursuing the goals that provide vigor to aspirations. Deficient mirroring produces the characteristic disintegration products of self disorders, including depression, anergia, and rage, as well as defensive grandiosity.

The examples such as the greatest airplane, the powerful force, or the boy who strives to become the greatest violinist illustrate the excessiveness of the grandiose wish. Beneath that surface excess or bravado is frequently faltering self-esteem. Thus, for example, the greatest airplane may have an association to a crash, or the powerful king is overthrown, or the boy fails as a violinist. More typically, projective test content referring to vigor or power does not take the form of exaggerated grandiosity like the preceding examples. Some examples are a Rorschach percept of a spaceship take-off elaborated in a way that emphasizes that the sight is majestic, or the abominable snowman described as impressive, or an imposing animal such as a lion described as strong or with a grand mane. Responses such as these emphasize the wish to be admired and sometimes have additional elaboration about a patient's feeling misunderstood or unheard or otherwise indicating empathic failure.

Other examples are more subtle. Consider the following Rorschach responses from a 37-year-old firefighter experiencing outbursts of anger. The acute reaction followed his inability to prevent his father's death in a car accident that he witnessed. This patient produced "the stealth bomber" as a response to Rorschach Card V. He elaborated this response on inquiry as: "Broad wide wings, the sleekness of it, the principle that it's an undetectable surveillance." Although not without connotations of secrecy, aggression, and immunity from detection, this response can also be seen as an image suggesting grandiose qualities such as being the best of its kind and most powerful. The response conveys a desire to be admired for its sleek looks. In terms of psychological development, it is not very different from the little girl showing off her Sunday best or a little boy wanting praise for the big fish he has caught or the proud owner of a new automobile remarking: "Isn't that a beauty!"

As an indication that fantasies of greatness can readily coexist with less flattering self perceptions, this same patient gave several responses indicating weakness or vulnerability. Thus, following his percept of the stealth bomber, on Card VI this man reported: "A microorganism. I can't relate to this thing. Like under a microscope, looks like it's being squashed between two sheets of glass." On Card VIII, the patient delivered a response of "two rodents climbing to something, a wall, just stuck to it, a foot's coming out and it kind of looks like he's falling away but yet he's still stuck there, like a cartoon," and on Card IV: "A beaver laying next to a roadway, looks like a flattened animal, the lighter color makes it look more frail like a crusted-up dried-up dead animal."

The flattened-out beaver percept was followed by an attempt to restore some resiliency to the weakened undermined self, but the effort was short lived: "It also looks like a space shuttle, the one that blew up. The Challenger." Thus, his attempt to invoke another strong, powerful image became the vulnerable shuttle that failed to function and exploded in a well-known disaster. In the psychopathology of self disorders, patients often give responses depicting prideful, buoyant imagery, such as this space shuttle or the example of the stealth bomber, followed by indications of an underlying devalued self.

This same patient previously reported a response on Card II as follows: "Looks like I've been working on my car and I banged my fingers again, and the dirt and grease and the blood," which he elaborated on inquiry as: "If someone's bleeding like that why don't you get up and do something about that, but like if it's me, I'd just as soon get the job done, it's obviously been bleeding a while and I'd just keep working right through it."

Despite the fact that several pathological Comprehensive System codes are apparent, notably, inflated morbid special scores, these alone do not fully capture the vulnerability of self-cohesion strongly portrayed in these examples. Whether bravado, grandiosity, invulnerability, or sheer brute tenacity, the responses of this man dramatically conveyed the price that he paid for walling off the intensity of the affect surrounding threats to self-esteem. Thus, prideful, vigorous imagery characteristically alternated with projective test responses suggestive of depletion.

On other projective tests, this patient continued to reveal aspects of how demanding he was for himself. His stoic, singleminded pursuit of fulfilling a responsibility served to sustain optimal self-esteem at any cost. The patient related a conventional TAT story to Card 1 in which the boy is told to practice the violin and he appears to obediently accept. The concern behind the story was not whether the boy wants to do the job, but rather what he must do to master the skills. Accordingly, "He studies and practices and is happy to make music for himself and others." The wish to present oneself as competent is well and good; it is the substrate for a self turning to the world for admiration. To this point, there was nothing particularly remarkable about the patient's response. When the patient felt he came up short, an intropunitive side to his expectation of accomplishment began to emerge.

Thus, on Card 3BM, the girl was "sent to her room for disciplinary reasons; she failed to clean it," and the girl felt like a "prisoner in her own room, she feels cold and alone and mistreated." As the outcome, he reported that she buckled under, completed the job, and faced responsibility. Later, describing his figure drawing of a person, the patient emphasized the "grown, mature" side of the person. He expressed concern about unexpected situations in which he had no control, such as "seeing wrongs he's not able to correct" or "not being able to do enough."

Together with the Rorschach examples, a picture emerges of a man with a strong need to be competent, responsible, and in command of himself. These traits can be seen as manifestations of the grandiose-exhibitionistic pole of the self, traits that emerged with every reasonable anticipation that mirroring selfobject responsiveness in the form of affirming his accomplishments would be forthcoming. Any perceived weakness that undermined the sense of joyful pride in a vigorous, accomplished self disposed him to feel affectively distanced from feelings of depreciation. This quality is not one of guilt-driven intropunitiveness characterized by wrongdoing; rather, this man's turning in on himself resulted from a predominant feeling of not measuring up. The patient felt underpowered rather than guilty. His difficulty in sustaining self-esteem was not essentially a problem of grandiosity. It was the failure to live up to the excessive standards he came to view as prideful accomplishment worthy of mirroring selfobject responsiveness. This failure produced the disintegration products of rage outbursts that dominated the clinical picture, perhaps mobilized by finding himself helpless to save his father from a fatal car accident.

The following series of clinical examples also highlights the close relation between the appearance of grandiosity and its underlying origins in self-depreciation. Like the previous vignettes, these examples include illustrations taken from the TAT and projective drawings in addition to the Rorschach. They also consider the matter of differentiating mirroring from idealization selfobject functions.

A patient, a 21-year-old woman hospitalized for an agitated psychotic reaction, gave the following response to Card IV of the Rorschach:

A giant, like Jack and the Beanstalk, and this would be the beanstalk he climbed to see if there's a castle up there, and the giant came out and Jack ran away and cut the beanstalk down and Jack fell from the beanstalk; he saves the town and he's a hero.

Heroic, yes; grandiose, perhaps; in either case, the risk was running away from something threatening and falling down. The appearance of a noble gesture, replete with all the greatness of being the conquering hero, is close to an associated fantasy of falling. Later, the same patient produced this percept: "It's like Merlin, some sort of magician, or maybe a witch talking out of something, it just looks like a witch, either bad or good, helps people or doesn't" (Card IX).

Although possibly an attempt to grasp at an image of Merlin as a mythic figure associated with great but benevolent powers, the image was short lived and quickly gave way to disturbing content. These two percepts were typical of much of the remainder of her Rorschach protocol, in which percepts of vulnerable self-esteem were common. Other illustrative responses included flies eating garbage, a squashed cartoon cat's head, and "a little bear's claw," which immediately followed her Merlin percept.

On Card 1 of the TAT, this patient told the story of a grandfather who gave the boy the violin as a present that has been handed down, and the story pertained to the boy's solitary attempt to figure out how to play. The boy appeared immobilized by his inability to play and felt "bored," perhaps a euphemism for depressed or, from the self psychological view, devitalized. The patient continued her passive inactivity on Card 2, where she was "waiting for a bus to take her to school to make something of her life" because she "wants her parents to be proud of her." As on Card 1 the girl passively waited to be taken somewhere. She anticipated that making something of her life to make her parents proud would just happen to her. The self as actively pursuing or attaining goals was not part of this patient's experience of the self. Rather, as a passive recipient of whatever came her way, she appeared to submit to what she was given. This picture is not one of a vibrant, buoyant self that feels full of itself or strengthened from within. The self psychological meaning of such passivity or dependency suggests inability to take steps to invigorate herself when necessary.

On Card 7GF, the patient described a nanny as reading to the passive little girl. The girl was seemingly unmoved by the nanny's ministrations. The girl then "goes off and plays," and although the nanny was described as attentive, the girl was "just off in the blue." When asked to elaborate her drawing of a person, the patient also lacked a firmed-up sense of who or what the person should be. Thus, she commented: "This is going to be sloppy, I'm just going to draw it like a kid. She's unhappy or happy, maybe. I don't know, she's looking off somewhere, waiting for something, maybe a car or someone to pick her up."

Her drawing of a male was described as "a character, not a real person, a fairy tale character from a book. In England in olden days and he was a prince and he's just that. He rides a horse, helps other people, defends them. If something goes wrong he saves the day." The emptiness and indecisiveness of the sense of self and the faulty mirroring of the vigorous strivings of the self for definition are particularly notable in this young woman's projective test responses. This picture is not that of a cohesive, invigorated self, but rather a possibly depleted shell of a self.

On Card X of the Rorschach, the patient attempted to depict lions as a figure of strength, but the percept became "lions on a crest, or a brooch, like my grandmother's brooch." Before assuming, however, that the attempted reach for a vigorous percept of lions cannot be sustained but instead became a design on a piece of jewelry, one must consider the possibility that the grandmother was a source of strength to be relied on for idealization. This possibility may also apply to the patient's previous Rorschach response of Merlin the magician. Nevertheless, this interpretation is unlikely; the patient failed to sustain an idealized wish for strength in her tearfully delivered references to the witch-like qualities of the percept as it was elaborated on inquiry. In addition, the previously noted responses of a valiant prince who was not real or the heroic Jack in the Beanstalk who was cut down are ominous. It is difficult to be reassured that the lions on the grandmother's brooch and the percept of Merlin can do much to come to her aid. Rather, these responses represented futile attempts to repair undermined self-cohesion. Recall again her passive anticipation of others to pick her up at a bus stop or take her to a place where someone comes along to "make something of" her.

Thus, the possibility of idealization as a compensatory structure is weakened by the emphasis in this patient's associations on failure or unavailability of potentially strong, idealizable figures such as Merlin or the heroic prince who becomes an unreal fairy tale character. Although the powerful lions on the grandmother's jewelry may suggest a possibility of a revivable, idealizable selfobject, the relative emphasis on helplessness rather than on potential sources of strength favors the view that deficient mirroring is the predominant self state.

These examples indicate that the appearance of clear or suggestive percepts of a grandiose nature, including descriptions of powerful figures, does not necessarily represent inflated self-worth. Indications of vigor and invulnerability often give way to other percepts expressing weakness, devaluation, or diminished self-esteem. Rather than attempting to portray psychological health, responses of a grandiose nature frequently represent ill-fated attempts to preserve whatever vitality can be managed. As these examples illustrate, the effort is often not well-sustained, and the patient typically caves in before very long.

ADMIRATION

My discussion of grandiosity examined the issue of how the surface appearance of exaggerated self-worth may have more to do with defensive concealment of an underlying self disorder. The defense is the way that people protect themselves from re-exposure to injuries to self-esteem. This response becomes particularly important when the injuries result from selfobject failures to respond empathically to the need to feel invigorated, appreciated, or understood. These needs are all manifestations of mirroring selfobject functions.

Several of the following examples of mirroring selfobject failures come from a re-examination of outstanding projective testing texts from other periods in the development of diagnostic testing. These classic case discussions are valuable in their own right and also demonstrate that the interpretation of projective test content followed from the theoretical approach in which it was originally framed. Some of these views can be reconceptualized in light of subsequent developments in psychoanalysis, such as the psychology of the self and various theories of object relations. I am including select examples in this chapter to demonstrate how a clinician with a self psychologically informed viewpoint might understand such material.

Schafer (1954) presented the Rorschach protocol of a woman who was diagnosed with conversion hysteria (Repression, Case 1, pp. 197–203), a diagnosis emphasizing the characterologic organization of the personality as hysterical and narcissistic. In his ego psychology formulation of the protocol, Schafer commented on the naive and egocentric themes, accompanied by feelings of inadequacy and a need for protectors who are depreciated but still admiring of the patient. This patient's initial response to Card I was an orchid, which Schafer regarded as an indication of the core narcissism and a symbol of a passively received tribute to a woman's attractiveness. The implication is that the patient's presentation of herself asking for adornment or praise represents a character weakness. Consequently, her seeking attentiveness is a defensive reflection of narcissistic vanity.

Clinicians adopting a self psychological interpretation might view this response as neutral with respect to psychopathology or even characterological defect. The orchid would represent the patient's normal need to be valued, as when a child turns to an admiring parent for a display of acceptance of the child's effort. The initial response to Card I may be compared to the beginning treatment sessions of a patient asked to associate freely. If the early associations in treatment are thought of as asking the question "How am I doing?" the central dynamic is a need to be seen favorably or as competent. The comparable question about beginning the unfamiliar Rorschach test can just as easily be "Is this orchid a good enough response?" Thus, the interpretation of a narcissistic character structure is not crucial for understanding the orchid response but may represent the dynamic of healthy mirroring needs striving for recognition.

The patient's next response of a woman's dress need also not be interpreted as another narcissistic-decorative indication as Schafer regarded it. Schafer considered that the dress as an adornment took precedence over the human qualities of the person in the central detail of Card I. The focus on the dress rather than on the person may show a continued need for recognition or admiration originating with the orchid percept, as if the patient asked the examiner to admire her dress or appearance as a symbol of herself. It is like asking again "How am I doing?" without necessarily implying a deficiency in failing to appreciate the inner qualities of the person.

By the time Card II was presented, this patient's percept of dwarfs attending Snow White signifies a failure of the patient's wish to be admired or noticed, at least from the standpoint of Kohut's understanding of mirroring needs. The image of dwarfs may indeed indicate a depreciating mockery of men, as Schafer suggested. The same imagery can also reflect the patient's feeling of herself as weakened. This feeling is reflected in her state of being attended by dwarfs, in the absence of a more suitable selfobject presence to confirm that the patient as Snow White is, in effect, the fairest of them all. (This association is mine, not the patient's or Schafer's.) This line of thinking considers the patient's desire to be the fairest of them all, as I view it here, not as grandiosity, but rather as simply asking for admiration or affirmation of herself as worthwhile. The characterization of Snow White as standing for basically normal expectations of an optimal level of selfobject responsiveness can represent just as plausible an alternative to the vain, hysteroid "Southern belle" of Schafer's ego psychological interpretation.

Much of the remainder of this patient's protocol consisted of imagery such as heavy boots, a stuffed animal skin worked on by a taxidermist, a rat, beetles, and a dead tree branch. By the time the patient arrived at Card IX and reported knights in armor, it is easy to imagine that she had described again and again her experience of an injured self in need of mirroring selfobject responsiveness, with the suit of armor representing her need to protect her brittle sense of self. From this viewpoint, the knights in armor response need not be construed as another manifestation of the Snow White and seven dwarfs image of Card II, which was Schafer's beginning to his commentary about Card IX, emphasizing "hysteric imagery, Southern-belle style" or his patient's need to ward off hostility.

On Card X, Schafer considered the percept of a caterpillar that the patient despises (and other percepts of bugs and beetles seen on Card X) as naive, egocentric expressions of phobic defenses. A clinician of a self psychological persuasion may consider these same responses as the patient's failure to sufficiently repair the injuries leaving her with feelings of self-loathing. The patient's other response to Card X was a flower bud, which Schafer interpreted as part of her concern about loss of youthful charms. A psychology of the self interpretation centers on this image of the flower bud as a revivable kernel of self-esteem awaiting a responsively empathic selfobject to help restore an enfeebled self. The difference between the clinical interpretations of the previously cited responses contrasting drive theory and the psychology of the self also illustrates the different viewpoints about whether human needs are essentially in the service of enhancing faltering self-esteem or are drives and their derivatives in search of discharge.

As just noted, Schafer's patient concluded her Rorschach protocol with the image of a budding flower emerging forward, much like the orchid she began with. This imagery can be understood as a representation of narcissistic-decorative needs, as Schafer recommended. It may also be understood from the viewpoint of what the patient needs to sustain viable self-esteem. The examiner's empathic response to the Rorschach percept is to the need it represents. The self psychological view of empathy is not the same as the customary meaning of empathy as concern for a person's plight. With this type of empathic understanding, in Kohut's conceptualization of the self, one then considers an image such as a flower to stand for states of the self. More characteristically, it represents what the self requires for its "flowering," that is, cohesion or vigor. Thus, the imagery depicts as much the idea of what the self needs for its buoyancy as it reveals its state of health or disrepair.

The initial response of an orchid can also be seen as the response of the self *expecting* to be valued, like the healthy child who turns to the mother after successfully practicing some skill with the expectation of praise for that accomplishment. This mechanism is precisely that of the mirroring selfobject response. Schafer's patient experienced disparagement as revealed in many of her responses between the orchid and the flower bud. Feelings of disparagement reflect empathic failures to the self's more or less normal expectation of accurate mirroring to the assertive display of its vigor, like the orchid response. The knight's armor may represent the self's attempt to protect itself from further injury, and the flower bud of the following inkblot can be construed as a revivable attempt to obtain an empathically responsive mirroring response. The prognostically favorable indication implied by this dynamic does not reflect the relatively inflexible characterologic or defensive position that Schafer described as narcissistic-decorative in type.

A similar example is supplied by a sequence of Rorschach responses reported by P. M. Lerner (1988, p. 81) in which a patient reported on Card V: "A bat ... beautiful, billowing, and showing its splendor ... yet there is pain in the wings, they look racked and crumbled." The next response, also to Card V, was "dancing girls you see in Las Vegas with costumes on, head gear and little feet."

Although Lerner regarded these examples as illustrations of Winnicott's concept of the false self, he noted that the patient initially emphasized the exhibitionistic aspect of the self "showing its splendor" to be admired. This reaction quickly led to the anticipation of not being responded to (or selfobject failure, in Kohut's view) and resulted in the "crumbling" depression of diminished self-esteem. Lerner viewed the dancing girls percept as a defensive manifestation of the false self on the basis of the reference to being in costume. An examiner with a self psychological approach based on Kohut's work might note that the percept of dancing girls in costume represents an attempt to repair a devitalized self that had "crumbled" and failed to sustain its greatness ("showing its splendor"). Therefore, the percept need not necessarily be seen as defensive, but rather as the healthy attempt of a self seeking what it needs to be reinvigorated and thus to forestall further depression.

It is instructive to examine another patient's response to Card X, similar in some ways to the previous patient's response of the dancing girls in costume or Schafer's patient's percept of the flower bud. The response is described much more expansively in the following example, also taken from Schafer (1954; Projection, pp. 305–306). This patient reported: "Springtime with budding and flowers ... a certain sort of exuberance to it ... a feeling of newness in it, beginning a new thing." In the Menninger scoring system, this response was considered to be a confabulation, with a CF score, although Schafer noted that it contains "elements of pure C, absurd F- and autistic handling of size relationships" (p. 306). Although there is some question that this response unambiguously satisfies Comprehensive System criteria for confabulation, there can be little doubt that an integration failure has nevertheless taken place. This interpretation casts a different light on the matter of whether references to budding and newness represent rejuvenated self states in the same way as in the previous examples.

The poor quality of the response, in its utilization of affect (C or CF), form demand, and cognitive organization, may compromise this view about the self state. The response should at least cause examiners to consider comorbid psychopathology. Schafer pointed out that the response comes as a surprise because of the emptiness and depression suggested by the rest of the Rorschach protocol. Thus, examiners must take into account the possibility of hypomanic denial in evaluating this response, which provides a useful reminder that the total record, including the assignment of major scores for form quality, affect regulation, and cognitive organization, cannot be ignored in the analysis of content. This point is crucial to guard against the danger of unrestrained interpretations considered in isolation of the total record.

In contrast, another response with exuberant affect, but without a cognitive-affective integration failure, and also to Card X, was reported by Athey (1986, p. 36):

> Martian creatures ... overall, it's very colorful and conveys to me a feeling of celebration, even jubilance or flight. ... I guess I'm thinking of fireworks like on the Fourth of July ... like the burst of color and light of fireworks, and there is an overall feel of lightness and airiness to it as well.

Unlike Schafer's patient, Athey noted that this potential pure C response did not inappropriately combine with form-based components, and the associative process remained task focused. There were no thought disorder or cognitive integration scores. Thus, there was no apparent perceptual-cognitive failure in this response, which permitted an analysis of the joyful affect unspoiled by a response of poor form quality. This response is more similar to that of the flower bud of Schafer's first patient, but not to the response of the flower bud from the hypomanic patient just noted.

The contrast between these examples also serves as a useful reminder that the content analytic approach I am emphasizing throughout this book follows after formal scoring. It is not my intention to argue that content analysis should represent the sole or even the primary basis for clinical interpretation.

DISILLUSIONMENT AND SELF-DEPRECIATION

The previous examples illustrated that deficient responses to normal selfobject needs for mirroring undermine healthy, robust self-esteem. Mirroring provides the foundation for sustaining self-esteem; if it is off the mark, poorly timed, or insufficient, the result is the symptomatic picture of narcissistic personality and behavior disorders, or more generally, of disorders of the self. One of the chief manifestations of self disorders is depression with its associated problems of emptiness, chronic boredom, or disillusionment with life. These problems are frequently expressed in the form of self-depreciation, although they may be defensively transformed into devaluation of others as well. The examples that follow indicate how disillusionment and self-depreciation may appear clinically in projective test content.

The following Rorschach responses are by a patient who is more self-depreciating than were Schafer's and Lerner's patients cited previously. Nevertheless, there remains an attempt to repair a self state that appears pervasively devalued. The patient is a 35-year-old man, hospitalized for a major depressive episode after several job rejections following a checkered work history in his professional field. He produced the following response to Card VI: "Two bison, small horns and a head, irregularly shaped legs." He followed this response with a percept of "two bear rugs with just one arm," to which he added on inquiry: "They could be sewn together to make one rug. (Q) two pieces trying to come together to make a whole."

Ego psychologists would naturally be attracted to the conflict–defense configuration and would perhaps consider the bison percept to be a manifestation of aggressive wishes (suggested by the powerful figure of the bison) that are threatened by the counterwish of retaliation (the diminished horns and irregular leg of the bison; the missing [castrated or amputated] arm from the bear rug). This interpretation very likely regards the punitive superego as influential in the patient's depression.

Alternatively, this patient's responses suggest a desire to present an appearance of strength represented by the image of a bison, but this image is immediately undermined by the reference to small horns and poorly shaped legs. The sewn-together bear rug response reveals a self state in which the patient cannot stand on his own. The response captures failing to sustain self-cohesion particularly well by indicating that the patient, in his defective state, feels malformed or incomplete.

Another example comes from Holt's (1978, pp. 312–317) discussion of the TAT obtained from a young male college student. One TAT story reads: "He is a broken man ... He tries to find research in a pulp mill but by now he has become an automaton. He has no initiative and no spark, and his mind is warped."

Holt interpreted this response as an indication of stereotyped conformity. The same patient went on to produce another story in which: "She is completely disillusioned with what she thought there was in life other than what she had so she comes home and marries ... and settles into a life style exactly like that her mother had ... she resigns herself to it." Holt's interpretation emphasized disillusioned resignation. He characterized this young man's passivity as defensive reactions to threats to self-esteem. Although this view is evident, it may not go far enough. With the benefit of Kohut's understanding about the fall in self-esteem experienced when the self is unresponded to, the hopeless giving up reflected in these TAT responses suggests more than defensive passivity. These responses capture not only how the patient undoubtedly feels, but also what he urgently needs. Specifically, the need is for the responsiveness of an alive, invigorating selfobject that can provide the necessary mirroring for this man to recover his assertive ambitions.

Further evidence that self-cohesion has been undermined in the absence of optimal selfobject responsiveness may be seen in another TAT story from this young man:

This fellow has been working in the lab trying to find a new form of gasoline that will revolutionize the market. After 165 trials he finds it; an oil company buys it, but the new gas is shelved, and the man realizes ... that he will have to start over again. He is disillusioned with science which has no more to offer him. He has given up the idea of benefiting man. He is a broken man.

Holt did not indicate TAT card numbers, so it is unclear whether this story precedes the previous story. It is not crucial, however, insofar as the main point remains unchanged: After much effort, the product of the man's work is "shelved," as are all his hopes for sustaining self-esteem. Unmirrored and unresponded to with the vitalization he needs to support a buoyant, alive sense of the self, his ambitions (of science and benefiting mankind) and self-cohesion (the reference to a broken man) fail to take root. Although not inconsistent with Holt's characterization of this TAT story as a lowering of the ego ideal, Kohut's enhanced description of a healthy, viable self as a precondition for ego ideals adds a further level of understanding to the relation between selfobject functions buttressing self-esteem in striving to accomplish life goals.

Two other TAT stories from this same patient illustrate the devaluation that has developed to protect him from the self-esteem injuries he apparently experienced repeatedly: "He's against everything ... and against what everybody else is doing in general because he can never be satisfied with the world as it is. He always has a chip on his shoulder and a grudge to bear," and "the sounds that came out just were not music to him; so little by little he began to hate music lessons ... practicing just became a bore and a burden ... He began to hate his teacher. He began to dislike his mother for making him take lessons."

Holt's descriptions associated with these stories highlighted negativism and resentment. A reactive (defensive) pattern of abasement serves the purpose of protecting the patient by letting him retreat to an unreal world in which matters are set right. Kohut would very likely call attention to the experience of feeling bored and listless, of mechanically going about the business of life in a joyless manner. This self state of devitalization is bereft of the needed mirroring selfobject experiences that provide energy or pleasure. The patient's incentive to pursue goals and to enjoy life is replaced with angry, resentful emptiness.

The need for mirroring has not disappeared entirely and may still be revivable, as can be detected in TAT stories in which the patient "gradually worked up until he owned ... a corporation ... so he was rather successful in spite of the fact that he didn't have his father's help," and "he was a great daydreamer and often thought of himself as a Galahad riding off on a white horse or a kind doctor who helps all his patients." In addition, the patient tells a story in which "the farm isn't yielding anything any more, but still they keep on ... their future is just nil ... but they'll try again, year after year." Holt's description of these responses emphasized the patient's fantasies of achievement, but it is not clear whether these form the basis for his interpretation of a "retreat into an unreal world where matters are set right" (p. 317). The Galahad story is no more an indication of a retreat than any normal striving of an injured self attempting to find whatever resources may still remain to keep afloat. To regard it otherwise is clinically misguided, from the self psychological viewpoint. Nor is it correct to view owning his own corporation as magical thinking or a grandiose fantasy. The joyless struggle to keep trying despite repeated disappointments can not be overlooked in this patient's ongoing experience of his struggles to repair injured self-esteem.

ARROGANCE AND DEVALUATION

One typical way in which mirroring needs may appear is in the form of criticism, faultfinding, or arrogant superiority. These represent aspects of grandiosity and appear sometimes with only a superficial defensive veneer that barely conceals an underlying aggrandized sense of self. In fact, on closer analysis, the arrogance appears to mask feelings of diminished importance. The haughtiness or sense of entitlement is often the surface manifestation disguising that patients with self disorders can feel devalued, sometimes painfully so.

Although Kernberg (1975) and the *Diagnostic and Statistical Manual of Mental Disorders (DSM-IV)-fourth edition* criteria for narcissistic personality disorder accorded entitlement a prominent place among symptomatic features, Kohut did not emphasize this quality in the self disorders. Kohut's preference for directing attention to cold aloofness or arrogance rather than feelings of entitlement did not minimize the importance of entitlement in his thinking on the subject, however. Arrogant faultfinding is not seen as originating from envy, as does the British object relations theoretical preference or Kernberg's position on devaluation. Rather, the self psychological emphasis is on vulnerability or self-denigration. Thus, consider a response such as "two pigs dancing snout to snout ... or Middle European peasants dancing in a folk dance—women probably, peasants" as produced on Card II by a Hispanic man (P. M. Lerner, 1988, p. 286) or similar examples such as content involving "talking down to" or giving "dictation" to the examiner as in several examples provided by Schafer (1954) and P. M. Lerner (1991). Responses such as these are understood in the self psychological framework as revealing a patient's vulnerable, undermined self-esteem rather than as arising from a primarily aggressive impulse or from a sadistic or envious introject.

Following an object relations interpretation of psychological dynamics, P. M. Lerner (1991) also considered devaluation as a major clinical phenomenon seen on projective tests. Devaluation, from this viewpoint, may represent envy. Some of Lerner's examples included distortions of the human form, such as a sinister-looking figure, a headless figure, evil witches, or figures from outer space. These examples characterize a self-image of incompleteness, distortion, or failure. These aspects of the experience of the self are not the same as Kohut's concept of devaluation. In Kohut's view, devaluation appeared as a defensive means of protecting the self from further injury by concealing how the patient experiences compromised self-esteem.

The following vignettes are from a 53-year-old depressed woman executive currently in her third lifetime hospitalization for a suicide attempt. The patient had a history of flight of ideas and decreased need for sleep, although there were no clearly documented manic or hypomanic episodes. Her initial Rorschach response was "a butterfly" (Card I), and on inquiry she stated:

> The dominant thing is the wings, not a perfect rendition of wings. This thing is not interesting, but calling it a butterfly gives it more validity even though it's not perfect, so I gave it its best name. Looking at it now I see these hands like maybe it's drowning, but at first I didn't see that.

Her next response to the same card is a frog, subsequently elaborated on inquiry by the comment: "Frogs seem like ugly witless things to me," which is then followed by a bat, to which she notes, on inquiry, that "it looks blind, no intelligence there." This same patient reported two butlers as her first of five responses to Card III; however her fifth response was "creatures talking to the butlers, they seem to know what they're doing, though, not like that woman we just drew, sort of a dumb ox" [the human figure drawings preceded the Rorschach]. She began her inquiry to this response by commenting: "It's like you'd just better do it right, you fellows [referring to the creatures talking to the butlers], this is a very important affair so don't screw up."

Responses characterized by haughty arrogance frequently coexist with other percepts denoting self-depreciation and finding oneself lacking. Thus, this woman produced percepts such as "antennae of a bat, something very sensitive, the vital center of the bat, the nerve center. If you destroy that you destroy the whole thing" (Card V), and "like an animal, perched, balancing" (Card VII), to which she elaborated on inquiry: "like all this kinetic stuff. I must be very lacking in fantasy. There must be this big void in me that I'm not that fanciful."

Even on Card III (between the butlers and the creatures talking to the butlers), the patient reported percepts of gnomes and "a decoration to fill in the picture. I could say it looks like a tie but that's not very interesting ... it's not doing anything, just hanging there." One final example from this same patient's record is a response to Card IV of "dry leaves, very thin and curled" to which she added in the inquiry: "I see a burst of glory, very dramatic, wondrous and warm, while everyone else sees it as everything dying." This response may provide a good illustration of hypomanic denial.

It is at the same time a good representation of the lengths to which she may need to go to preserve a vibrant, buoyant self in the face of a self state more accurately experienced as diminished.

This patient's combination of bravado and devaluation extends beyond the Rorschach. Several instructive illustrations from her TAT and figure drawings continued the same themes noted on her Rorschach. Thus, elaborating on her drawing of a person, this patient stated:

> It's devoid of a projector who could project it well. This poor person is not attractive and not very interesting and she certainly has no style. That's a feminine line there but I don't know how to make her pretty, she's sort of stuck with this funny body. Sort of a stupid expression, a flat, featureless face: the cortisone look.

By her critical, mocking tone, this patient attempted to distance herself from this projection of her depreciated self. Her response was consistent with the previously noted Rorschach percepts in which the patient attempted to stand above her percepts, such as an uninteresting tie or an imperfect butterfly. Her effort was not entirely successful, as in her remarks about a void in herself so that she was not "fanciful" in her imagination. In the projective drawing, she tried to avoid identifying with the person who was unattractive, but her only recourse was to fault the projector who is not able to project the figure well. On Card 1 of the TAT, the patient told the story of a boy who is told to play the violin but "he couldn't care less, so he pulls out the violin in both boredom and exasperation, he puzzles how he can be expected to get anything out of this contraption." Her outcome was that the boy breaks the violin "with his hands in his pocket and a shrug of defeat ... although the mother is disappointed."

After inquiring about the mother's disappointment, the patient changed her tune: She concluded her story with the boy "dejected" rather than the previous defensive shrug of defeat. Once again, and by now on three different projective tests, this patient showed that a defensive bravado, critical arrogance, or distancing herself from shortcomings readily evoked feelings of shame or disparagement. Her vulnerable self-esteem was repeatedly seen through images of diminished intellect, attractiveness, or talent.

Schafer (1954) reported the Rorschach records of two patients in which a similar dynamic appears to be evident. One patient's (Repression, Case 3, p. 213) response to Card III is that of two little men, about which Schafer noted the condescension, but which he also conceptualized from the drive theory position of oedipal rivalry or masculine strivings. Similarly, another patient's (Denial, Case 1, pp. 255–268) response to Card I was the sinister-looking image of a figure with a small head, big body, and "short hands lifted up like this, as though he needed elongation for strength ... with no mentality: that's why you could go back almost to prehistoric ages with it." On Card III, the same patient reported dead limbs of trees, "an old hobo ... gives the impression of rags and tatters," and a monkey hanging from a tree.

Commenting on these responses, Schafer considered the reference to the male figure seeking strength on Card I as the patient's unstable conception about masculinity and devaluation of the male figure. He noted: "She may be unsure whether masculinity implies strength or weakness, i.e., whether to be awed by it or to sneer at it" (Schafer, 1954, p. 256). He continued in this vein by interpreting the hobo–caricature figure as an indication that men are ineffectual failures. Schafer included the dead limb response as a further representation of masculine deterioration and the inadequacy of men as providers. Clearly, although devaluation by no means went unnoticed in Schafer's interpretive remarks, these themes are cast squarely in a drive theory framework. From this perspective, oedipal rivalry is superimposed on oral hostility in the patient's complaints about the inadequacy of men as nurturant providers.

Schafer's patient continued to deliver responses of a similar nature, with percepts such as "little gnomes" and a "horrible old man" (Card V), a "weird figure" and "the Old Man of the Mountains carved out in the rock, not by a good sculptor" (Card VI), "the face of a baboon" (Card IX), and "a child's drawing ... but the house is too small" and "an old telegraph pole that was partly cut down and grayed with age; not painted the way modern ones are" (Card X). The devaluative content and tone of many of these responses revealed this patient's preoccupation with underpowered figures. In this regard, the projected aspects of her feeling concerned her own ineffectualness.

This same patient displayed indications of idealizing selfobject functions alongside her responses with a devaluing tone. I return later to the clinical significance of mirroring and idealizing selfobject functions coexisting in the same person. For the moment, it is sufficient to note that these selfobject functions need not be mutually exclusive. Indeed, the relative balance between them and the capacity for one selfobject function to achieve self-esteem regulation more successfully than another are further important considerations in the interpretation of projective test findings.

In regard to Schafer's patient, Kohut's view would not ignore the possibility that men are seen as incompetent, although the dead tree limb, the hobo in rags and tatters, and the figure with the small head in need of elongation need not refer exclusively to men. Schafer's patient's faultfinding is well-noted and is seen as her attempt to defensively protect herself from being re-exposed to feeling inadequate. The same dynamic also applies to the patient with grandiose-sounding criticisms delivered repeatedly.

Thus, grandiose bravado or complaining on projective test responses may be understood as externalizations of what is at root a prominent self state of feeling defective. Theoretically, the exaggerated grandiosity and devaluation seen in Schafer's patients' responses cited previously may be understood as originating from an unmirrored self. The empathic responsiveness of a selfobject environment capable of understanding the self's requirement for vitality and cohesion has chronically been absent, has left patients vulnerable, and has caused them to defensively fall back on haughty arrogance to protect the devitalized self.

Schafer (1967, p. 116) also reported a sequence of TAT stories from a 52-year-old male patient with a chronic alcohol problem. The stories represented admixtures of bravado and devaluation alternating with self-depreciation. The patient began on Card 1 with a story about a boy practicing the violin who "hadn't brought off, what will we say, the Scarlatti exercise to his satisfaction. He is a sensitive, thoughtful child who, like myself, needs a haircut. ... Okay, that takes care of Buster. Oh, you put everything down" [noticing the examiner's verbatim recording].

Schafer's clinical interpretation took full account of the theme of failure but emphasized the defensive tone in which the patient presented himself as cultured while flippantly remarking about the haircut. The nonchalant detachment about the examiner's work barely concealed the patient's devaluation. This devaluation extended to the condescending reference to the boy of his story (with whom he identified) and continued throughout successive TAT responses. Schafer commented: "From a characterological point of view his style of defense—facetiousness, condescension, transient identification, status seeking, nonchalance—is steadily narcissistic" (p. 122). The self psychological view would focus on the injury and the patient's image of himself as small and insignificant. From this viewpoint, unattuned selfobject responsiveness to the self-esteem loss is the central dynamic feature.

The issue of compromised self-esteem runs throughout the rest of this man's TAT protocol. Thus, for example, the story for Card 7BM showed the degree to which the patient alienated himself from the needed soothing responsiveness in the selfobject milieu, as the patient told of being in trouble with the law and "his patient, understanding father is appearing with him in court and trying to offer a bit of paternal advice. The boy, both remorseful and defiant, is listening to papa but it is too late. He is sent to a prison term ... for further details, see page three." Schafer certainly noted the "sarcasm and detachment concerning human involvement and morality" (p. 125). It is clear, however, that the central interpretive points were "intense fear of destructive, authoritarian punishment for the aggressive, sexual, and oral aspects of oedipal strivings, and fear of being cut off from maternal supplies, of which he feels very much in need" (p. 127).

The focus of a self psychological interpretation is rather different. The grandiose bravado is a thinly disguised smokescreen attempting to conceal the injury from an unavailable, unresponsive, or unattuned selfobject milieu. The story's description of an understanding father whose advice arrives too late to help the boy betrayed the absence of a selfobject environment in which normal exhibitionistic strivings were tolerated and affirmed. Injuries resulting from momentary failures might have been eased by timely, empathically responsive calming, which might have forestalled the patient's need to develop such hypermetabolized grandiosity and sarcasm. The patient's need to depreciate much of what he came in contact with preserved his faltering self-esteem.

It should be apparent from all these illustrations that grandiose images are closely related to depreciation. On suitably vigorous inquiry, these grandiose responses readily expose the self injury that undermines a cohesive, firmed-up mental structure. The inferential strategy assumes that a reference to the condition of an object seen in a Rorschach percept alters the nature of the response itself in a psychologically important way.

The same observation is true of descriptions of the mental or physical state of a character in a TAT story or of a human figure, house, or tree drawn on command. The description does not refer only to an object with good or poor fit to the form demand of the inkblot, and the perceptual function is not seen as the primary task. The elaboration about the condition of the object or person is taken as a projection of some aspect of the patient's internal state. In particular, the experience of the self is crucial insofar as it is felt to be cohesive, vigorous, or able to withstand threat. The predominant selfobject need is typically one in search of a potentially available or responsive selfobject to repair defective mirroring.

CONTENT ANALYSIS AND SELF STATES: FORMULATING INFERENCES

To this point, I have sketched several principal clinical features characterizing the mirroring selfobject function. I have attempted to show that mirroring selfobject responsiveness is fundamentally a normal rather than a pathological need. It is both necessary and expectable that accurately timed empathic mirroring leads to healthy self-cohesion in normal development. Only when normal mirroring needs are derailed, through deficiency, inappropriate timeliness, or inaccurate responsiveness, is self-esteem undermined. Mirroring selfobject failures prevent the feeling of admiration that promotes healthy pride, buoyancy, and a feeling of being valued. The results of defective mirroring are self-depreciation, haughty grandiosity, or devaluation previously described in addition to the more pronounced disintegration products that Kohut described.

I proceed now with further examples, which were obtained by pursuing a more vigorous inquiry than is often the case. Some of these examples represent subtle features of mirroring selfobject functions. These illustrations are all the more notable because the subtle manifestations of defective mirroring emerged from the detailed inquiry that becomes necessary when considering content. The inquiry that I illustrate here probes in depth to reveal selfobject failures that often result from empathically unattuned mirroring. People who feel devalued attempt to hide this self state in life, on interview (particularly when they feel unsafe with a therapist or interviewer), and also on projective testing. Patients with resilient defenses conceal their depreciated self states more effectively; they often drop hints rather than expose their problems like an open wound. These hints may not be detected sufficiently with formal scoring. It requires a probing inquiry, conducted sensitively and judiciously, to reveal the self state in depth.

The strategy of vigorously pursuing elaborations and associations on inquiry comes as no surprise to seasoned clinicians, including those whose preference is to favor empirically supported inferences. The purpose of provocative inquiry is to bring to the foreground the internal experiences mobilized by projective stimuli. Provocation in this sense does not mean that thoughts or affective states are suggested or induced. A clinician's judgment determines where to draw the line between unearthing what is there and planting the seed of what an examiner wants to see emerge.

The first example presents a series of TAT responses and figure drawing elaborations that suggest important aspects of the self state. The patient was a 21-year-old unmarried woman hospitalized for a depressive episode after an unsuccessful job search following her college graduation. Her drawing of a woman was described as happy, autonomous, and joyful, but her drawing of a man shifted to an image of someone indifferent and unattainable. Her earlier verbalization about the autonomous and confident woman changed when she was queried about what she meant by the man whom she drew as unattainable. She commented: "Girls would have to feel like you have to get someone, something I always felt I'd never attain. He's looking away, not interested in what I'm doing." It is of more than passing interest that her devalued self-esteem came forward in her elaboration of the male drawing. This response casts doubt on her original statements about the female drawing. This skepticism about the healthy self-image based on the female drawing would not have arisen in the absence of the additional comment that emerged after a thorough inquiry about the male drawing. This patient reported a number of other responses that revealed the same self state so that the interpretation is not tied to a single response. The patients who can conceal deep internal states are precisely the patients who require special efforts to provocatively reveal what an examiner needs to understand about this level of the personality.

The TAT continued these concerns about failure, measuring up, and attempting to assert her own wishes: The boy of Card 1 "failed to do as well as he should have," the girl of Card 2 "feels left out because she's obviously not part of the more simple farm life," and the character of Card 3BM is "like a puppet who fell. All her strings got cut. In the end, she stands up again." The predominant imagery of failure and isolation is also associated with the feeling that "her mother is not into what the daughter is doing" (Card 2) and "the girl wants to do something but the mother is hovering over her being overclawing" (Card 7GF). These responses suggest deficient mirroring of the patient's autonomous wishes. The mother's selfobject failures, lacking in empathic responsiveness as these appear to be, contributed to the patient's concern about measuring up. Although a few of these elaborations were supplied spontaneously by the patient, just as many appeared only after a follow-up question. It is well worth repeating that it takes time to conduct a thoughtful, careful inquiry.

The following examples are taken from the Rorschach of a 16-year-old girl whose parents were divorced; she had been hospitalized following a suicide attempt precipitated by her father's recent remarriage. In each instance, the patient was asked for an association by way of testing the limits after the scoreable response features were obtained in the standard manner of administration. On Card I, the patient reported "a dog, a Brittany spaniel, a puppy," to which she added upon prompting after the formal inquiry for determinants: "Looks dead or sick or unhappy, just kind of there, no emotion." On Card II, she responded with "a big diamond in the middle, like an engagement ring," which was elaborated on inquiry as being "surrounded by junk, it can't shine because no one could see it because there's so much other stuff surrounding it that it's just buried. It's sad because no one can see the beauty of the ring unless they dig through all that stuff." On Card III, the patient reported "a bloody frog," which she explained in the inquiry as: "blood smeared all around it and it just runs, like someone stepped on him." The patient produced "a dragon" on Card IV and elaborated further on inquiry: "Funny-looking like his front feet are bent over and the back feet are up here, a flexible dragon. (Q) looks sad to me, like he can't blow out a fire any more. He's old and he's rotting away."

Some of these percepts are notable because of the juxtaposition of striking contrasts, such as an engagement ring surrounded by junk or a dragon (even a "flexible" dragon) who is old and rotting away. The psychological meaning of a powerful but impotent dragon or junk obscuring the glitter of the diamond is relevant for understanding the patient's self state.

The image of junk alongside a shining ring points to a condition in which the self is very likely experienced as devalued. It also contains some degree of preserved self-esteem, because a valuable object is still viable however demeaned it is. This response also provides a good example on projective testing of Kohut's belief that the injured self is invariably experienced alongside the selfobject function that it needs for its recovery. In this instance, the devalued self as expressed through the reference to junk is potentially revivable in the form of the diamond, which represents, therefore, a vigorous self wanting to be seen, admired, or valued. The reference to the engagement ring might also connote disparagement of marriage or intimacy as the ring is described as surrounded by junk.

The percept of the dragon may be understood as a symbol of strength to be taken seriously, regardless of the hostile or menacing connotations it also has. The play of children, especially boys, is replete with fantasies of overcoming powerful and frightening figures, fantasies that have more to do with affirming vigor than with aggression. This patient's dragon may also represent a self wishing to be admired for strutting its stuff as if to say "Look at what I can do." The self is represented as weak, however, regardless of how face saving the defense of a "flexible" dragon may seem. This attempt to buttress a self state shows more vulnerability than vigor. Similarly, the stepped-on frog and the sickly dog are also indications of an injured, depreciated self. At least three of the four responses would not have yielded the self state interpretation denoted here without the testing of limits after a standard inquiry.

This patient's TAT stories take on a significance that is not only consistent with the just-mentioned self psychological interpretation, but that also casts a different light on how conventional interpretations of common TAT themes might be construed. On Card 2, the patient described a situation in which the man plowing the field, who is married to the woman in the background, has an affair with the woman in the foreground. He leaves the woman because he prefers his wife, and the woman "feels she's been used and hates the guy, but eventually it doesn't bother her." To Card 3BM, the patient's story is that of a girl crying because her mother, who had promised to sew a new dress for her, "gets caught up in other things so she has to do it herself, and like cutting the dress she gets it uneven and ruins the dress. She wears something else and lets it go by." The patient relates the following story to Card 4: "She's in love with this man but she moved away and just came back after a long time and finds him married to someone else. She tries to make him come back to her but he won't. Then she finds someone else."

All three stories have a theme of rejection, either by a man in favor of another woman or by the mother who appears to forget about the patient. All three stories end with an apparently flippant disregard for the affective reaction of being rejected or ignored. It is not difficult to infer oedipal rivalry and defeat interpretations from these stories. The patient seems inclined to favor defensive operations that allow her to wall off or minimize the emotional impact of rejection.

From a self psychological standpoint, however, the themes in these three stories indicate a normal-enough seeking of admiration, appearing in a way that suggests that she should be valued for her qualities. She asked for a mirroring responsiveness that would enable her to feel vibrant. The stories are a TAT analog of the diamond to be admired or the vigorous dragon demonstrating its strength as these were seen on this patient's Rorschach. Moreover, the TAT stories are a clearer statement of the wish for mirroring selfobject responsiveness. The spurning of the female figures in the stories, together with the mother who became distracted and forgot about her, points to the patient's experiences of devaluation associated with the thwarted mirroring selfobject need. These experiences are echoed on her Rorschach, in which the diamond cannot shine because it is surrounded by junk and the dragon is no longer powerful because it cannot blow out a fire and is in danger of rotting away.

Thus, the wish to be treasured or seen as desirable, vibrant, and valuable emerges in these projective test responses. This wish can be viewed as representing the normal manifestation of the grandiose-exhibitionistic self that presents itself to the world, like the normal toddler asking to be admired and affirmed. That the patient experiences mirroring selfobject functions as absent, inattentive, or unresponsive to her can be seen in the diminished feeling of buoyancy of the self, producing feelings of inadequacy. This feeling is also evident in the patient's story about making a dress that is ruined because the mother was too uninvolved to help her and in her stories of men seeking other women as love objects. These responses recapitulate the percept of junk obscuring a diamond and the response of a dragon rotting away. The defensive walling off of painful affects associated with the mother's neglect or the men turning away from the women of the TAT stories also appears. This imagery reveals the distance that this patient attempted to create to minimize experiencing narcissistic injury to her vulnerable self-esteem.

Even the example of the bloodied frog suggests something more about the experience of self-depreciation because the patient reported that the frog was stepped on. This comment is as compelling as the strong association between the red color and blood; it reaches beyond the aggressive connotation of stepping on a living thing as expressed in this response. Probably hostile in intent, although not necessarily always, being stepped on is also a prominent metaphor for how people feel when belittled or criticized insensitively. The consequent injury to self-esteem is a dimension of personality that should be considered in addition to the propensity for rage. Finally, the examples of falling in the water and the sick or unhappy dog without emotion also suggest self states associated with injury. These less striking images are consistent with the psychological meaning of the patient's responses of a stepped-on frog that is bleeding or a diamond ring that is degraded by junk that hides its brilliant sheen.

These two cases illustrate the importance of considering richly elaborated verbalizations. Examiners must conduct a cautiously provocative inquiry when necessary to expose a patient's inner life as much as possible. Usually all that is needed to provoke or unearth an association is simply singling out a word or phrase and asking for elaboration, such as "An engagement ring?" or "A flexible dragon?" Often, provocative inquiry is not even necessary: A patient may freely provide useful associations, such as the TAT responses or the bloody frog Rorschach percept cited previously. Examiners must permit verbalizations to come forward beyond what is needed for formal scoring to hear the deep psychological meaning.

CONTENT ANALYSIS AND SELF STATES: IDENTIFYING MIRRORING AND DRIVE DERIVATIVES

This section addresses the matter of drawing inferences about self states, particularly those arising out of defective mirroring. I discuss differentiating between interpretations derived from self psychology and ego psychology by using projective test content and begin with a discussion of some problems about how mirroring may be accurately identified.

Mirroring

The first example illustrates how a self psychological explanation of a Rorschach response may be misapplied. This vignette is taken from one of the few reports in the published literature about a self psychological approach to projective testing. It provides a particularly good illustration of the need to exercise care in clinical interpretation. At the same time, this report by Arnow and Cooper (1988, p. 58) contributes several excellent examples of a self psychologically informed interpretive approach.

Arnow and Cooper (1988) provided the following Rorschach response from Card VII: "Two statues facing each other but without much expression on their faces." Their interpretation of this response centered on the formality and coldness of the statues. They emphasized the patient's experience of the mother's difficulty in providing sufficiently enthusiastic mirroring. Arnow and Cooper suggested that the patient hid behind a controlled exterior. They also suggested that this response characterized one of Kohut and Wolf's (1978) typologies, referred to as the contact-shunning personality.

Arnow and Cooper's (1988) interpretation of this response should be seen as tentative. Although the interpretation is appealing, the response of statues without expression does not unambiguously characterize mirroring. The affectively removed statue figures may well refer to an important aspect of the patient's experience of his selfobject environment, however a more compelling case could have been made if the patient's verbalization involved turning to the statue percept for affirmation that was rebuffed. A percept of a statue may sometimes connote unavailability when the statue is specifically referred to as expressionless as in this example. Unavailability is not, however, the same thing as deficient mirroring, particularly in the absence of an indication that a need is frustrated. Furthermore, the clinical validity and conceptual utility of Kohut and Wolf's (1978) subtypes have not been uniformly acknowledged.

This fact does not necessarily weaken the basis for assuming that a mirroring selfobject need for empathic responsiveness is present. The percept as it stands, however, is too ambiguous for one to conclude that a mirroring need is mobilized for the patient at this time. In treatment, the selfobject need is less certain when it is inferred from its absence. Selfobject functions are most clear when seen through rage reactions and depression or depletion anxiety arising from frustration of the selfobject need. These functions are perhaps best illustrated by Kohut's (1971) case of Miss F., summarized in chapter 1.

The same consideration about inferring selfobject functions through the absence of a reaction or evidence for disintegration products is applicable in psychodiagnostic testing situations. The most reliable indications of faulty mirroring are references to a rebuff of the need for mirroring selfobject responsiveness. The response to that rejection (such as somebody or something's being depleted, in ruins, or rotting away) becomes crucial for identifying the selfobject need. Responses based on absence of a reaction, even stiffness or coldness, are less reliable because they are nonspecific to mirroring. They may still be accurate, but other substantive evidence is needed to make a compelling case.

The problem with Arnow and Cooper's example is compounded by attributing the mirroring deficiency specifically to a maternal figure. Perhaps their reason was that the response occurs on Card VII, but this gratuitous interpretive link is a well-established error in clinical inference. Their attribution may be applicable to the patient on the basis of the total protocol, but as a clinical vignette considered out of context, this example is ill advised. It is also unclear whether Arnow and Cooper regarded the statue, with its associations of reserve, as an indication of an unresponsive mother, the patient's defensive coldness, or both. Finally, Arnow and Cooper's (1988, p. 59) view about the patient's defensive reserve may not be well-supported by the available evidence. Kohut did not inevitably imply that a surface veneer of coldness or a controlling manner represents a defensive transformation of defective mirroring.

In contrast, Arnow and Cooper (1988) provided a better reasoned example of a Rorschach percept of a chandelier coming close to the mark: "Very, very warm, of the past. Grandmother's house. To bask in the warm light of a radiant smile." This response sustained their interpretive hypothesis of a mirroring need, represented by the chandelier as something to be admired.

The chandelier as a representation of the grandiose-exhibitionistic self is thus a more understandable interpretive suggestion, in contrast with the statue–mother–Card VII link of the previous example. With this interpretation built around the association between warmth and the grandmother, the longing for the grandmother in connection with a mirroring selfobject function can more readily be appreciated.

As with grandiosity, responses with references to mirror images or reflections do not automatically connote mirroring selfobject functions. For example, P. M. Lerner (1991) cited a Rorschach response of two men "mirroring each other ... a man fixing himself up in front of a mirror" (p. 216). This response was intended to illustrate narcissistic mirroring, as an illustration of Kwawer's (1980) scale of borderline interpersonal relations. This mirroring is not, however, the same as that described by Kohut. Similarly, Sugarman (1986, p. 67) reported the following response to Rorschach Card VIII: "This looks like some sort of a jungle animal looking at its reflection in a pond." Neither example indicates that the patient felt devalued or experienced a need for empathic responsiveness. The examples highlight the caution necessary when extrapolating concepts from one theoretical system to another to avoid introducing unintended implications. Although it is true that mirroring is a central concept in Kohut's psychology of the self, it is equally true that casual indications of reflections in a mirror do not by themselves connote Kohut's specific meaning.

The following response, from P. M. Lerner (1988), contains an image of mirrors that is consistent with mirroring selfobject needs. Lerner's patient reported a clown making a face in a mirror so that there seemed to be two people when there was just one person (Card II). Lerner commented about the patient's difficulty in differentiating her own internal states from those that the patient attributed to others. From this point of reference, her preoccupation with mirror images represented her way of seeing herself in others. The patient thus attempted to know who she was and what she felt. Her imagery also represented the need-gratifying quality of her relationships.

This interpretation may illustrate a theoretical difference between Lerner's conceptualization of the patient's diffused sense of self and Kohut's interpretation of mirror imagery as the patient's need to sustain a clear experience of the self as cohesive. Nevertheless, the need for mirroring selfobject experience seems to be well-sustained in this Rorschach response. This percept and other examples that Lerner reported, contain more than the mere mention of mirrors and mirror images. There are sufficient elements of an experience in depth with regard to the sense of the self and its requirement for a mirroring selfobject function to sustain feeling firmed up.

Mirroring and Drive Derivatives

To this point, I have described the circumstances in which Rorschach response imagery may represent mirroring. The examples that follow are concerned with a different matter: whether a Rorschach percept best lends itself to a classical drive theory interpretation or to one from an alternative framework, that of psychoanalytic self psychology. I illustrate self psychological interpretations alongside those derived from ego psychology. Multiple examples from the same patients offer the possibility of sequence analysis for examining consecutive responses.

The examples in this section are all taken from Schafer (1954, 1967), who has provided some of the richest and most complete protocols in the existing literature. Schafer's interpretations are valuable because they are conceptualized solidly in the ego psychological tradition.

The first patient (Schafer, 1954) began Card I with a bat, followed by "the continent of Australia after an atom bomb hit it," and concluded with "a map of Shangri-la." It is understandable that Schafer stressed the aggressive content of the bomb; so, too, does a self psychological frame of reference. The difference, however, is that in the self psychological interpretation, this response is a disintegration product announcing that the patient's self-cohesion is undermined so seriously that it is in danger of being devastated.

In a drive theory interpretation, the destructive rage is a manifestation of the patient's aggressive drive. In contrast, the self psychological position regards the response as the patient's saying "I have been destroyed or shattered" rather than "I am angry or enraged." The patient does not reveal his hostility so much as he reveals his vulnerability. In addition, as considered in this context, the percept of Shangri-la is not thought of as a denial of aggression in the form of passive-regressive wishes as Schafer advised. Rather, it is an attempt to repair the devastation by achieving some semblance of restorative calmness.

Self psychology has been criticized for minimizing aggressive urges, but this criticism is often misplaced. Aggression is not ignored but has a different clinical meaning. Instead of being seen as a fundamental drive, anger is more typically understood as a disintegration product that indicates the presence of a self that is either vulnerable or endangered. The self seeks a means to restore cohesion. The response of Schafer's patient illustrates the dilemma well. Shangri-la is not the patient's attempt to escape from destructive rage; instead, it represents the hope to find a source of soothing calmness in which the patient can recover from the injury to which the self has been exposed.

Subsequently, this same patient gave the response on Card IV of "a bearskin rug charred in a fire." Although Schafer's interpretation included the patient's destructive impulses, he also commented on the overriding sense of devastation that the patient experienced. He noted that it is of "more immediate significance" when he stated: "The patient appears to feel in ruins." This feeling is close to the self psychological viewpoint.

Before the response of destruction in a fire, the patient reported birds with boxing gloves and ballet dancers, then Scottie dogs chasing a butterfly (Card V), and, still later, cherub figures and an island that suggested a safe harbor (Card VII). The patient concluded Card VII, however, with a decomposed pelvic structure. He became appreciably flustered in his initial inability to deliver a response to Card IX, an inability accompanied by bravado and defensive arrogance. The patient at last admitted failure when he stated that "it doesn't bring to life a single thing, so we might as well say so."

His feeling of being incapable of bringing a response "to life" may be a plausible metaphor for this man's core experience of the self state as devitalized and his fear that it cannot be revived. He did succeed, however, in delivering responses of South Sea island natives kissing and wearing fluffy ostrich feathers and a Mardi Gras scene that he named "I'm forever blowing bubbles." In a similar fashion, after an initial response to Card X of "My God! They finally blew one apart here!" he concluded the protocol with sea animals and another Mardi Gras scene.

Thus, Schafer's patient alternated between a self state of devastation and attempts to repair injured self-cohesion. He attempted to ease his way out by either defensively amusing himself or searching for some source of calm amid the inner storms he experienced so powerfully. This man attempted to repair an injured self by seeking calming selfobject responses, although this attempt was sometimes concealed behind a frivolous off-putting surface presentation. This case is included here, in a discussion of mirroring, because soothing images are frequently a manifestation of mirroring selfobject functions. In this sense, ministration or nurturing is sought not as an expression of dependency, but as an attempt to repair injuries to an undermined self. Thus, responses such as those cited, representing oral needs in the framework of drive theory, may alternatively be viewed from a self psychological viewpoint as indications of mirroring needs.

Another example, from a later work by Schafer (1967, p. 129), may make the point more clearly. A depressed patient reported the following TAT story on Card 5:

> This woman is taking a last look at her living room. She has invited her husband's boss for dinner and she is not ready ... she is worried that the room isn't neat enough because her husband always says she is messy ... she does have time to go upstairs and change and it is a very successful party.

Schafer's (1967) interpretation centered on oral needs, yet the protagonist of this story may have been primarily concerned with how she appears and how she is judged. Her self-esteem seemed to depend on the affirmation resulting from performing successfully. From the vantage point of self psychology, concerns with oral needs surrounding food and a dinner are considered less crucial features. Although not commented on by Schafer, anal preoccupations derived from criticism around messiness are also of minor interpretive importance. At most, the dynamics of such oral or anal conflicts are secondary to the central need to preserve self-esteem.

Pathological or pronounced oral needs or anal preoccupations are therefore disintegration products rather than drive states. The need is for the self to be experienced as robust and cohesive. This experience is sought by securing selfobject responsiveness based on acknowledging the need to be judged as competent. In this sense, the specific selfobject need is that of mirroring. Like the Rorschach examples quoted previously, calming, soothing, and reassuring responses are usually considered to represent central aspects of Kohut's broad interpretation of mirroring.

FURTHER PROJECTIVE TEST INDICATIONS OF A DEVITALIZED SELF

These examples provide illustrations of defective mirroring needs that are subtle. In other manifestations of faulty mirroring seen frequently in moderately well-compensated patients, self-esteem appears less overtly pathological. The essential characteristic of this category of self-esteem dysregulation concerns a person's experiences of him or herself as small, insignificant, or unresponded to along with feelings of tentativeness about facing the world with confidence.

In everyday life, patients may describe transient states such as shyness, timidity, generosity to the point of selflessness, unfailing availability to others' needs, and admirable humility. Sometimes viewed as virtues to others, these subtle manifestations of an often asymptomatic self disorder are best thought of as characterologically ingrained features, at times associated with subclinical dysphoric mood, or with chronic but intermittent states of dysthymic moods that fall short of full criteria for a major mood disorder syndrome.

Although less frequent, striking, or provocative, the projective test features of these subclinical states are similar to those of patients with more overt self disorders. A diagnostic testing examiner may either fail to notice such responses or may be uncertain of their significance and dismiss them as a momentary anomaly, particularly if such responses do not recur. Responses like these are more difficult to interpret because they can be fleeting and barely noticeable, as if, on an airplane, turbulence passed so quickly that there was not time for the captain to request that passengers fasten their seat belts. As with the airplane turbulence, a problem arises when there are more than just a few such isolated moments or responses.

The customary criteria for judging adequacy of inferences can lead to a decision to minimize the validity of subtle signs of self state disruptions. I am hesitant to argue strongly for paying great heed to fleeting responses of this nature; the criteria for taking them into account are usually impression-istic and therefore difficult to defend convincingly. My main recommenda-tion, therefore, is for clinicians to note their presence and potential significance as a tentative indication.

Some examples of the types of responses that I refer to describe dimin-ished or underpowered figures, such as "two men facing each other; cartoon faces, old crusty types with a cigarette dangling out of the side of the mouth, playing patty-cake" (Card II) or "a hint of a couple of faces, humanoid, child-like, almost a cherub. The smallness and delicacy to the features" (Card VII).

These two responses are from the protocol of a 34-year-old male physi-cian who was receiving disability benefits while claiming that he was unable to return to the practice of medicine. The percepts were not notably unusual for these card areas, and the form quality and determinants were also unremarkable. The percept of men playing a child's game is likely to be seen as an indication of impotence or insignificance, a regression originating perhaps from oedipal defeat. This cartoon image may also be a thinly disguised self-devaluation deflecting attention from the self state of one feeling infantilized, as the cartoon image of adult men reduced to child's play suggests. The percept of a cherub is also not particularly unusual, although the tendency to emphasize the oedipal theme of smallness can obscure the fact that the delicacy of a child-like figure suggests fragility of the self.

In contrast, neither of these responses is as unambiguous as, for example, another patient's percept of "some kind of flower, the leaves are dying, they're wilting over" (Card IV). Here, the devitalized self state emerges in a clear and undisguised manner.

This same patient began the figure drawings with the comment: "You're attacking my weakest skill," a remark conveying his fear of being re-exposed to a vulnerability in which he might appear deficient. His drawing of a man, in which he "drew his hair like my own," was immediately criticized in statements about a receding hairline, too-long arms, and being young "but not real young." Much of his elaboration referred to fears that the person in the drawing "[is] found out to be not good enough," "trip[s] and fall[s] and the roof falls in," and is "walking but not really going anywhere."

On TAT Card 7BM, the patient described an interaction between a father and son in which the father was a successful attorney who wanted the son to follow in his footsteps. The son attended the same college and law school as his father, who was "reasonably pleased, but the son is not. He does what his dad wanted him to do. Now he's into it and it feels pretty hollow." This might be looked at as an unsatisfying resolution of an oedipal conflict by accommodating to the powerful father's wishes. The response also can be interpreted as in keeping with Kohut's (1977, 1984) preference to favor the self-esteem component of oedipal dynamics as crucial. That is, the patient may have acquiesced to the oedipal parent, but if the boy was not responded to with joyful pride, as a "chip off the old block" to use Kohut's metaphor, the self was driven underground. Consequently, the patient was re-exposed to feeling devitalized, and, as the patient said, "It feels pretty hollow."

The self state that results from devitalization, a state that Kohut had termed depletion depression, may be inferred from projective test responses such as those just described, in which the experience of depletion is subtle rather than unequivocal. As with cases of more pronounced selfobject failure, the most telling characteristic is the persistent absence across responses of some sense that a vitalizing selfobject is sought. The issue here is not primarily one of diagnosis, centered on differentiating, for example, among a self disorder, borderline personality disorder, or another characterologic condition. Instead, the question is how the patient finds himself or herself alone with the experience of the devitalized self, with no hold on the possibility that an appropriate selfobject is available to revive the depleted self.

Sometimes, there is a tentative hint of a potential selfobject available for mirroring, as in the following example: "A flower, dropping two petals" (Card VIII), which is elaborated on inquiry as: "It's getting rid of petals that are dying, it'll give out new ones soon." Although initially sounding like a percept representing deterioration, perhaps as a result of defective mirroring, this inquiry elaboration also suggests the potential for repair of an injury to the self.

At other times, however, the person representing the selfobject function may be seen as flawed and thus is not approached with hope to revive an underpowered self. This situation recalls that of a small child who does not turn to the mother with animation and expect her to pick the child up, fuss over him or her, or somehow respond in an empathically attuned way. It is rather the look of mild surprise, distanced curiosity, or even disinterest that a child shows to occasional, unpredictable displays of a mother's empathic responsiveness. Most of the time, however, there is little expectation that the mother can provide the mirroring selfobject responsivity to stimulate a feeling of joyful liveliness in an ongoing or sustained way.

The phenomenon I am describing here does not occur in an isolated way on an occasional Rorschach or TAT card but is a persistent, repetitive theme appearing regularly across TAT stories and sometimes in the narrative inquiry accompanying human figure drawings. It is sometimes captured in the ebb and flow of brief spurts of hopeful anticipation alternating with disappointment or dashed hopes. Because it resembles depression or dysphoria, it is often mistaken for the subjective mood feature of a major depressive disorder. To regard this as a depressive sign, however, contributes little more to understanding the clinical state in depth than the diagnostic interview already provides.

Some good examples of this phenomenon may be seen on the TAT stories obtained from a 25-year-old man with a psychotic disorder, reported by Holt (1978, pp. 164–174). On Card 1, this young man described a child, sick in bed, who has been given music to study; the boy preferred an adventure story "that interests him more than the music." The boy was described as studious, regretting missing school, and "He is not too happy, though not too sad. His eyes are somewhat blank ... reading a book without any eyes or knowing what is in the book without reading it."

The boy disregarded the music and fell asleep reading the book. Holt noted the theme of passive-resistant counteraggression in the boy's not studying what the parents wanted him to. He also introduced the theme of castration based on failure to refer to the violin in the picture. Holt commented on the boy's difficulty in sustaining interest in the adventure story that he chose to read and felt that his parents would not mind. Holt also noted that the story concludes in withdrawal, as the boy fell asleep.

Apart from the conflict–defense interpretive framework favored by Holt, it is also possible to approach this story from the standpoint of self psychology. In this view, the boy's seeking an adventure story represents his attempt to revive an uninvigorated self, in view of the predominant affect state of being sick, alone in bed, missing school, and assigned an uninteresting task to study. The absence of the parents in an empathically involved way cannot go unnoticed. The boy is thus left to his own devices to provide the needed stimulation to an uninvigorated self in this context of parental selfobject failure. In the end, the boy's efforts to revitalize himself ultimately fail, he cannot sustain the interest any longer, and he withdraws into sleep. The deficiency in selfobject mirroring responsiveness can presumably account for the boy's ennui or inner emptiness.

Later, this patient told a story to Card 7BM in which the young man, depressed by poor health and feeling hopeless, was told by his father to find the will to cure himself because otherwise the father and mother must care for the young man's wife and children. The outcome was that the young man moved to a healthier climate with his family, but still failed to recover. His children were old enough to support their mother, and the young man had no further contact with his father. Holt emphasized the moralistic position of the father in addition to his guilt and lack of nurturance. This situation accounted for the son's feeling that he can resort to passive rejection and aggression only by discontinuing any further contact with the father.

From the viewpoint of the psychology of the self, there is hardly a clearer illustration of empathic unresponsiveness. Not only does the father fail to notice the son's distress, but he lectures him about his responsibilities and further ignores the son's need by making sure that the son realizes the burden that the father himself might have to bear. This interpretation about failed empathic mirroring is not based on whichever aspect of the moral position one addresses, but rather on the father's responding to the son without any apparent awareness of the son's precarious state.

Even more telling, in the present context of diminished expectation of selfobject availability, there is no indication that the son attempts to persuade the father to attend to his injured self. The son's passivity is not so much a rejection of the father as a reflection of the son's inability to stand on his own. He fails to recover from his illness and does not thrive. The illness of the young man represents the devitalizing self disorder from which he suffers and reveals compellingly how he has come to expect continuing and ongoing selfobject failure. Like the previous story in which the boy withdrew into sleep, the young man of this story withdraws from his unempathic father who fails to provide the encouragement or mirroring to revitalize the young man's faltering self-esteem.

Holt's patient continued with another TAT story. On Card 13B, he related a story set in "a very poor farmhouse in an isolated part of the country" in which the boy's mother is about to deliver a baby and the boy "has been told to stay out of the way." He turned to the father but "since he cannot get much affection from his father who is too busy working in the fields to even be kind to him, the boy, in his small mind, comes to the conclusion that it's a hopeless case." At this point, the mother needed the boy's help, "which makes him feel very elated and he decides he will never leave home. He had really done more than his father."

Holt used the term *oedipal fulfillment* to refer to the "elated" victory the boy "in his small mind" ultimately achieved. Feeling needed after the initial rejection by his parents counteracts the boy's feeling that he is unloved. From a self psychological position, however, the boy seems to tell the examiner that he feels forgotten about and must keep out of his overburdened mother's way. Understandably, patients who feel themselves to be a burden can hardly expect to experience the gleam in the mother's eye, one of Kohut's favorite metaphors for the developmental origin of normal mirroring. The fact that this boy recovers so dramatically, notwithstanding the underlying meaning of his wish to never leave home, points to the level of selfobject admiration that he craves.

It is of more than passing interest that in the face of deficient mirroring from one parent, the person experiencing faulty empathic responsiveness attempts to turn to another potential selfobject. Compensatory structures to counteract mirroring selfobject failure may emerge in this way. In this story, unlike the previous two stories from Holt's patient, the young man shows some indication of what he seeks in the way of selfobject responsiveness. He also conveys how much he is at the mercy of what happens to randomly come his way.

That the brief hope for empathic mirroring was too transitory to sustain adequate self-esteem may be seen in the patient's story to TAT Card 16 (the blank card). A settlement's inhabitants suffered in an environment in which they could not survive:

> Entirely reliant upon themselves and no one was reliant upon them. Because of the reason that they were alone was also the reason that they came to their doom. If they had had one line of contact ... they could have perhaps been saved.

From the standpoint of drive theory, Holt's comments emphasized the oral deprivation and cravings underlying this image. Holt also referred to narcissistic withdrawal in the patient's desire for human contact that he found unattainable. The inner deadness and devastation of the self were not overlooked in Holt's remarks. Holt may have anticipated Kohut's emphasis on the special significance of a psychologically alive selfobject environment to sustain the self through disillusionment or threats to self-esteem. Accurate empathic attunement from selfobjects is regularly needed for sustenance and "psychological oxygen" throughout life.

These examples show that a self state characterized by inner deadness develops from marked selfobject unresponsiveness. There is a near-total abandonment of hopeful expectation that mirroring selfobject responsiveness is even possible. The patient seems to have given up, which is not the same as subjective depression. In Holt's example, this entrenched characterologic position is comorbid with a severe disorder, in this instance a schizophrenia-like illness. No presumption about causality is intended. These responses show that a profoundly injured unmirrored self may be detected even in severe psychopathology. In chapter 7, I present the full protocol of a case illustrating a similar degree of defective mirroring in a nonpsychotic affective disorder syndrome.

For other indications of subtle self state manifestations of defective mirroring, several examples pertain to patients' finding fault. Often, the patients' criticism is confined to references about irregularities of the image rather than to overt complaints about its inadequacy. Examples of this dynamic may be seen in the following: "A large furry animal like a badger, crawling along the ground. Its front paws aren't quite right" (Card IV); "these don't go together down here, it's made out of paint on one side of the paper and they took the paper and smashed it together because it's the same on both sides" (Card I).

Faultfinding responses such as these reflect patients' complaints that the world has "done them wrong" or mistreated them. These patients' role in life is to collect grievances that show how they have been slighted. At one level, they are correct insofar as accurate empathic responsiveness has been lacking, but correcting wrongs is hardly ever therapeutic, although the patients' understanding their feelings of being shortchanged may lead to a salutary outcome. As for the psychodiagnostic use of projective test responses of this type, faultfinding complaints are often best understood as deriving from a history of mirroring selfobject failures.

Other subtle examples of faultfinding may be seen in responses such as "the shadow of a tree, it has no leaves and no branches, because the color's fading here" (Card VIII); "an old bone, the bone is chipped and it's got little holes" (Card IX); "a daisy. I don't like daisies, they look too plain, I like more color" (Card III). Criticisms or complaints such as these nuances of projective test content can provide indications about self states that are otherwise difficult to discern in a clinical interview. Many patients manage to conceal character pathology through a well-defended and compensated clinical presentation, but projective test comments about irregularities suggest the underlying devaluation or self-depreciation. The veiled criticism conceals an inner feeling of diminished self-esteem, not unlike the way that people feel after purchasing store models or "demos." Although these products are not necessarily damaged goods, many people still consider them less than optimal. Patients with subclinical self disorders feel this way internally, and this feeling arises from deficient mirroring selfobject experiences.

Another subtle feature of projective test content related to mirroring selfobject experience takes the form of creative, novel, or even playful responses. Consider, for example, the following responses: "A turtle, looks like it has little socks on. Maybe turtles get cold feet, too, but the rest of his body's kept warm by his shell. Needs to keep his feet warm, too" (Card II); "a flower, but the stem's not big enough for the flower. Either the flower has to shrink or the stem has to get bigger" (Card II); "a butterfly. His wings are down like he's tired. He's been through a lot" (Card V). In the absence of hypomanic indications, responses of this nature may be only one step removed from a deep concern for the integrity of the self.

Finally, a need for mirroring may be contained in responses in which an amotivational state predominates. For example, Schafer (1967, p. 139) reported the following TAT story to Card 20: "Well, it looks like somebody taking a walk in the park. Maybe he was sitting at home and got tired of doing nothing and wanted some fresh air and went out for a walk."

Schafer's comment about this story centered on the motivational state of feeling bored and inactive. From the vantage point of the psychology of the self, the search for fresh air is an indication that the understimulated self is seeking revitalization to enliven or invigorate itself. Although not specifically denoting a self state in need of mirroring selfobject responsiveness, an unsatisfied mirroring need often turns out to be involved in many patients' amotivational states.

All these instances deserve note because they portray elements of important self states, albeit understated and subtly expressed. The self states in these responses may not often be the most prominent characteristics of clinical psychopathology, but they are no less important because self-esteem regulation is of concern in a broad range of clinical conditions, including psychotic reactions, mood disturbances, character disorders, and even normality. Either a self disorder or a muted vulnerability to disturbed self-cohesion may constitute the central psychopathology.

A disorder of the self can appear as a primary disturbance in narcissistic personality or behavior disorders. It may also be secondary to other psychological disorders with a self-esteem disturbance as one important aspect. In both instances, subtle manifestations of self states can be readily detected in projective test responses. Psychodiagnostic clinicians may find utility in being alert to their presence in the content analysis of projective test material.

6

Clinical Indications
of Selfobject Functions:
Idealization and Twinship

In this chapter, I continue the discussion of projective testing indications of selfobject functions. The previous chapter was devoted to the clinical indications of mirroring. Here I consider the clinical findings indicating idealizing and twinship selfobject functions on psychodiagnostic tests.

IDEALIZATION

Theoretical Considerations

The second major form of selfobject functions that Kohut (1971, 1977) elaborated was idealization. I begin this section of projective testing illustrations of idealization with a summary of the principal conceptual and clinical features of this selfobject function. The points I have selected to restate are particularly salient for interpreting the vignettes from the psychodiagnostic test material that follows.

Idealization appears clinically in a variety of forms, including admiring or looking up to others, holding them in awe, or turning to others for calming strength or to restore equilibrium. The center of greatness shifts from oneself to an idealized other to whom a child or adult turns with the hope of bolstering self-esteem. Idealization does not imply attributing omnipotence or excessive greatness to the idealized selfobject. Thus Rorschach or TAT responses can describe an admired figure, like a parent or favored teacher, without attributing exaggerated qualities of greatness to the figure.

Idealization may ultimately strengthen ideals or values, although the primary psychological function of idealization is restoring calm or giving solace. Projective test content referring to soothing or protective figures is likely to connote idealization, albeit subtly and sometimes silently. A calming presence is probably more common or clinically relevant for

156

identifying the mobilization of an idealizing selfobject function than are descriptions of more obvious indications, like religious or inspirational figures. Often, an intensification of idealization selfobject needs follows an experience of disappointment or injury resulting from deficient mirroring. This response may be corrective or palliative for faltering self-esteem if the insufficient mirroring has not been too traumatic, chronic, or premature.

Idealization represents a more or less normal maturation of a selfobject need for someone to look up to and treasure. This experience fosters renewed vigor of the self by transferring greatness from the self to a figure who can be respected. Idealization thus strengthens or enhances self-esteem. Psychodiagnostic test content can readily refer to admired figures, but it is more important to note that the admired figures reinvigorate the self.

In the face of injury, idealization may revive a self in need of another route to sustain its cohesion when it has been interrupted or disturbed. Although not an inevitable consequence, idealization may be another direction to repair the self, as a compensatory structure, if mirroring has been insufficient but not seriously undermined. Thus, a projective test protocol that contains responses alternating between depreciation and admiration suggests the possibility that a compensatory structure is present. The content also indicates the success of this mechanism. I previously cited Bacal and Newman's (1990, p. 232) metaphor of the self "walking in the shadow of his admired object"; this image is useful for looking at projective test content to reveal an idealizing selfobject function.

Silent idealizations may obscure the clinical identification of an idealizing selfobject transference for some time in treatment, although veiled references suggestive of idealization may be discerned in the clinical history. Projective testing may reveal muted idealizations more clearly than does the diagnostic interview. In all clinical methods, however, idealization, like mirroring, makes its presence known through selfobject failures that predispose patients with self disorders to depletion depression or anxiety or more serious disintegration products. These symptoms are well-known to clinicians treating narcissistic personality or behavior disorders and should also be familiar to psychodiagnostic examiners.

Responses whose content denotes disappointment or humiliation, such as falling from grace, are important, subtle indications of an idealization selfobject function. Disappointment at the hands of an idealized selfobject seen either as faltering or defective characteristically thrusts a patient into a vulnerable state of narcissistic injury. Still worse, rejecting or trivializing a patient's idealizing overtures only compounds the problem. The discovery that an idealized selfobject is ill, weak, or diminished may be sufficient to re-expose a patient to the devastating injury to his or her own self-cohesion.

From psychodiagnostic testing material, precisely this sequence of describing the content of Rorschach percepts or TAT figures in an idealized manner, followed by an elaboration of the image as devalued or depreciated, defines the idealizing selfobject need most convincingly. The one without the other is certainly possible, but the most definitive test indicators are simultaneous evidence for the idealizing wish, the failure of the selfobject function, and the patient's ensuing reaction (such as rage, demoralization, or sullen injured withdrawal).

Clinical Examples

Consider the following example from a 55-year-old photographer-writer hospitalized for a depressive episode. This episode was precipitated by the patient's wife's recent onset of illness. On figure drawings, his drawing of a man was elaborated as follows:

> I am a camera. This is a photographer and he sees the world as it is, sometimes it's pretty painful. Sometimes he sees that his wife has cancer and he doesn't know how to deal with that. Sometimes he's not able to have any control of things.

The next drawing, that of a woman, was described as the patient's wife:

> [She] tends to feel pretty good about herself, coping with cancer much better than I am. She's a professional woman, a speech therapist, she enjoys her work and manages her job on a professional basis. Her relationships with her students and fellow therapists are good. She's observant, extremely honest, affectionate, and complimentary.

I chose this example to open the clinical illustrations for this section on idealization because it demonstrates a fundamental premise about what people seek in an idealized selfobject function. This example, which contrasts the description of the two figures, is deliberately not the clearest or most self-evident I could have chosen, because it does not highlight an exalted person or a quality of exaggerated greatness or importance. Rather, it illustrates a subtle but crucial point about idealization.

The patient cast himself as floundering and his ill wife as managing gracefully despite a life-threatening illness. He did not describe his wife in glowingly idealized terms as god-like or as perfect or even powerful. That is precisely the point: Idealization is not necessarily detected from aggrandized images, such as all-powerful or bigger-than-life figures, royalty, or gods. Idealized figures are often seen as having a quality or ability that the patient lacks, a quality leaving the person feeling depleted or underpowered in its absence. Idealization represents one way that a person attempts to repair this aspect of diminished self-cohesion. The self becomes strengthened through the calming reassurance felt in association with the selfobject.

In a relatively undramatic way, the patient described himself as beside himself, as feeling out of control in his distress. The contrasting image of his competent, well-functioning wife provided the calmness or sustenance that he cannot provide for himself. The idealized image appeared in the context of this patient's experience of himself as being overcome and passively floundering. His fearful anticipation of loss suggested the need for the idealized selfobject to sustain or bolster self-cohesion. The idealization occurred in the patient's search for something that he himself lacked, not in references about bigger-than-life images.

The example just cited also demonstrates that the primary diagnostic indication of idealization is not a specific image, such as a Rorschach percept of a giant, but the quality attributed to the percept, such as its strength or power, poise or composure, or calming function. The crucial consideration is the patient's elaboration or association about what the image connotes. Certain Rorschach images such as wizards, ballerinas, or angels may frequently be construed as indications of idealization. These are thought of as representing a wish for strength or vitality, as possessing special or unique powers, or as simply being out of the ordinary compared with other human figures. Such imagery may be considered to represent the Rorschach counterparts to invoking thoughts of admired people such as Albert Schweitzer, Jacqueline Kennedy Onassis, Arturo Toscanini, and to bring it closer to home, Heinz Kohut or David Rapaport. Responses such as wizards or angels may not necessarily reflect any of these qualities. Many percepts like these may or may not be of acceptable form quality on particular blot locations on the basis of normative frequency compilations such as those of the Comprehensive System.

As I observed in chapter 5, another reason for the need to inquire thoroughly but judiciously has to do with the frequent observation that many responses are elaborated in ways indicating that an idealizable object, admired for its beauty or greatness, may simultaneously be perceived as defective or wanting. Deidealizations of this type occur in responses such as a ballerina with a broken leg or an angel with torn wings. Examiners need to inquire for such deidealizations to emerge; merely eliciting a percept suggestive of idealization, like a ballerina or an angel, does not adequately convey what is truly being expressed.

For example, one woman with depression described, on inquiry, a wizard like the Wizard of Oz (Card IX):

> A phony, he staged the whole thing, he just seemed like a crook, he has to be something other than what he is, a big facade, like my father. Now he's caught, everyone thought he was so great. He seemed like a real nice man, some softness under the scary image he portrayed.

The patient also produced a Rorschach percept of "Arthur Fiedler from behind, leading his orchestra" (Card III). The inquiry to the Arthur Fiedler percept revealed that "he's dead, he died an old man." The patient later produced this TAT story:

> A girl who wishes she could be a ballerina, her mother reads her a story about a ballerina, she fantasizes obsessionally about being a ballerina, she tries on her first pair of shoes and dances as if she had magic shoes and dreams about a beautiful ballerina she imagines. (Card 7GF)

The story concluded with the girl "sad now, she hates everything about everything. She's just depressed, stares a lot."

As these examples indicate, idealized selfobject needs may appear alongside expressions of failed responsiveness and sometimes unavailability or loss. The idealization is frequently revealed to be transitory and fragile. The selfobject need is clear, but the unavailability or inability of the selfobject to provide the needed vigor has been transformed into disappointment, depreciation, or rage, as these responses suggest.

The previously discussed patient's responses are not rare or uncommon, particularly in those with severe conditions such as borderline personality disorder. Idealizing selfobject needs frequently appear in the form of their breakdown rather than in anticipation of being achieved. The failure or interruption of the selfobject function indicates the presence of the need.

At other times, the idealization is sufficient to sustain the possibility that the need may be responded to and the idealized figure remains available. The need for carefully probing inquiry should not be minimized, both when the idealization is self-evident and when a surface appearance of idealization gives way to a deeper sense of devaluation or rejection of the empathically unresponsive idealized selfobject.

It is of some interest that the previous patient, who used drugs, produced a TAT story about Valium, a story conveying that the substance may have sustaining or restorative properties. Consider her story to Card 3BM:

> A woman who discovered the world of Valium, a doctor started her on it. She just came back from a session, took too many Valiums, she's exhausted from the session. She just sat down to relax, hopes everything would just go away. Eventually she just wakes up and goes on, she lives from appointment to appointment and Valium to Valium. Eventually through AA, someone helps her get her life together, then she helps other people and is very good at it.

The craving may be thought of as an idealization of the drug as selfobject for its calming properties. This example demonstrates that the critical selfobject need for people or objects is the function that they serve for people.

As I have been emphasizing at several points thus far, the evaluation and assessment of idealization offer persuasive reasons for obtaining a detailed Rorschach inquiry that goes beyond ascertaining determinants and location scores. As with mirroring, but less consistently so, idealizing selfobject needs can be expressed in a direct and straightforward manner. But idealizing selfobject needs may initially appear as subtle and easy to overlook. Paradoxically, idealization may also seem compelling as an interpretive suggestion, when in fact it can conceal dissatisfaction with idealized selfobjects. Thus, a reference to a figure such as an angel is by itself not informative. Only through a judiciously curious and probing inquiry (I use the term *judicious* to mean "nonleading") does the quality of the selfobject need become sufficiently clear to reveal its idealizing character.

For example, a 19-year-old depressed female college student began her Rorschach with: "Two angels, some godlike power. Moses in the middle, with his arms raised" (Card I). Following inquiry about location and determinants, the examiner asked this patient about her reference to godlike power, to which she responded: "I assume someone who would raise their arms would be like an appeal to a god." Initially, there could be some uncertainty that the reference to godlike power referred to the grandiose-exhibitionistic self or represented a desire for an idealizable figure to whom she can turn to buttress a vulnerable sense of self. The added elaboration on inquiry clarified that the reference to godlike power suggested a wish for an idealizing selfobject.

Besides thorough inquiry, the analysis of sequence is another important means to understand idealization. A 14-year-old depressed suicidal girl reported "an angel, very big wings" on Card I, and, on inquiry elaborated by saying "someone in heaven. They die and become an angel, it represents good." This benevolent-enough response would not have been so remarkable had it not been preceded by "a bat with a mean smile, laughing at someone." The angel response was followed by "the flying monkeys in the Wizard of Oz, carrying Dorothy." She described the reference to carrying Dorothy in the inquiry as: "they're what the wicked witch uses to get things for her, she wants the ruby slippers because they're magic. It's the evil side of the Wizard of Oz that kills people and steals things."

I suggest that this adolescent girl sought a protective figure (the good or benevolent angel) to shield her from what she saw as malevolent forces (represented by the mean bat). The idealized good angel failed to function for her, despite its enlarged (and possibly strong or safe) wings. Thus, she was left unprotected, in the hands of the witch who stole Dorothy's magic shoes. She sought insulation of the self from harm, but this help did not appear to be available for her.

This theme emerged again on Card VI in this patient's report of "what Jesus is, a crucifix" to which she added on inquiry: "People didn't like him, he said he could do miracles and they didn't believe him and they killed him, they didn't think he was telling the truth." This use of a probing question, together with the sequence analysis of Card I, produced the conclusion that the patient did not believe in a strong, benevolent figure who can be counted on to provide an idealizable selfobject function. The weakened Jesus, like the angel of Card I, lacked the vitality or resilience to save himself. This image implied the girl's concerns about being vulnerable to malevolent figures.

Her disillusionment with potentially idealizable selfobjects also appeared on the TAT. Here, she described figures to whom she might look up to for sustenance as impotent. For example, on Card 13MF, she told the story that "a doctor tried to save this patient but couldn't and he's very ashamed" and on Card 18GF, "someone's holding their lover who just died." Although idealizing selfobjects have not overtly abandoned her, there is little depiction of effort or concern to show the girl that someone was trying hard or putting forth effort on her behalf. Through her disappointment that a responsive idealizing selfobject environment did not seem to exist for her, it becomes possible to see that an unsupported, devitalized self might well dispose this adolescent patient to the suicidal urges associated with her depression. This notion of a disappointing idealized selfobject environment is compounded by feeling neglected by parents she might wish to have function in that way but who have, instead, forgotten about her. Thus, she supplied a TAT story describing parents who: "would like him to learn the violin but he doesn't see that she [the mother] understands and he feels he's letting her down" (Card 1). In another story, the parents: "are out working on the farm, the mom doesn't care about her and all the dad cares about is if the crops come out during the harvest ... the mom is self-centered and only cares about herself and the dad doesn't really understand her because she's a girl" (Card 2).

These examples represent evocative responses with richly productive inquiries. A large number of patients, however, tenaciously guard their vulnerable self-esteem in the form of terse verbalizations. It is important to avoid misunderstanding these patients' apparent withholding as defenses against hostile impulses. For instance, the following example of idealization comes from the projective testing of a 41-year-old unmarried woman. She lived with her parents and was hospitalized after a suicide attempt following arguments with the parents, related to the failure of her effort to start a dressmaking business. This off-putting woman gave the impression of an arrogant-sounding malcontent, and her projective protocols were generally tightly guarded efforts in which requests for elaborations were responded to as challenges or affronts. She attempted to conceal as much as she clarified when asked about suggestive or provocative aspects of her responses. Nevertheless, her figure drawings unwittingly revealed a glimmer of idealization of the sort often resisted or defended against by patients with fiercely maintained fronts of self-assurance or arrogant pride. This patient's first drawing was that of a woman, which she elaborated as:

> A woman meditating so she can deal with the world. She's getting ready to go to work, very happy with her job, it's tedious work, she has a lot of responsibility, but she gets paid very well. Life is beautiful, but there can be trouble, it can be empty. Her motivation in life can be pleasant. She's not married, has no children, she could have an easy life. She donates her money to charity to help others.

The inquiry following the drawing of a man began:

> Did I put pants on that other drawing? He's an aggressive business-type of man, he'll take care of his family and love his wife and do things to make

her very happy and she could do whatever she wants. He's dominant,
arrogant, self-centered. She'll look up to him.

Although the female figure reflected at least some measure of ambivalence in regard to her self-image, the assurance she wished to feel about
herself was more unambivalently experienced toward the male figure. The
wish for an idealizable selfobject who can provide the selfobject function
to invigorate a vulnerable self may be detected in her remark about looking
up to the man. The patient seemed to let this comment slip indifferently at
that vulnerable, revealing moment.

Patients like this woman are difficult to evaluate, and their style of
responding to inquiry requests characteristically leaves an examiner feeling
as if he or she is attempting to extract blood from a turnip. Although there
is no simple solution to this dilemma, attending carefully to passing comments or slips that these patients produce is important. At the same time,
an examiner must be mindful of potential overinterpretation based on
limited content.

Conducting a Probing Inquiry

This example also underscores another difficulty often associated with
projective test administration. The problem is determining what constitutes
adequate inquiry or elaboration of a response, whether on the Rorschach,
TAT, or figure drawings. Examiners must obtain the data necessary to either
score a response or infer something about its meaning without conducting a
too leading or provocative inquiry or extending inquiry indiscrimately
beyond the customary, controlled conditions of test administration. They
must balance the merit of obtaining potentially useful and clinically interesting information against implementing a procedural variation that can be
construed as "not part of the Rorschach" (Exner, 1995, p. 4).

This issue is admittedly controversial, particularly in Rorschach psychology, and theorists have not reached agreement on this point. The extended
case report of Mr. L. in chapter 8 demonstrates one potential solution, based
in part on a second Rorschach inquiry devised to test the limits of verbalizations and associations. The other full case report in this book, Ms. T.
(chap. 7), is an example of a standard inquiry, one that is provocative but
does not require the testing of limits undertaken with Mr. L.'s protocol.

Some projective testing examiners are interested in identifying selfobject functions and self states that are meaningfully (and not superficially)

in keeping with Kohut's in-depth understanding of these phenomena. These clinicians understand that a pure administration style deviating little if at all from focusing the Rorschach inquiry on information necessary for accurate coding is too limited. More problematic is carrying over the tendency to conduct a conservative but limited inquiry on other projective tests; such sparse inquiry can yield little more than stereotyped, hackneyed psychological insights of limited depth or be overly influenced by perceptual detail rather than fantasy. This approach is probably inspired by the need for pristine or uncontaminated inquiry that is now customary for the Rorschach. Examiners struggle, therefore, between seeking results that provide an understanding of personality in depth but which run the risk of invalidity, and obtaining results that remain close to the behavior and verbalizations but are too superficial in their validity. If clinicians who refer their patients for psychodiagnostic testing, to clarify subtleties of diagnosis or characterology, can expect little more than trite superficiality, they are not likely to be consoled by the fact that the simplistic interpretations they receive were the result of our best efforts to ensure reliable and valid measurement. It has long been my impression that the low regard clinicians in some quarters hold for psychological testing reports is well-deserved when reports are filled with obvious and superficial findings that contain a lack of thoughtful reflection beyond the narrow specifics of the basic data.

Although criteria for the extent of TAT and figure drawings inquiry have never been formally established, the available literature on the issue is quite limited. The lack of consensual criteria for inquiry on tests other than the Rorschach, as well as for testing the limits as an expanded method of Rorschach inquiry, becomes particularly problematic for a self psychological approach to psychodiagnostic testing because projective tests with limited inquiries reveal little more than speculative hints about the self states that form the centerpiece of the psychology of the self. A further discussion of this matter and one potential suggestion to remedy the situation is illustrated in the extended case of Mr. L. presented in its entirety in chapter 8. The results of this protocol demonstrate that aspects of idealization or twinship could not have been detected in the absence of a carefully conducted testing-of-limits inquiry.

In respect to the other side of the dilemma, vigorous or interested inquiry need not be provocative, inappropriately leading, or culminating in spurious findings bordering on wild analysis. I remain convinced that joining the contrasting temperaments of in-depth inquiry and empirically-based scores ultimately requires a disciplined, thoughtful clinical strategy based on a coherent theory of personality. Just as the optimal qualities that make for good psychotherapists have yet to be described, the definitive characteristics combining meaningfully sensitive and clearheaded thinking are yet to be specified for clinicians engaged in psychodiagnostic evaluation.

For the moment and in the present context, I simply comment that the clinical identification of idealization and twinship selfobject functions with projective tests poses a particularly challenging test of this dilemma, one far more difficult to resolve than is the case with the generally more transparent or easily elicited projective test indications of mirroring selfobject needs.

Differentiating Idealization From Grandiosity

Grandiosity, in its conventional implication, connotes expansiveness and is sometimes delusional in nature, as in the case of bipolar syndromes. Kohut, however, did not think of grandiosity with that implication in mind; rather, his intended meaning was that of a self putting itself forward to be affirmed or acknowledged. Kohut's use of the term *grandiose-exhibitionistic self* is not what most clinicians understand the term grandiosity to mean.

Kohut, probably unfortunately, continued to use the term *grandiose-exhibitionistic self*, which had been his term for narcissistic pathology, to indicate (in his broadened view) turning in eager expectation to the world to be admired or responded to with pleasure. He did not primarily regard grandiosity as exaggerated self-worth, arrogant pride, or self-righteousness. Kohut understood that these surface manifestations occurred, although he regarded them as the narcissistic pathology resulting from a selfobject environment that is chronically or traumatically unresponsive to a normal, expectable need for admiration.

Schafer (1954) provided a basis for the customary interpretations of Rorschach responses of grandiosity, such as coats of arms, emblems, crests, and similar imagery. From a somewhat related viewpoint, it is not difficult to consider that examiners familiar with Kernberg's (1975) views on narcissism are inclined to regard such percepts as manifestations of entitlement or special position. From this position, a percept such as "some screwy design: not quite a coat of arms but some water color monstrosity of some nature" [Card IX] (Schafer, 1954, p. 297) could readily be interpreted as devaluation. The percept could also represent self-depreciation if the coat of arms is thought of as self-aggrandizement. An interpretation of hostile devaluation or rageful envy could also follow from drive theory or object relations theory.

Another possible formulation comes from the psychology of the self. This line of interpretation is unrelated to grandiosity, aggression, or devaluation. It stems from people's efforts to put themselves forward with pride (but not necessarily with arrogance) in expectation of mirroring or in wishing for a strong, idealizable selfobject. This suggestion does not resolve the difficulty of distinguishing between these two selfobject needs, but it does point to an interpretation that is not frequently considered when this imagery is observed on projective tests. The "coat of arms monstrosity" response cited previously may represent either the disappointment in the idealized selfobject or the inadequacy of the self state.

The response provided by Schafer was preceded, on the same inkblot, by "a stain of meat wrapped up in a piece of paper, like blood in a package of meat comes spread out." It is not difficult to see the aggressive connotations of such an image, and the devaluation of the coat of arms can be viewed as a continuation of the same psychological dynamic. It is also possible to view the sequence of these two percepts as the patient's attempt to recover from the gory "bloodied-up" or defeated self state, represented by the bloodstained meat. The coat of arms can represent this patient's attempt to turn to a strong, idealizable figure in the hope of repairing the injury to the self. The attempt was unsuccessful, however, because the patient felt disappointed and then critical of the idealized selfobject as capable enough to restore the self-cohesion that the patient required.

Schafer (1954, p. 404) also interpreted a patient's Rorschach responses, both from Card VII, as grandiose images. These two percepts were a temple or monument and domes such as that on the national capitol. In addition, Schafer regarded another patient's response of a crude monument resembling a religious cross (Schafer, 1954, p. 385) on Card VI as consistent with other indications in the patient's protocol about rebellion against internalized superego authority and values. These interpretations are quite understandable from the vantage point of the ego psychological framework. Even though I present these three responses here in isolation, Schafer's interpretations are internally consistent with the full protocols from which these vignettes were taken.

From a self psychological view, however, an image such as a monument, as in these examples, can be seen as a manifestation of idealizing selfobject needs. Responses such as monuments and temples or similar religious imagery may also be present in patients with a self disorder, who hope that previously thwarted attempts at mirroring are satisfied through idealization. The examples cited from Schafer are instructive because idealization is suggested regardless of whether the imagery is primarily that of greatness (such as the capitol monument percept) or of devaluation (such as the crude religious cross monument).

Thus, in summarizing the self psychological clinical significance of percepts such as a monument, coat of arms, crest, or emblem, one need not automatically assume that such responses represent grandiosity. Sometimes, larger-than-life images such as a giant or an angel may also be difficult to distinguish from grandiosity. The possibility of idealization may be a viable alternative; an appearance of devaluation of the idealized selfobject represents the failure of or disappointment in the idealized selfobject, particularly when mirroring selfobjects have been chronically unresponsive. Aggression, whether conceptualized in a drive theory or an object relations framework, is also not a definitive or exclusive basis for a critical, hostile, or depreciating tone expressed in projective test responses when it is considered from the self psychological position.

Self psychology offers another viewpoint for understanding these responses. The previous sequence of responses, in isolation, does not enable an examiner to decide whether the monument or coat of arms percept represents grandiosity (either in the conventional sense or in Kohut's view) or idealization.

Differentiating References to Idealization From True Idealized Selfobject Functions

In view of the type of imagery often reported on projective tests, it is not surprising that images such as religious symbols, totem poles, crests and badges, and similar percepts rich in symbolism suggest idealization. This idea is based on the compelling associations surrounding omnipotence, strong powers of a religious or quasireligious nature, or even symbolic references to abstract ideas such as chaos, doom, and creation. From the vantage point of drive theory, imagery of this nature might give rise to interpretations of grandiosity, narcissism, or hostile impulses. Related examples include less exaggerated images like statues, chandeliers, or alien beings in protective suits, such as some of the examples that Arnow and Cooper (1988) gave as indications of a self disorder.

Although fertile ground for generating propositions about idealization selfobject functions, such interpretations require more than the customary degree of caution. My main reason for recommending a particularly conservative approach to such material stems from the obvious, understandable associations between images containing powerful symbolic content and interpretations of omnipotence or power. The associations are often accurate, but the associative link must rely on a greater burden of proof than simple content or the connection stimulated by such imagery. In reference to self psychology, the connection between powerful or exalted imagery and idealization requires a further link specifying that the projective test imagery provides or is needed for restoring vigor, calmness, or self-cohesion.

Thus, the restorative properties of the figure or object described in projective test responses must be clear. This requirement of greater precision is illustrated here in several instances of false positives. The examples implicate but do not sufficiently sustain a link between references to power, greatness, or larger-than-life images and an idealizing selfobject function.

Consider, for example, the following two Rorschach responses: "Like a church, a steeple, the cross. People going out the door to see if anybody's coming in" (Card VI), "a totem pole" (Card VI), to which the patient said on inquiry: "They worship it and carve faces of people who died on the totem pole, worshipping after the dead." These responses, from the same patient, occurred in a protocol with indications of devaluation and morbid preoccupation such as "a reflection in the water" (Card II) subsequently elaborated as "it's a man, he looks like a monkey," "a tombstone" (Card II), and "a leaf drying up" (Card IV). Even the response: "Angels, like on the Flintstones, telling the two women what to do" (Card III) lacks the full import of angels as self-cohesion–building or protective figures. These angels are not so exalted as controlling, and they represent comical figures at that. Thus, they can hardly represent strong idealizable figures.

Similarly, Schafer (1954, pp. 255–267) presented the Rorschach record of a patient who gave several responses suggestive of idealization, but the figures repeatedly failed to come through for the patient. For example, this patient reported a percept of fire and brimstone on Card II, followed by a cathedral with a little steeple, indicating its smallness or powerlessness against the overwhelming imagery of the fire and brimstone image preceding it. On Card IV, this patient produced no less than 12 responses, dominated at the outset by an emaciated cat-like figure, a villainous character, and a disfigured mermaid. This patient also delivered a percept of a citadel–church image "in the distance" seen in a minute detail on the blot, followed by "an old warrior." Neither the distant, minuscule citadel nor the weakened, one-time warrior-protector (to which the patient also added: "Shadowy, of course") was likely to do much good and must be considered to represent feeble efforts to secure needed, idealizing selfobjects to little avail.

Other examples from Schafer's patient included small male lions, another temple "from a distance," still another temple as drawn by a child, and two torches from the days of Charlemagne or King Alfred as "carried by a man but the man is not here." These percepts are consistent with the impression of misguided attempts to mobilize potentially idealizable selfobjects. The patient's efforts failed to produce a sufficient degree of vigor to sustain an overwhelmed and vulnerable self state.

In chapter 5, I cited examples of defective mirroring by this same patient. At that time, I commented that the appearance of both mirroring and idealization selfobject needs was not conceptually inconsistent but can illustrate the appearance of one type of selfobject function as an attempt to create a compensatory structure when another selfobject function (usually mirroring) had failed to bolster an injured self. In the present example, however, Schafer's patient provides an illustration of her apparent failure to secure mirroring and idealization selfobjects to sustain a weakened self. This idea conveys the seriousness of the self disorder when compensatory structures fail to take hold or when there is chronic or massive empathic unresponsiveness in more than one sector of the self. The case of Ms. T., reported in detail in chapter 7, also illustrates defective mirroring with unsuccesful efforts to develop idealizing selfobject functions as a compensatory structure.

The following example illustrates a sequence of three Rorschach responses to Card VI, in which the middle response apparently represents an idealizing selfobject need if considered out of context. The sequence of these responses unambiguously shows that an interpretation of this sort is incorrect. A 34-year-old female inpatient produced this sequence of responses to Card VI: "A thing, a living object, I'm beginning to get to know this ink blot better. The head of a snake, a penis," followed by "it's a star now, a six-pointed star," which was spontaneously elaborated on inquiry as: "Judaism, the Star of David. My faith is more spiritual versus religious. I believe in a divine plan but I don't go to temple." This patient concluded Card VI with the percept of "an ass," which, on inquiry, was seen because of the appearance of a split that gave rise to an association of constipation. By itself, this patient's Jewish star percept, with her associative elaborations about faith and spirituality, suggests mobilization of an idealization selfobject need. Preceded and followed by the snake–penis and anality responses, however, this interpretation of the Star of David response may be implausible.

Subtle Indications of Idealization

This section provides examples of projective test responses other than images such as exalted figures like royalty or religious symbols to indicate idealization. The examples that follow contain few if any illustrations of provocative or suggestive indications of idealization such as wizards or angels. Here, the images are deceptively simple and subtle, but on close scrutiny, represent idealizing selfobject functions.

A 30-year-old Black female accountant, who was hospitalized with depression accompanied by homicidal and paranoid ideation, produced a projective testing record characterized by notable disorganization. The patient's projective protocols revealed considerable preoccupation with rage and abuse. In addition, other responses indicated idealizing selfobject functions. These responses represented figures whom the patient turned to for idealization, but whom she ultimately experienced as disappointing. For example, her response to Card II from the Rorschach was "a lamp or something, like a genie lamp." She clarified "genie lamp" when asked about this reference as follows:

> There's something inside of it. A person. She's in this thing and can't come out until someone helps her out. It's cramped, there's no room to breathe. Someone comes by, rubs the lamp and she's free for a while until she goes back in the lamp.

The patient elaborated that the woman inside the lamp was sensitive or hurting and was being punished by being trapped inside the lamp because she had done something terrible. Apart from the implication of wrongdoing of potentially delusional intensity, the crucial reference to idealization, however, pertained to the wish that some magical, benevolent figure would emerge to ease her distress.

For the same reason, this patient described "a flying animal" (Card VI), about which she said upon inquiry: "I guess he's connected to something, maybe a bigger butterfly, a mother butterfly or something. [Connected][1] He needs him for support, he can't do it by himself."

This patient's TAT stories complemented and expanded on the idealizing selfobject needs suggested in her Rorschach responses. On Card 1,

---

[1]Examiner's queries during testing appear in brackets.

the patient described "a little boy that loved to play violin, he played it wherever he went. One day his teacher said he couldn't play it anymore because he wasn't doing his other work. It made him very sad." When asked what sad meant, the patient stated that "he's trying to understand what she's talking about." Thus, the affect of sadness results from disappointment in a potential idealized selfobject, represented by the teacher, who has let the boy down by failing to recognize his need. This interpretation may be more decisive alongside that of a teacher who is also seen as depriving or punitive. The teacher need not be seen as great, powerful, or on a pedestal for the idealizing selfobject function to be present.

This same patient continued with a story on TAT Card 2:

> [A] girl . . . loved to go to school but they lived in this house, it needed a lot of work. The mother was pregnant so she couldn't do a lot of things. So the mother made her do chores every day and look after the other kids. This went on for seven years, then she ran away to the relatives' house, and there she obtained the education she needed.

In the next card (3BM), this patient reported that "a child's been abused. He's praying to God to help him stop being abused and to stop his mother from doing it, but still she abused the child and he just got up and ran away."

That these stories contain references to abuse or neglect is a matter that I am sidestepping because it is secondary to understanding the patient's depth psychology. These two stories contain clear references to the central figure's feeling psychologically ignored, and the self remains unresponded to in the context of neglect or abuse. Without trivializing or dismissing the sociological or public policy question of child abuse, I emphasize in the present context that the more important psychological issue is the patient's hope for an idealized figure to come to her aid to restore self-cohesion. The patient needed the selfobject function of a strong presence to turn to, not so much for protection as for repairing self-esteem.

These themes continued in the patient's stories to Cards 7GF and 7BM, in which the girl of Card 7GF was consoled by a neighbor and the young man of Card 7BM was consoled by his grandfather. That the idealizing selfobject function repeatedly failed this patient may be detected in her resolution to these stories, as well as in the stories cited earlier. Thus, the girl cannot be reassured by the neighbor because "she learned adults lie ... she doesn't trust the neighbor," and the young man does not believe his grandfather: "The grandfather may be genuinely concerned about the boy but the boy doesn't know that, he don't [*sic*] know where to go or who to turn to."

In his expanded formulation of idealization, Kohut considered idealizing selfobject functions to include fostering or bringing about a vigorous and buoyant sense of self-esteem. When sustaining optimal self-esteem is compromised, TAT responses such as these represent the failure of an idealizing selfobject need. The patient turns to someone in the hope of the person's providing this restorative or rebuilding function, but the need either goes unrecognized or is rebuffed. The patient then feels abandoned, ignored, and ultimately diminished. This interpretation is ultimately more important than are descriptions of figures as strong, exalted, or powerful.

The following case also illustrates the wish for idealizable selfobjects as seen through either empathic unavailability or failed responsiveness of the figures to whom the patient turned for repair of his self disorder. The patient was a 31-year-old male who developed a depressive episode after he had been discovered in a pattern of chronic lying in which he greatly exaggerated facts about his education and work. On TAT Card 1, this patient described:

> A little boy, he looks frustrated, he can't understand his instructor and why he can't play it. He's not asking advice from his parents because they think he should know how to do it, he doesn't know where to turn. He asks his parents if he can give it up, and he gives it up, they don't care.

On Card 3BM, this same patient told the following story:

> That little boy is me. Lots of times I'd go in my room and just cry because I didn't know what was going on in school that day. I couldn't go to my parents. I didn't think they'd understand, that's why I left school.

Later on, he commented about Card 7BM: "That's not our home but it's a father giving the son advice. He never showed me how to do things that a man should know. This man looks like he's giving the son good advice and the son appreciates it."

The noteworthy aspects of these responses concern the predominant need for an idealizable figure who is portrayed in a position of teaching, advising, or consoling. In each instance, the sought-after figure failed to fulfill the idealizing selfobject need that was aroused. This situation predisposes to a self disorder with a symptomatic expression in depression, characterized throughout many projective test protocols as devitalization or defeat. It is not the grandiosity or the prominent wish to be admired, adored, or otherwise mirrored that the patient longs for or seeks. The problem illustrated in these responses is the empathic failure of a figure to serve a selfobject function of bolstering undermined self-esteem. The idealization selfobject need remains, therefore, driven underground, thwarted or unrecognized.

The following two Rorschach responses may seem to represent idealization, but only one of these examples properly reflects this selfobject function. The case is from two adjacent Rorschach responses to the same card (Card III) from a 15-year-old adolescent, hospitalized in connection with his unmarried mother's inability to manage his behavior at home and school. The first response was "two little spirits," which this young man elaborated in the inquiry as:

> Conan the Barbarian. They put all kinds of paints on him to keep the spirits from taking him to wherever he was going to go in his next life, heaven, like the utopia, where he's destined to go. They loved him, didn't think he deserved to die yet. This girl sacrificed herself to the gods so that he'd live.

It is not difficult to detect that being protected is of utmost concern in this boy's response. It is emphasized in his verbalization coupled with his wish for a benevolent figure to provide for his safety or well-being. Although it is unclear from the content of this response that a vulnerable self requires this selfobject function, there are such indications in other places in the projective protocol.

This boy's next response to Card III was "two genies playing cards, both look like they're reaching in their back pockets to pull out an extra card, they're cheating."

On inquiry, he added:

> They're like misty, like coming up out of their bottle, and form into some humanistic thing as they go up their body. Some magical type of thing or person, another type of being, almost like from another world or something, like this fantasy kind of thing. They're almost like gods. Something that doesn't conform is a type of god, mythologically. These don't look too honest, trying to cheat at cards, neither one likes to lose.

Contrasted with the previous response from this adolescent boy, his percept of a genie seems to suggest that the patient may admire the figure for its ability to cheat. The genie is also couched in imagery that the patient described as magical and god-like in quality, unlike his previous spirits percept in which he had turned to them for calming reassurance or vitalization of the self. His response is also different from the genie response of another patient (cited previously), in which someone helping her was the crucial aspect bearing on idealization.

These two responses from the adolescent boy highlight that his responses required attention to the verbalization that distinguished them with regard to the specific or unique idealizing selfobject function that each response identified. The spirits provided a self-restorative function but the genies were not seen as needed in a similar way. They might be, and the possibility of idealization should not be ruled out entirely. Nevertheless, the contrast between these two responses in respect to the selfobject function is still instructive.

Interpretive Cautions About Idealization

The examples described in the previous section show clearly that content alone can be misleading. Content together with its associative elaborations reveals the selfobject function. The crucial associations may frequently require vigorous but unobtrusively elicited inquiry. These examples also parallel the way that selfobject functions are recognized in treatment. That is, it is not merely the praise or admiration of great or powerful qualities in the therapist or analyst or in the people in the patient's life that is decisive for idealizing needs. Rather, the disappointment in their empathic failures reveals that the admired figure or transference object is vitally necessary for the patient to feel buoyed up or thriving. This quality indicates the brittleness of the patient's self-esteem. Likewise, in psychodiagnostic testing, idealizing selfobject needs are usually revealed by their absence or by their failure to protect self-esteem.

This last point highlights a caution to bear in mind when the relevant sign or marker is the absence of a clinical feature. There is always a potential risk in a clinical examination, whether based on diagnostic testing or interview, that interpretations may be spuriously built up from the absence of signs or symptoms or the failure of a psychological function to be present. Several examples of idealization already presented demonstrate this point. The solution to the problem requires examiners' vigilant attention to ensure that Schafer's (1954) criteria of logical consistency and regularity or frequency of the sign in the total protocol are kept in mind.

Data of the type I am referring to do not necessitate abandoning an inference because it may be too "soft" to be sustained. Rather, they require particularly refined clinical acumen for a seasoned and well-disciplined examiner to decide whether an interpretation can be sustained or supported.

Responses that suggest idealization are less frequent and recurrent in a projective protocol than are those concerning mirroring. It is also more difficult to attend to the absence or lack of a feature than to note its presence. The clinical function calls for examiners' full empathic listening skills and for immersing themselves in the response content, and frequently in its subtleties or nuances.

The problem I refer to is not one that is infrequent, too unreliable to assess with sufficient confidence, or too atypical to be detected. It is also not just one of diminished sensitivity or of too many false positives. Its resolution is not easy. Not only are Schafer's (1954) criteria for interpretation helpful in this effort, but they are indispensable in guiding clinicians' impressions. When one is in error, the result may be clinically and scientifically indefensible, but when on the mark, the clinical yield is nothing short of powerful.

TWINSHIP

Theoretical Considerations

The twinship selfobject function is the most difficult to discern both clinically and on psychodiagnostic testing. Kohut (1971, 1984) originally considered twinship to be a subtype of mirroring, but in his final thoughts on the subject, he regarded twinship as a special function deserving its own status.

The difficulty in identifying twinship selfobject needs is not that of detecting possible signs or indicators such as responses related to twin figures or symmetrical objects. These indications are easy to note on projective tests. The problem, however, is in deciding whether superficial references of this sort truly represent twinship selfobject needs. There is no lack of Rorschach percepts about twins or symmetry of the inkblots. Even TAT stories have references to perceived or fantasied twin relationships. The overriding consideration must always be one of determining whether a selfobject function is present. To be judged as present, there must be an indication that the selfobject exists fundamentally to sustain or bolster the cohesiveness of the self.

The rarity of this selfobject function is one reason that Kohut's use of the term *twinship* leads to confusion, especially when interpreting projective test content. The many references to twins that arise, particularly on the symmetrical Rorschach blots, can more often mislead than amplify Kohut's intended meaning of the twinship selfobject function. Percepts about twins, even conjoined twins, are no more than suggestive or speculative. The companionate or "soulmate" qualities expressed in these interactions are the crucial elements necessary to accurately characterize the selfobject function in sufficient depth.

Most projective test responses pertaining to twins have little more than speculative or weakly supported bearing on twinship selfobject functions. The necessary evidence to best make the case lies not in simple or superficial percepts, but rather in the richness and depth of their elaboration. Unfortunately, such responses are not frequent, and several responses are often necessary to be confident that a twinship function has been mobilized.

The twinship selfobject function does not appear prominently in many interpersonal interactions, including those occurring in psychotherapy, particularly during short-term treatment. True twinship selfobject function is nuanced and often subtle. Its clinical presentation may appear relatively late in treatment, even during intensive psychotherapy or psychoanalysis. It is often initially mistaken as idealization or mirroring. Sometimes, twinship is simply unnoticed until a patient is understood in depth. Thus, for projective testing indicators to identify true twinship selfobject functions is a challenge that is difficult and prone to error in view of the brief sampling of the patients' internal life characterizing psychodiagnostic examinations.

Rorschach content is often the best source for identifying twinship selfobject needs. The TAT may be too structured to permit deviations from conventional responses to a story line, and indications of twinship may not readily appear. Even more important as a consideration than structured format, the types of stories that the TAT elicits favor themes of mirroring or idealization. As a result, subtle differentations between mirroring and twinship can too easily be obscured, particularly when the inquiry is not sufficiently probing or when a patient is especially defensive, withholding, or uncommunicative.

In addition, the verbalizations required for the TAT or human figure drawings inquiry do not characteristically provide sufficiently sensitive access to a deep level of patients' selfobject functions. Patients are often at a loss for words that come close to indicating twinship companionate needs. This is the case even among the most verbally articulate people, who may actually experience more frustration than usual in attempting to convey the specific quality of the alter-ego twinship function that they seem to seek. For this reason, the nature of the Rorschach technique may reveal twinship needs in their most direct or unconcealed form. The inkblot method makes it difficult for people to obscure, defend against, or otherwise distance themselves from, twinship selfobject needs. There are exceptions, and I have included a number of TAT examples in the vignettes that follow. Quite a few are from the projective protocols of articulate adolescents.

In my opinion, superficial references to twins or twinning are best ignored, unless compelling elaboration across several responses can substantiate such references as genuine indications of a twinship selfobject function. Thus, projective test references to twins or pairs should be reserved for only the most clear-cut instances of twinship selfobject needs. In the next section, I provide illustrations of both good and insufficient examples.

Psychodiagnostic testing clinicians need to contend with the fact that the best evidence for twinship needs does not emerge from conventional content analysis in the way that mirroring or idealization is detected. The twinship selfobject function is often deduced from a clinically well reasoned analysis of the test material in relation to clinical theory and in-depth understanding of psychoanalytic self psychology. Conventional thematic cues are of limited use in the completed interpretation. This approach requires appropriate caution tempered by the most conservative scrutiny of customary test evidence, not to mention a thorough and accurate understanding of Kohut's self psychological views.

Clinical Indications

My first example vividly demonstrates the essential features of the twinship selfobject function and illustrates the difficulty in eliciting the twinship selfobject function when inquiring about projective test responses. The response is to Rorschach Card II, from a 22-year-old depressed inpatient: "Two people pressing their hands together, I think they're two women. They have those big old hair styles." To this point, the response is ordinary, and the beginning of the inquiry is equally commonplace: "The arm's here, the left arm's up to her. Their palms are together. Looks like they have gloves on, another reason I thought they were women. Here's the heads. This down here is menstruation." On being asked further about the reference to menstruation, the patient continued in the following way:

> It just is. [Q] I guess they are. They're menstruating. How long have you been a psychologist? [Q] They're friends and they know what's going on, they're combining ideas, they're giving each other the same idea. [Q] They

understand each other's life experiences, they're very happy. [Q: Menstru-
ating?] It's just about their sexuality. Actually, it's not menstruation, it's
more like the feeling they share. Oneness.

Apart from the question of whether a color determinant should be
assigned to this response, there can be little doubt about the selfobject
need that it reveals. This patient defensively attempted to protect herself
from elaborating further about menstruation and its associations. Thus,
after making reference to menstruation for the first time only at the close
of the inquiry, she responded defensively to a question about what made
it appear that way by saying "It just is," followed by silence. Her
distracting tangential question about the examiner's experience represented an attempt to deflect her anxiety. She then took me to task for
exposing her to a vulnerability with which she struggled, and largely
unsuccessfully at that. It is as if her question to me was really: Don't you
know anything about respecting defenses?

There are two main points to emphasize about this response. The first is
that it demonstrates the core characteristics of the twinship selfobject need.
It reveals an experience between people centering on intimacy and shared
understanding in depth. It captures a feeling of oneness or a deep and close
bond. Although the two figures might have been designated as a pair, the
patient did not describe them so. The fact that two figures, even human
figures, are seen on Card II is not crucial to the identification of twinship.
It is merely incidental to the essential feature of the response, which is the
wish for an experience in depth of significant mutual understanding, alikeness, or oneness.

The second important point is that it is easy to miss this very feature of
the response. It is not alluded to at all in the association proper; the inquiry
begins conventionally, and only at the point that the patient might have been
expected to conclude the inquiry did she introduce the reference to menstruation. Before any elaboration or clarification by the patient, the examiner might understandably be tempted to think that this association
expressed concern about somatic or sexual matters, illness or fear, or even
aggression. One might have to settle for these speculations had the patient
gone no further than her initial defensive "It just is" remark when further
inquiry became necessary.

Only by pursuing the association, despite the patient's apparent discomfort, did her profound vulnerability about the need for twinship selfobject
responsiveness become apparent. This need probably gave rise to her

tentativeness or defensiveness and ultimately caused her to feel exposed. Twinship selfobject needs are frequently seen in just this way, as passing comments or casual elaborations to the central response. It sometimes becomes difficult to elicit further clarification about these additions, as the present vignette illustrates.

Twinship as a Companionate or Shared Bond: The Problem of Twins

The next several examples are projective test responses based on images of twins. The symmetry of many Rorschach blots, in particular, readily elicits pair responses, and it is not uncommon for some of these responses to describe twins. In a discussion of a self psychological approach to psychodiagnostic testing, it is inevitable that percepts of twins are thought of as potential indicators of twinship selfobject functions. Paradoxically but not surprisingly, this is rarely true.

A careful reading of Kohut (1971, 1984) shows that the psychological features represented by twinship are based almost totally on the communion in depth, companionate functions for calming or soothing that are essential for repairing an injury to self-esteem, or a shared bond or world view that becomes a central requirement in the self-selfobject relationship. I have emphasized precisely these qualities of selfobject functions in general throughout this book, and these qualities are especially important for the twinship selfobject function.

The following two examples, both of which involve Rorschach percepts of Siamese or conjoined twins, are analyzed from the viewpoint of the crucial features that characterize twinship. The first illustration comes from a patient who produced the following Rorschach response to Card II:

> Siamese twin animals, like puppy dogs. I can see their snouts. They're cute. They're joined at the nose. They could be thinking the same thing. These are maybe thought waves. They could be kissing. There's a smile.

On inquiry, this 33-year-old woman, referred for evaluation of the psychiatric component of a hyperventilation syndrome, stated:

> Here's the feet, body, ears, eye, snouts. These snouts have a horned effect which I don't want to look at, because it makes them look like they're not real, like from a fairy tale. They're cute. [Q: Joined?] They're probably very

close, they're kissing. They're transmitting with one another. Because they're happy and dancing.

This patient offered an indication that a twinship selfobject function might be evoked, not so much by her reference to conjoined twins as by her comment, during the association phase, about thinking the same thoughts. This idea becomes elaborated further in the inquiry as transmission of thought waves. This interpretation of twinship needs, although suggestive, still falls short of being compelling. The best way to explain what is missing from the response is to contrast this percept with that of the previous patient who produced the response of menstruation.

The previous patient referred to a deep degree of involvement between the figures in the form of combining ideas, depth of understanding, and a sense of oneness, as stimulated by the reference to menstruation. The present patient's references to conjoined twins transmitting thoughts, thought waves, or thinking the same thing did not have the same degree of compelling alikeness. It lacked the "soulmate" quality of a faithful replica or an intimate bond.

The nature of this contrast is instructive: Twinship selfobject needs are experienced (and expressed on projective tests) with a measure of *depth* and *intensity*. References to transmitting thought waves or having identical thoughts, in and of themselves, do not hit the mark, despite the quality of similarity represented by the concept of twins. Many references to conjoined twins, for example, als·) warrant this caveat, even though it is certainly possible that a twinship selfobject need could have been simultaneously mobilized.

For example, Kwawer (1979, p. 521) reported the following Rorschach response to Card VI: "Now it looks like a Siamese twin ... this is half of the Siamese twin and this is half of the Siamese twin. Separating them ain't nothing, but putting them together makes a person even." The quality of requiring both parts to make the whole is the crucial comment that qualifies this response as an indication of a twinship selfobject function. Had the patient stopped with the reference to conjoined twins, there would not have been a compelling reason to assume that a twinship selfobject function was strongly suggested.

Other examples of Rorschach responses that illustrate Kwawer's (1980) borderline interpersonal relations scale were provided by P. M. Lerner (1991, p. 216). The first example, under the descriptor of narcissistic mirroring, is "These are two men mirroring each other, two little mimes" (Card II). This response approximates a twinship selfobject function but remains, as it stands, insufficient to represent the quality of a faithful replica. This example also shows, parenthetically, that a patient's use of a word like *mirroring* does not mean that the patient's selfobject function corresponds exactly to the term. In this example, as the word is reported with no additional elaborations, mirroring rather than twinship actually might be the relevant selfobject function to consider.

Two other responses supplied by Lerner come closer to the mark; both are categorized under Kwawer's (1980) descriptor of separation-division: "These two things appear to have been at one point connected and broken apart. ... It's as if on the inside there was some continuity between the two" (Card IX) and "Looks like a cell in separation. ... One has divided and two haven't quite joined together" (Card X).

The component of separation or coming apart appears in these two examples, which represent a crucial characteristic in the quality of intensity of the bond. The reference to continuity in the first example and the idea of a single-unit cell joined together in Lerner's second example are consistent with the suggestion or impression that a twinship selfobject function may have been revived. Further indications of the depth of the bonds implied in these examples constitutes more persuasive evidence on this point.

Another example of a suggestive but still not quite fully convincing illustration is taken from Lovett's (1988, p. 124) description of his scoring system for narcissistic identification. He provided an example of a reflection response as follows: "Two people working on something. The red shows that they're thinking exactly the same thing" (Card III).

The previous examples were even more subtle than are responses of twins as illustrations of the problem of interpreting obvious-sounding responses as indications of twinship. References to separations, disconnections, and thinking similar or identical thoughts are on the right track. Responses like these still require inquiry to clarify whether the essential quality is also contained in a patient's experience—a clear indication of a unique or intimate bond, the special significance of the faithful replica, or the companionate or silent presence providing calm reassurance. Just as simply referring to twins means very little about the twinship selfobject function, references to activities such as miming, mimicking, or copying may not capture the definitive psychological character that the twinship selfobject function is intended to convey.

The problem of identifying twinship function arises frequently on the Rorschach, because of the moderately compelling pull for references to identical figures that are sometimes actually presented as twins, based on the symmetry of the inkblots. I close this section with an illustration of two responses that demonstrate this point. These Rorschach percepts described twins but lacked the psychological quality of alikeness; as a result, the responses cannot by themselves represent twinship selfobject functions.

The first response, to Card II, was: "A couple of bears fighting things out. My twin brother and myself." A second example was given to Card VII by the same patient: "Female twins. Probably in the kitchen, using a microwave oven for the first time."

Neither response contained inquiry material revealing anything of note beyond the standard information about location and determinants. These two responses might well have been viewed as examples of twinship before the discussion in this chapter, but examples like these do not meet the crucial test. The responses require a more urgent quality of alikeness, shared similarity, or bonding as an exact or faithful replica to genuinely represent the in-depth sense of twinship that Kohut had in mind. The content must give clear indications beyond a reference to identical or twin objects. Because of this requirement, the twinship selfobject function is seen only infrequently in psychodiagnostic testing.

This quality provided a potent psychological moment in the New York stage production of *Side Show*, a musical about the autonomous but tragically conflicted strivings of a pair of real-life conjoined twins. The twins realized that their separate and different aspirations could not possibly succeed if they were to remain as one consolidated living unit. Indeed, their ultimate strength was their synchrony as a unit. Despite this rebuff to the twins' individual hopes, their immutable need for each other provided the strength that sustained them psychologically. Here is the essential quality of Kohut's twinship selfobject function: It is not being similar or identical that really matters, but the mutuality of need or psychological oneness. Similarly on the Rorschach: Percepts of twins or conjoined twins must clearly indicate mutuality in the need for the twin for the person's psychological survival or sustenance (that is, self-cohesion).

Twinship Selfobject Functions and Adolescence

Some depressed adolescents, prone to sullen withdrawal, isolation, and loneliness, may be particularly disposed to experience pronounced twinship selfobject needs. Forming intense relationships with one or a very small group of friends, they share close-knit bonds based almost totally on similarity of thoughts and feelings. Such attachments provide cohesion to brittle self-esteem by demanding almost exact matching of affect states. This strong requirement of matching or similarity seems vital to preserve the relationship, not to mention the cohesiveness of the self. The intensity of these relationships is so great that even minor breaches are barely tolerated and can give rise to rage reactions or depression, sometimes accompanied by suicidal gestures or self-mutilation.

Breaches or ruptures of this sort frequently result from withdrawal by the "twin," sometimes because the other person has formed another attachment fulfilling a different need. Alternatively, the "twin" may have managed to progress psychologically to a level of relatedness no longer based so completely on the experience of the faithful replica of the twinship selfobject function. The patient, however, feels left behind and abandoned, and his or her self-esteem falters. I give two examples of projective test responses from such patients as illustrations of how this dynamic configuration may be detected.

One patient, an 18-year-old man, was hospitalized following a suicide attempt after a male friend had rejected the patient and attempted to develop other relationships. The patient was overcome by experiencing his life as meaningless and had some indications of subsyndromal depression. This man's response to Card II on the Rorschach was as follows: "Two turkeys, sitting on a table, taking a drink, trying to understand each other's thoughts by placing their hands together," and on inquiry:

Their hands in the background, heads, like sort of contemplating. [Q] Just their face. I do that with my friends sometimes. Just for fun. We already know each other's thoughts, but sometimes we'll put our hands together to try to understand it better. And we're usually right, that's because we understand each other so well.

The indication of intimacy and understanding based on an unspoken capacity to divine each other's inner states seems evident and represents another form of the essential characteristic of the twinship selfobject function. This quality was close to the surface in this patient, as is often the case with young people compared with adults. The same indication of a twinship selfobject need can also be noted in the young man's TAT response to Card 3BM:

This is Sandra and she has a very close relationship with her girlfriend Sally, but they're not sexual. They understand each other so well, that could best be understood as like one-minded. She begins to depend on

Sally too much as the only person who can understand her, so she deliberately cuts off from her other friends to be with Sally. But Sally has other friends too and doesn't want to devote her time purely to Sandra, and she confronts Sandra and tells her she can't deal with Sandra being too dependent on her and says she's sorry but she can't be friends with her anymore. Sandra gets depressed and contemplates suicide; there's the gun. She'll shoot herself because only her friend could understand her instead of anyone else and she latched on to that. They're two distinct people but they think the same. That's what she needs, a feeling of total understanding.

Another adolescent patient, a 15-year-old girl, was hospitalized following a suicide attempt when her boyfriend withdrew from her after an abortion. She produced the following TAT story to Card 7GF:

It's Jane and her mom. Jane doesn't have any friends so she holds on to her doll and pretends it's a real person. One day her mother told her she didn't think she should use the doll as a friend. Jane said she didn't want any friends. One day the mother threw the doll away, Jane got angry with her mother and said she'd run away. She forgave her mother because on the way she met a new girl who's now her best friend.

This example is more subtle. The story is somewhat uncommon for this card, but is not particularly unusual. The notion of using a doll to compensate for lack of friends or inner emptiness is not exceptional. Holding onto the doll with such exclusivity or for dear life, as it were, suggests that the doll has come to substitute for a friend or has become (in an intimate, vital sense), her friend. It raises the question that a twinship selfobject need may be operating in maintaining this adolescent patient's self-esteem. Although the story also suggests regressive elements, it reveals a capacity to replace a detached, inanimate relationship with a real one. Clinicians must wonder about the nature of the selfobject need that predominates in that relationship.

This example is not as evident an indication of a twinship selfobject need as is the previous example of the boy putting his hand against that of his friend to intensify their level of intimacy. Nevertheless, I have included this girl's story alongside that of the boy to highlight the exclusivity that is expressed. The story represents an important indicator of a twinship selfobject need. It also shows, as in the previous examples of the depressed adult patients, that a range of certainty about the presence of twinship selfobject functions in projective test responses is frequently more evident than is the case with other selfobject functions. This range of confidence about the revival of the twinship selfobject function is often based on indications of single-minded commitment to achieve a strong sense of oneness or kinship. The adequate evidence, on a case-by-case basis, for twinship selfobject needs relies on the projective test protocol in its entirety.

For example, another adolescent girl, referred to evaluate the reasons for chronic truancy and poor academic performance, produced the following story to TAT Card 3BM:

> This girl found out her best friend died. She thought she couldn't live without her best friend. She's thinking of killing herself. But instead, she cut her hair so she'd look ugly and always be left alone by others. She finds another best friend and is happy again. [Q] They were close, they told each other everything, she didn't have anybody else she could count on. Her friend did everything for her, like a mother.

Considered alone, a twinship selfobject function might be a plausible interpretation of this response, largely on the basis of the degree of involvement with the friend. The intensity in the relationship is greater than expected in a mirroring or idealization selfobject function. It is something more than "like a mother"; not only is there a sense of complete need ("her friend did everything for her"), but doing "everything" adds a quality of an archaic infantilizing dependency.

The same patient, however, related the following story to Card 6BM:

> The mother has shocking news for the son. His father was killed in the war. The son can't see how he'd live without his father who he's admired through all the years. He finds a woman to take the father's place.

Here, the intensity of the relationship seems to be based on idealization. Both stories described a quality of desperation in the face of loss of the needed selfobject. The hint of a total or exclusive bond on Card 3BM raises the question of a twinship need, but this response may be just as readily understood as idealization, because of the story told to Card 6BM.

Note, however, the similarity between this patient's story to Card 3BM and the previously cited story by an adolescent girl to Card 7GF, in which the mother attempted to dissuade the girl from forming a bond with the doll. In the former case, the relative absence of other selfobject functions supports the possibility of twinship as the primary selfobject need. In contrast, in the present patient, her stories to both Cards 3BM and 6BM indicated at least some ambiguity about the nature of the selfobject need.

There remains a question, at least, about the primariness of one selfobject function over another.

Alikeness, Shared Similarity, and the Faithful Replica

The following examples provide two illustrations of responses that point to a patient's need for a selfobject to resemble oneself. The first response reflects a wish to be exactly alike another person, and the second response represents the need to have another person become what the patient wished she might have been in her own right. In both instances, the twinship need is expressed but then quickly renounced. It remains unclear whether the wish is actually satisfied, rejected, or defensively concealed behind a facade of mature acceptance. Phenomena that connote merger longings or boundary disturbances can also be conceptualized from several object relations viewpoints. My discussion of these responses is from a self psychological framework.

The patient, a 38-year-old woman in a psychotic reaction precipitated by self-withdrawal from antipsychotic medication, gave this response to Rorschach Card VII: "It looks like two women looking at each other making silly faces, or maybe distorted faces." On inquiry, after describing the form-based features of the human figures, the patient stated, in response to the examiner's query about the silly faces:

> The faces are sunk in there like maybe an old-fashioned type or a dumb-looking hat, maybe they're trying to put on the same type of clothing to maybe look like a twin or something, and then realized how silly it was. No matter how they're dressed, they're still the same person. My psychiatrist said that to me. You could admire the person but couldn't be that person.

The second illustration from this patient was her story to TAT Card 1:

> Looks like my older son when he was taking Suzuki violin lessons. He hated it. The first thing he said was I don't want to do that, and someone said it was what I wanted to do and not him, and I shouldn't have forced him. I wanted to play the violin, my father does, he's very accomplished, he's very perfect. I'm more slipshod, I don't like doing things perfectly, it would be too much of a strain because everything has to be done rush, rush. [Patient continues in this hypomanic digression until asked for the outcome to her story.] He doesn't take any more violin lessons and he's glad and he's happy. He's glad he could finally voice an opinion.

In these two examples, the need for the selfobject to function as a faithful replica resembles twinship, but there is some question whether this interpretation is accurate. In earlier examples of the patients discussed previously, the twinship selfobject function was characterized by a quality of kinship or a close bond as the basis for the selfobject responsiveness sought by those patients. In the present examples, the two figures were seen as exactly alike, as if they were the same person. The wish for shared alikeness or similarity is more than a perception of resemblance based on looking alike or thinking the same way. It seems to run deeper than surface similarity and is close to the core of the experience of the self. No matter that the patient dismissed her selfobject need as silly or trivial; that problem is different and suggests that she might feel unworthy, ashamed, or undeserving. More to the point, however, is the question of whether the response expressed the possibility of admiring another person without having to become that person.

Herein lies the difficulty in the differential diagnosis: Is this response essentially or primarily a twinship selfobject function, or is it a need for a level of selfobject responsiveness based on idealization to buttress self-cohesion? The answer to this question requires the full projective protocol to decide the clinical issue accurately. Rarely, if ever, does a single response contain a sufficiently clear or unambiguous basis for deciding among various possibilities. The issue of a twinship or idealization selfobject function is the critical question that an examiner must consider by using the entire protocol to decide the matter and to determine how to view this patient's first response.

The patient's second response suggests a vicarious experience of attempting to enhance self-esteem. Vicarious gratifications or wishes on projective tests are not rare. They usually imply some degree of using another person in the service of fulfilling an unmet need, thereby sustaining self-esteem. Sometimes, the narcissistic extension is seen as exactly like the patient (the faithful replica). It may also appear closely bound up with the patient's need to achieve a goal by imitation or by becoming a duplicate of someone else. Both mechanisms should be considered to represent potential indications of twinship when the heart of the experience is based on the need for merging with the selfobject.

The patient's response in which her son was expected to become an accomplished violinist in the way that her father was but that she could not achieve comes close to meeting the criterion of shared similarity. In the end, however, it falls short because the focus of the response is the patient's failed expectation of herself rather than the compelling need for her son to be like her or like what she wished herself to become. The vicarious experience must go beyond someone who does something for the patient. The selfobject must in some central or deeply felt way embody or be the same as oneself. This experience should not be confused with merging or loss of self–other boundaries, as occurs in transient psychotic states.

It is always possible that this patient did indeed hope that her son, by taking up the violin, would become an extension of herself or that his need would parallel her own need. Through the son, the patient might earn her father's admiration, despite the story outcome in which the son managed to discontinue lessons and the patient allowed him his wish. Her hypomanic digression in the midst of her delivery of the response adds further uncertainty as to where she might have gone with her story. The answer to the clinical question at hand remains uncertain; the questions I have posed, however, illustrate the clinical issue that examiners must decide about this response as an accurate representation of twinship or some other selfobject function that has become mobilized.

The patient's primary concern centered on her own failure as she went off the point of her story about the son, but her story does not afford an examiner a clear indication about the central selfobject function. On the basis of this single response, even in light of the patient's Rorschach response noted previously, the most conservative approach to interpreting Card 1 does not rest on a twinship selfobject function. The possibility of twinship is worth noting, but the ultimate basis for an interpretation of this type requires scrutinizing the entire protocol for more persuasive evidence to sustain the idea of a twinship need.

The following example illustrates that a projective test response signifying a particular selfobject function prepares the way for understanding other test responses. These subsequent responses might not otherwise have led to a particular interpretation of a selfobject function. The example is from the projective testing of a 44-year-old male anesthesiologist hospitalized with an acute depression. This patient produced an agitated Rorschach protocol, beginning with "two priests holding up their hands in some kind of benediction" (Card I), which he elaborated further on inquiry by stating that "benediction is wishing well, it makes me feel good, part of a community, connected with others."

This same patient made a figure drawing of a man that he described thus:

[A] high school student, with girls and cars on his mind, he probably works part time at McDonald's or some such place. He's very much worried about his self-image, what he looks like, he just wants to look like everyone else, to be just one of the guys.

He also made a female drawing of someone "ten years older than him, out of high school, happily married, responsible, looking forward to sharing a life together. Most people that age are optimistic that everything will work out just fine."

The Rorschach response illustrated here is consistent with a twinship selfobject need surrounding the desire for kinship and the calming strength that this provides. As in several of the examples previously considered, a reference to twins, identical figures, or even similarly appearing figures is not essential for the identification of the twinship selfobject need. The crucial characteristic in this response is the reference to belonging to a community from which he derived a sense of human connection, regardless of the reference to the priests. This response prepares the way for understanding the two figure drawing responses in a way that was not otherwise apparent.

Without this patient's response about priests communing, the examiner would very likely consider an interpretation of the male drawing as being centered on regression, immaturity, or insecure identity when a middle-aged adult, who is a successful physician, appears to identify with a teenager working at McDonald's preoccupied with girls and cars. This impression is pronounced in view of the sharp contrast between this patient's drawing of an adolescent boy and that of a mature woman undertaking expected adult responsibilities. Understanding this patient's twinship selfobject need, derived from the Rorschach response, provides an insight about that aspect of the figure drawing inquiry pertaining to the boy's desire to be accepted by his peers. This interpretation offers another aspect to consider, as an alternative to or alongside that of a regressive pull or a problem in achieving mature adult identification.

One can readily see this man's difficulty as his struggle to sustain a twinship selfobject need. His struggle addresses his need for a meaningful connection with others, a connection through which he could draw on this resource to feel at one with or at home with the people in his surroundings. As a result, self-esteem regulation and the repair of an injured, undermined self can be strengthened by needed twinship selfobject wishes. From this viewpoint as well, the figure drawing of the older mature woman meeting adult responsibilities that he felt incapable of facing also suggests the possibility that the patient aspired to restore mature adult functioning, perhaps through twinship.

By now, it should be clear that the mere reference to twins, human or animal figures that are identical, or any other reference suggestive of unequivocal alikeness indicates nothing more than that one should consider that the possibility of a twinship selfobject function has been mobilized. The critical criterion for an interpretation of twinship must still remain the clearly expressed or implied psychological quality of alikeness or similarity. Twinship should be based on a need for a "twin" figure to restore or enhance self-esteem in a compelling manner with some degree of substantial depth.

7 MS. T.: MIRRORING

A CASE OF FAULTY MIRRORING SELFOBJECT RESPONSIVENESS AND UNSUCCESSFUL ATTEMPTS TO ESTABLISH COMPENSATORY STRUCTURES THROUGH IDEALIZATION

In the previous two chapters, I examined the clinical indications of selfobject functions on projective tests and illustrated the three selfobject functions with vignettes from selected Rorschach, figure drawings, and TAT responses. This chapter and the one that follows present the complete test protocols of three projective test instruments for two patients to illustrate mirroring, idealization, and twinship selfobject functions.

The difference between this material and the previous clinical examples centers on three important points. First, selfobject functions often appear in admixtures rather than as clear and discrete forms, although one typically emerges as predominant. Second, not all responses in a protocol refer to selfobject functions. Third, the clinical appearance of more than one selfobject function serves an important adaptive purpose for maintaining self-cohesion. The alternative selfobject routes formed to repair a devitalized self appear as compensatory structures in the regulation of self-esteem.

The case reported here illustrates the projective test indications of mirroring selfobject needs and demonstrates that because these needs had been chronically rebuffed, the patient's internal experience was predominantly devalued. The case also shows an unmirrored self in which inadequate responsiveness to normal mirroring selfobject needs led to pronounced and nonremitting devitalization. The patient attempted to revitalize the self through idealization in an effort to build compensatory structure, although this idealization too was thwarted. My comments emphasize the formulations derived from self psychology. Other interpretive remarks based on either an ego psychological or an object relations framework are noted briefly, if at all, to keep the focus of the clinical illustrations centered on the insights derived from Kohut's formulations.

Ms. T. was a 30-year-old White, single, female inpatient in her first lifetime psychiatric hospitalization. She was hospitalized to treat a depressive episode with prominent suicidal ideation, accompanied by associated problems of decreased sleep, significant weight gain, bulimia, and dissociation. Ms. T. had trouble concentrating on her work when she was employed as a production coordinator in charge of publishing an industry periodical. She felt herself excluded from social interactions with co-workers. The patient had a college education and had no previous psychiatric history. At the time of diagnostic psychological testing, the patient was maintained off psychotropic medications.

Human Figure Drawings

I begin with Ms. T.'s figure drawings to provide an overview and to set the stage for a self psychologically based conceptualization. The predominant self state was clearly conveyed in the verbalization on inquiry about her initial drawing.

The patient first drew a woman, for which she provided the following description when prompted to imagine what the person was like:

> Let me start over. All we have is clothes with no person yet. I always knew I didn't have a very good body concept. A very icky hair style. The only thing that's sturdy about this whole thing is the outfit. She's a real disaster. [Why is that?][1] Because I don't know how to fix it any better. As long as you said it's okay, it's your mess. Nothing's real clear, it's very sketchy, nothing's real organized here. Everything's out of proportion, everything's awful. And ugly. [Awful?] The fingers aren't right. I know how to make fingers. [Describe the personality] It's like a zombie. No expression on her face. [Doing?] On this side, she's leaning on a rail, holding on to something, she can't support herself. So she doesn't have everything fall apart and collapse.

The elaboration of this drawing as a representation of diminished self-esteem comes as no surprise to any clinician regardless of theoretical persuasion. The self-depreciation in this verbalization is clearly evident; indeed, it is difficult to imagine a better description of a frail and barely thriving sense of the self. The absence of a firm, well-formed human figure

---

[1]Examiner's queries during testing are enclosed in brackets.

(at least in the patient's eyes, because the drawing itself was not seriously compromised) was accompanied by her perception of the figure as out of proportion. Her response revealed a self state as devalued as the "awful and ugly" representation that Ms. T. described.

The "zombie" reference to the personality, together with the figure's difficulty in supporting herself to prevent her from collapsing, suggests inner depletion, diminished self-worth, and a mirroring deficit even though there is no specific reference to failure to provide affirming or comforting sustenance. Such indications appeared later; a markedly devitalized self state such as this verbalization implies that insufficient mirroring is involved in producing a self state so devalued.

A depleted self state expressed in this way suggests that the absence of a sense of the self as vigorous or buoyant results from an inadequately responsive selfobject environment. The patient may struggle to conceal the self state from others because "the only thing that's sturdy about this whole thing is the outfit." Thus, what the world sees externally barely concealed the internal state of disrepair that is not "sturdy."

This description of an injured self is just the beginning, however. Kohut would argue that it is also important to make sense of how the patient went about repairing the devaluation that was experienced so acutely. Through understanding selfobject needs, one can understand how the patient attempted to restore the enfeebled self. In continuing to analyze the ongoing clinical material, it is crucial to bear in mind that Kohut's understanding of the self as struggling to preserve its vitality extends beyond simply characterizing the phenomenology, such as that in the previous description. In this clinical example, the salient question becomes not so much one of identifying the self state (which is already intuitively obvious), but rather of discovering where the patient turns to replenish what appears to be missing. This level of understanding requires reconstructing what went wrong with the selfobject environment that faltered for the patient.

Considered in this light, Ms. T. appeared not to seek out anyone beyond herself. The best she could manage was to steady her footing by leaning against a rail to prevent herself from "falling apart and collapsing." At first, she revealed her own underpowered abilities, and there was no indication of her anticipating that her distress could be empathically understood, let alone of expecting that any need for support or cohesion could be accurately mirrored. It is not that the patient was depleted and therefore bereft of resources. Rather, it is a question of what selfobject resources were potentially available to Ms. T., and what did these provide, or fail to provide, to bolster her devalued self state. The way that this patient made use of her selfobject milieu is a continuing focus of this diagnostic study.

Ms. T.'s second human figure drawing, a person of the opposite sex, was described as follows:

> Neither one of my people has very good hands. I'll just eliminate the problem because I'm going to put this guy's hand in his pocket. I'd do these stereotypical things like a tie, which is too wide, a shirt and trousers. [*Describe his personality.*] Probably a professional person, he looks like a preppie. He thinks he's going to decide what he's going to do and do it. He's got big feet so he must be pretty well-established. [*How's that?*] Because he's standing pretty firmly on the ground. Since you said draw someone of the other sex, I gave him a beard since not many women have beards.

Her playfulness about the beard and her handling of what she considered the problem of concealing his hand by drawing it in the pocket are probably ways to appear engaging. Yet, the defensive solution of eliminating the offending body part (deficient hand) is transparent. Ms. T. seemed to feel that there were more options for repairing the drawing of the male figure than were available for her drawing of the female (by inference, of course, representing herself). This second drawing depicted a man who was decisive, sure of himself, and firmly rooted—the very picture of healthy self-esteem by anyone's definition. The experience of herself in her previous drawing as enfeebled, unable to overturn an injured self state, and with no resources besides a "rail" to keep her from "collapsing" contrasted sharply with the surefooted representation of the male figure.

The patient's second drawing may also indicate that a potential revitalization of the self was possible. Ms. T.'s sense that there was a way out and that one need not hold on to a rail for dear life implied at least a possibility that she could turn somewhere to prevent collapse and to find the means by which the self could become revitalized as a secure structure.

Rorschach Thematic Content

As I have attempted to demonstrate, the human figure drawings can provide a broad overview of the personality structure or the lay of the land. The content analysis of the Rorschach protocol that followed enriches the general hypotheses raised by the human figure drawings inquiry. Ms. T.'s complete Rorschach protocol is accompanied by commentary from a self psychological perspective after each card. Comprehensive System codes or scores are not provided, to emphasize the augmentation that content analysis provides. Thus, the self psychological viewpoint is intended to be an addition to the main formal analysis of scores, ratios, and cluster interpretation strategies, to provide an expanded conceptual view.

Card I

1. *An angel leading a chorus, but she lost her head. (W)*

   Maybe because Christmas is coming up. Trying to get everyone to sing together so it turns out right.

2. *Two elephants drinking out of a fountain. (W)*

   Two ears, the tail, their nose. It looks like Dumbo. [Dumbo?] They're cute little pink elephants. I think Dumbo could fly, he could go wherever he wanted. Actually he was a freak and he had to get out of there.

3. *A Christmas bell and Christmas tree. (D4)*

   The white is the branches. Everybody's supposed to be happy.

The first response of an angel could initially be construed as an indication that an idealized selfobject need has been mobilized, because this image might connote a turning toward a benevolent but powerful figure. The angel has been rendered impotent, however, and has not only lost its head but tries to accomplish the task of leading others without any clear sense that it has been successful. The presumably warm or affectionate association to the Christmas season creates the impression that a selfobject need for someone to make things "turn out right" was evoked. That this need fails to be satisfied in a dependable manner to sustain a degree of cohesion of the self might also be seen in the reference to the angel as headless.

The patient continued on Card I with an elephant, although her associations emphasized its "cute little pink" quality. The animal was further diminished in potency by a reference to a children's cartoon character who is at once given magical powers (flying) but in the next breath is portrayed as a freak. It is not possible at this point to decide between two interpretations of the elephant percept. On the one hand, the percept may be an indication of a strong, hulking image providing the vigor to sustain an idealizing selfobject need. The elephant as Dumbo may also represent something diminished or cut down to size.

The possibility of hostile impulses, either in the form of the beheaded angel or the diminutive elephant, may be suggested in a classical drive theory approach to these images. An ego psychological framework may suggest an interpretation of a passive-dependent position based on the references to drinking and Christmas. From the perspective of psychoanalytic self psychology, aggression or dependency is secondary in importance. Rather, the disempowering of the angel and elephant is understood as an indication of a weakened self. The passivity or dependency interpretation is also secondary and represents the sequela of a devitalized self rather than a need state. Finally, the halting anticipation of happiness of the Christmas bell and tree may be understood as restating the theme of longing for revitalization of the self.

Card II

4. *Two people dancing. Here's their heads and their hands touching. (D6)*

They have on kimonos, like in Fantasia. [Q] It's magical, having everything come to life and match the music. Everything's well organized and orchestrated.

5. *A top in the middle. (DS5)*

How it's shaped here. I had one when I was little.

6. *Or a rocket with the jet propulsion. (DS5 + D3)*

A jet blasting off. All the smoke and debris. The rocket's off to places unknown. [Rocket?] No one ever thought rockets would be blasting off. You never know what will happen. Maybe like the one E. T. came in.

7. *A seamstress' model. This manikin doesn't have a head. A very long neck. It's a pretty dress. Mainly to show the dress off. (DS5)*

A sketch for a dress. It's all ready for somebody to take it, for something real special. A special occasion for a special person. It would have to be for a skinny person, so it's not for me.

8. *A monument in Arizona: a monolith. Very pretty colors. It looks like a Navajo painting. (D2)*

Like in the art fairs. A desert scene. [Pretty colors, a desert scene?] It's foreboding, isolated. Bleak.

The responses to Card II are very productive. Evidently, Ms. T.'s perceptual processes and imagination were compellingly engaged here, particularly by the center white space, because three of her five responses emphasized the DS5 area of the blot. Beginning with a percept about festive dancing and ending in a bleak desert scene, Ms. T. revealed wide oscillations of affect. These could easily be considered to reflect the lability of a borderline disorder or, in a previous diagnostic era, hysteria. Nevertheless, the diagnostic issue is a separate question from that of the psychodynamic interplay of conflict, anxiety, and defenses. A self psychological view of labile affect is understood as indicating that the self is in a state of unstable cohesion. This view reveals as much about defective selfobject responsiveness as about the diagnostic condition giving rise to this degree of affect dysregulation.

From this vantage point, Ms. T.'s percept of people dancing with their hands touching evoked her desire for a stabilized self, "well-organized and orchestrated." The "magical" fantasy reference could partially stem from her final response to Card I (a Christmas tree), as a continuation of the hope for securing a revitalized self. Like the succeeding response of a top and its association to a childhood memory, this percept of well-organized dancing can be seen as a wish for a vulnerable self to be repaired. This view is at variance with a typical interpretation of regressive wishes.

The theme of her need for restoring the self persisted, despite her third response about a rocket blasting off and leaving a trail of debris and smoke. The association on inquiry was not to falling apart or destruction; rather, she marveled about the achievements of space science. This response repeated the wish to restore a sense of calming stability. (It is an error to automatically equate an image of debris and smoke with an interpretation of a distintegration product.) The desire for stabilization holds even though it is experienced with the child-like, wondrous appeal of the familiar benevolent character of E. T.

This same sequence of responses might well be viewed differently by followers of drive theory; they would emphasize the extensive defensive layering to contain the hostile images of a rocket creating debris. The view of self psychology, however, is that interpretations about aggression or rage are misguided. The ego psychological view fails to take full account of the patient's expression of a self that she attempted to preserve as viable or animated. This patient sought to restore some measure of calmness in the aftermath of a disruption to self-cohesion as inferred from her association to debris. It is not the rage that is fundamental, at least in Kohut's view; the rage represents a byproduct of the failed attempt to preserve self-cohesion when the self state is threatened. Ms. T. was not blowing up; she has been blown away.

Her response of a seamstress' model of a headless manikin that displayed a pretty dress "for a special person ... not for me" began a downward spiral from her earlier percepts. These had included optimistic wishes such as dancing in a magical setting, a top like one she had as a child, and a wondrous appreciation of rocketry and the benevolent imagery of E. T. Later, she failed to see herself as the intended owner of the pretty dress and was no longer the special person she might wish to be; ultimately she ended with the self state conveyed in the isolation of the bleak desert scene. As Ira Gershwin wrote in the song lyric "They're writing songs of love but not for me", so, too, does Ms. T. convey this sentiment by her comment that the dress was for someone special "but not for me."

Ms. T.'s capacity to present a stable, invigorated self continued to waver, as already noted on her figure drawings and on Card I. Indeed, by the end of Card II, little was left but bleak isolation of an unstimulated self as represented by the desert monolith percept. Even her attempt to introduce "very pretty colors ... like in the art fairs" failed to work well for her. Her inquiry response was dominated by the desolation suggested by this percept. Whether hypomanic denial or an indication of her symptomatic dysphoria, the response pointed to the difficulty that Ms. T. experienced in her effort to preserve a consistent, ongoing level of self-esteem.

Her faltering effort in this regard implies that the desolation in these responses represented a disintegration product. In this context, the rocket's debris may now be considered to be part of this self state of desolation, but not for the reason that it connotes enraged destruction. Instead, debris as a disintegration product might belong with the devastated self state dominated by affects such as bleak emptiness and isolation.

With regard to the question of selfobject function, in this sequence of five responses, potential saviors of her faltering self were unavailable or impotent. Thus, the headless angel of Card I, the headless seamstress' manikin, and the benevolent figure of E. T. cannot apparently prevent her final percept of the bleak desert monolith, which was the manifestation of unavailable or inadequate responsiveness to legitimate selfobject needs. It is, by inference, profoundly deficient mirroring, despite a feeble attempt to seek idealizing selfobjects such as the imposing rocket, a magical, Fantasia-like quality, or the angel of Card I. Her rocket ended in debris, and her angel was headless. Even the animated Fantasia scene and the top could not prevent her final response of the bleak desert scene.

Such responses are significant indicators of deficient mirroring. Patients who are chronically left too much to their own devices ultimately wind up feeling ignored or forgotten. Ms. T.'s responses are notable for the absence of figures who might provide the selfobject mirroring function of affirmation. The other pathway to detecting faulty responsiveness from selfobjects is the more easily visible expression of disappointment. Here, the emphasis is on figures who fail in one way or another to come through for the patient. Ms. T. displayed the pattern of deficient mirroring characterized by being unnoticed or left too much alone for her own good, unable to hold up a cohesive sense of self to the world. Her devitalized self became like her percept of the top on Card II; had it been seen as spinning, its momentum would wind down and, like her brittle self, come to a grinding halt.

Card III

9. *That's stereotypical: two African people, pointed face, the Afro hair styles. Beating on drums, trying to get a message. (D1)*

It's just the bodies of the two people, beating on drums right here.

10. *Neanderthal people. They both fell out of a tree. This is what they were hanging on to, it probably broke. (D2)*

They're cave people. [How does it look that way?] It looks like a cave painting. They're hunched over like gorillas. They're primitive, not very smart. That's why they fell out of the tree.

11. *A bust of Beethoven. A big red bow tie so it'd be cute as a button. (D3)*

I'm looking at a negative image. Beethoven because his hair is sticking out. He's all jazzed up with the bow tie. [How does it look that way?] You mean sophisticated, class and culture? A desired goal. In the midst of this primitive stuff: Neanderthals falling out of a tree because they're stupid.

The popular response of the opening percept (No. 9) was conventional enough. The variation on this response in the next percept (No. 10) confirmed any indication of primitiveness suggested by the image of people beating a drum. Although a percept of primitive figures is often interpreted in classical drive theory as indicating the activation of a drive, usually aggression, this notion is rarely uppermost in the self psychological view-point, in which it more likely refers to denigration. Ms. T. attempted to minimize the primitive aspect of the percepts cited here by making them a piece of art ("a cave painting"). This attempt failed as a defense when she referred to the gorilla-like, hunched-over appearance. She noted that the figures fell from the tree because they were not smart. It could be argued that for Ms. T., smart was her way of saying fortified. She was telling the examiner that she cannot hold her own very well. In effect, she could fall down and find herself unprotected.

In drive theory, this response is an indication of diminished ego resil-iency, in which defenses are weakened, anxiety is not sufficiently contained, and adaptation becomes compromised. A self psychological interpretation takes the position that the patient is speaking here of the vulnerability of a self that cannot sustain itself and lacks strength or endurance. Its very cohesion feels threatened, and the selfobject need is for something external to come to the aid of a self that experiences itself as "primitive" or brittle.

Even in her "cute as a button" bust of Beethoven, Ms. T. could not resist referring still another time to an enfeebled self "in the midst of this primitive stuff." Her attempt to introduce a "jazzed up ... cute red bow tie" on a figure not infrequently referred to as a titan among composers was insufficient to repair the injury to the self. One cannot know all that underlay Ms. T.'s association to Beethoven or be sure that she realized Beethoven was often scorned during his lifetime, despite the esteem his music engendered. It is not too speculative, however, to consider that the percept of Beethoven represents a figure suitable for idealization. In this regard, it probably cannot provide what Ms. T. sought in the way of an idealizing selfobject function when it was portrayed as "cute as a button" instead of as a giant.

Card IV

12. *A big monster. Here's his head and his hands. An ac-tion shot because his feet go up and down.* (W)

His hands fell off. Here's his tail. [Hands fell off?] The worst thing he can do is step on you. His head is pretty small.

v13. *A medieval castle. All this protection. It's very danger-ous down there. To keep peo-ple out.* (Dd99; lower half of D1)

This is how it would look, here's the top right here.

v14. *Like Georgia O'Keefe, it's*   *The nasal cavity and horns. It's real*
     reminiscent of some of her   *neat. A dead buffalo and they made*
     works. It reminds me of a buf-   *something pretty out of it.*
     falo skull in the desert. (W)

v15. *A king. His crown, his head,*   *His outfit, the beard, his head and*
     all this is pomp and circum-   *hair. It reminds me of the emperor's*
     stance. (W)   *new clothes. They were all just*
                                            fooling him.

Ms. T. did not describe her monster as threatening, although she referred to his large size from the perspective of an "action shot." She wasted no time in immobilizing the monster, first by removing his hands and later by referring to his small head. Perhaps severing the hands was sufficiently immobilizing so that this figure did not also need to be beheaded, as Ms. T. had already done on Cards I and II, but she had not thereby protected herself from injury because the monster could still "step on you."

There followed a percept of a medieval castle, fortified but still not invulnerable. In needing "to keep people out," Ms. T. had expended so much mental effort on protecting herself and staving off injuries to the self that she became deadened in the process by the time she reached the percept of the buffalo skull. No matter that she tried to defensively represent this state of depletion and mental exhaustion as an artistic product. Even her closing percept to this card, that of a king, was undermined, because the power expected from a king was weakened and illusory. Ultimately, the king too became an unreliable basis for establishing idealization as a compensatory structure. The percept continued her reference to the bigger-than-life Beethoven as diminished and "cute as a button." As with her association to the fairy tale about the emperor's new clothes, one is not fooled by her diversionary kings, castles, Beethoven, and big monsters. She could not conceal that the king was just "pomp and circumstance," the castle held danger, the monster's hands fell off, and Beethoven was reduced to a "cute as a button" statue.

Card V

16. *Two people sleeping. (W)*   *The legs here, the elbow. Like at the*
                                            beach, resting. It's calm.

17. *A mythical animal getting*   *It's mythical because there's no ani-*
    ready for a take-off. (W)   *mal like this. His feet are getting*
                                            ready to run and take off. He's fine
                                            once he gets going, but taking off is
                                            hard.

I don't like this one very well.
[Q] It's not too exciting.
There's not too much happen-
ing.

Ms. T. began her responses to Card V with the appearance of what seemed like a recovery from the preceding upheaval. By psychologically "sleeping," she managed to feel "calm." Inasmuch as her vigilant efforts to protect the self from depletion consumed so much of her psychological resources, she seemed to be alone in this attempt. There is barely any indication of selfobject responsiveness that she could rely on. Her mythical animal percept could refer to a feeling that no one else seems to have to work this hard ("there's no animal like this ... taking off is hard").

She might be sleeping her way through Card V, but her comment about not liking the card became, in effect, a powerful quasiresponse: She did not like the quietude that was the price she paid for feeling calm. Thus, hardly a "sleeper," this response was a good example of a situation on the Rorschach when less is more.

The excitement that she missed here perhaps reminded her too much of the inner deadness suggested by the buffalo skull of Card IV and the desert scene of Card II. If so, did this reminder re-expose an unresponded-to self to a sense of dread about the threat of depletion? Could a sense of calmness also be intolerable because feeling comforted might prove to be illusory or undependable? These possibilities must remain tentative, however compelling they are at this point in the protocol. Speculation about these dynamics raises the question of what happens when it becomes necessary to self-protectively drive one's selfobject needs underground to protect the self from further devitalization.

This phenomenon may represent a milder form of the pronounced withdrawal states associated with the schizoid or depressive positions to which patients defensively retreat to protect themselves, similar to the states emphasized in the writings of Melanie Klein (1935/1975) and Guntrip (1969). Kohut did not attach the same significance to this phenomenon that Klein and Guntrip did, nor did he conceptualize clinical material in the same way. Nevertheless, there may exist some commonality between these points of view.

This patient's comment about the lack of excitement on Card V, coupled with her earlier responses of the desert scene and the buffalo skull of a Georgia O'Keefe painting, revived the fear of dissolution of the self. This reaction is reminiscent of the disintegration anxiety that M. Tolpin & Kohut (1980) believed to underlie several forms of self disturbances. Her animal who seemed to need a push to get going was still a "mythical" animal. Thus, feeling "fine" was illusory because the push (that is, selfobject responsiveness) of a suitably mirroring or invigorating selfobject was absent or in some vital sense not real or present for her. It was in this sense that "it's not too exciting."

Card VI

v18. *A buffalo skin hanging on a wall for decoration. (D1) I don't feel like doing this anymore.*

The front, his back legs, the spine is curved, the tail here. I feel sorry for the buffalo: Where does that leave him? You're supposed to be nice to them, they're an endangered species.

19. *Waves coming in, slopping all over the place. (D1)*

The foam hitting the beach. Soon the water will be all over, there won't be any land left. [How do you see it?] The way the foam goes over the beach. It's like writing messages in a sand castle and they're erased away, they're only left in your memory. The waves wash everything away. It's night.

20. *A kiwi fruit that somebody splashed. All the seeds exploded all over, just gushed out. (D12)*

This black looks like the stripe down the middle of a kiwi fruit. [Stripe?] It's something special, unusual. It's just coincidental.

I thought these were in colors.

Ms. T.'s remark at the end of Card V was restated even more strongly after her first response to Card VI. Evidently, she was becoming increasingly perturbed by some quality of the blots that made her wish to withdraw from the testing situation. Her earlier response of a buffalo skull now became a buffalo skin, and the mythical animal of Card V became endangered. She seemed to complain that the buffalo, an endangered species, was maltreated. Even her attempt to make the skin a wall decoration was no more convincing than her earlier attempt to turn her bleak desert scene into a Navajo painting.

At the conclusion of Card VI, Ms. T. complained further of her need for color in the cards, a response perhaps signifying that she was growing overburdened by the bleak task that the Rorschach had become for her. Her response seemed to capture how she experienced much of her life. The understimulation signified a self that was desolate, unresponded to, and ultimately devoid of the buoyancy required to sustain itself in a psychologically alive manner.

She felt drained ("I don't feel like doing this anymore") and perhaps frustrated with an examiner who continually re-exposed her to the devitalization of her self-esteem. She appealed to me and expected understanding or sympathy ("I feel sorry for the buffalo; where does that leave him?") as if to say to me: "What's wrong with you? Can't you see how much I'm hurting? You're supposed to be nice to someone like me who feels so endangered." My restatement of her inquiry comments practically defined this patient's complaint about an unresponsive or unavailable mirroring selfobject environment that did not notice her distress and needs.

The theme of an understimulated, unresponded-to self seemed to pervade the rest of Card VI and was captured in the melancholy tone of lost, unpreserved, or erased "messages." This theme foreshadowed a forgotten-about self in danger of eroding or being "washed away." It was reminiscent of her other castle (Card IV) that was in danger. Is the danger that something imposing or vigorous is elusive or transitory? Can it be "washed away"? Note also her comment about the castle on Card IV ("this is how it would look") as if she were reconstructing something from a memory; she repeated this image in her "memory" of the sand castle on Card VI.

Even the "special" quality of the kiwi fruit was problematic: A black stripe "exploded ... gushed." As much as she craved it, is gushing excitement or enlivenment too hot for her to handle ("exploded")? Perhaps self-protectively, Ms. T. contained this upsurge of affect by converting something "special ... unusual" into something merely "coincidental." (Recall again how her dress from Card II for someone special to show off is "not for me.") Perhaps, alternatively, the kiwi, with its associations of tropical colors, revived the wish for the enlivening of a depleted self. Its failure or disappointment might have disposed Ms. T. to comment about missing the color on the ink blots. Was she giving the examiner another chance to enliven her, only to have her hopes dashed?

On this card, characterized as it was by the most compelling indication of decompensation to this point, there was still no indication of a clearly stated selfobject need. This patient craved mirroring, complained about its absence, but finally felt that mirroring was too unsafe or unreliable to tolerate, and withdrew into a self state of depletion depression. This is the fate of the unmirrored self (M. Tolpin, 1993). There is some risk in making a point by reasoning from the absence of a function rather than from an interpretation about an actual percept. I nevertheless argue that what is seen here is a self state experienced as forgotten about and depreciated. It seems as if this patient could only complain about continuing the Rorschach at this point or wonder about why there was no color in the blots. This reaction is either a defensive withdrawal from a situation that has become too burdensome to bear or an expression of a veiled statement expressing a need for a selfobject to become available to enliven, revive, or otherwise add "color" to her depleted self.

That the selfobject need is expressed in only a veiled manner does not, however, mean that it is absent. If it is concealed by being driven underground, the examiner's task becomes more difficult; he or she must make something of so little. Sometimes, the selfobject function is not contained in the elaboration of the percept itself but may appear in a patient's indirect, associated comments in reference to the task itself. Thus, Ms. T.'s remarks about not liking a card, not wanting to go on, or asking for cards with color managed to convey what the response proper did not. Transference manifestations directed to the examiner could reflect the selfobject needs that characterized much of her life. Undergoing projective testing represented a microcosm of the patient's life and re-exposed her to the draining ordeal of her devitalized existence. When Ms. T. said in effect, "I don't like this any more, I want to stop, you don't give me anything with more color to work with," she perhaps expressed a wish for a selfobject to bring her back to life.

One does not see here the specific selfobject transference represented by mirroring, idealization, or twinship, but rather the general manifestation of a self state in disrepair. The specific selfobject function may not often be clearly indicated on the Rorschach but may appear vividly on a task such as the TAT, which evokes relationships among figures and ways that one figure fails to provide some selfobject function for another. Similarly, figure drawings may suggest depreciation of the figure and sometimes also contain an indication of what is needed to repair the defect in self-esteem. The Rorschach, on the other hand, more often captures the push and pull of conflicts, defenses, and anxiety, and reveals more about ego resiliency in the process. In a similar fashion, the Rorschach may often indicate more about the self state than about particular selfobject needs.

This is the case with Ms. T., whose clear manifestations of selfobject needs do become evident on the TAT. I describe this process more fully later, in the discussion of the material about Ms. T.'s TAT. The tentative speculations noted here, however, provide a way of thinking about the probable selfobject functions underlying the self states that are so richly evident in the content analysis findings from this Rorschach protocol.

Card VII

v21. *Two people bending over backwards. Their arms reaching out. (W)*

They're women, on tippy-toe so you know they'll fall over for sure. The arms have to be out. You balance so not to fall over. Also, they're balancing on their brains because that's the only thing that's touching.

v22. *Napoleon. His head, collar, the funny hat. (DS7)*

The hat part. He was a ruthless leader, a military genius, and powerful. A little guy who got where he wanted to, even though he ended in exile. So, he gave it a go, and got as far as he could.

23. *Two people balancing on the very edge of the top of a rock. They're trying to communicate either by using their arms for gestures or their heads coming together. (W)*

Here's the ponytail. Balancing on the base so they don't fall over.

By now, there was little new. Most responses essentially restated earlier themes. Beginning with people precariously balanced to avoid falling down, Ms. T. proceeded to the diminutive but powerful Napoleon who wound up defeated. Thus, she ended as insecurely balanced as she began. Ms. T. never managed to gain a solid foothold for her precarious self state. Her elaboration at the end of the inquiry to Response 21 was unclear; in an otherwise non-thought–disordered record, she seemed to struggle with headless or brainless imagery, and with desperation. This statement is another instance of a self state that lacks what is needed for its cohesion or stability.

Card VIII

v24. *Somebody's brain. Some of the parts are rotted out. A lot of the parts are missing. (W)*

The pons, midbrain, cerebrum, medulla oblongata.

25. *Noah's ark. Rocking on the*   *It doesn't exist. The boat that was*
    edge of a mountain top, kind   *supposed to save everybody.*
    of tipping. Even though it's
    been there thousands of years
    I think it's going to fall off.
    Everything there is petrified.
    (D4)

26. *Two bears climbing up the*   *They're supposed to have big*
    side with their hand reaching   *strong hands, so they're non-func-*
    out but it doesn't look like a   *tional, sickly.*
    bear hand. The fingers don't
    look good. (D1)

v27. *Two unicorns. Maybe just be-*   *Here's the horses' heads, the sad-*
     cause they're white. I   *dles. They're comforting, rocking*
     changed it to rocking horses.   *back and forth.*
     (Dds99=D5 + Dd33 + DdS28)

The neuroanatomical sophistication was surprising, but Ms. T.'s opening response to this card did not obscure the theme of rotting away. The theme continued the precarious "balancing on their brains" from Card VII, extended her reference to missing parts of a structure as vital as the brain, and persisted with the failure to keep afloat in the Noah's ark percept. The ominous-sounding petrification became more predominant as Ms. T. experienced the profoundly distressing devitalization of the self over and over again. Perhaps there was a hint of an idealizing selfobject need emerging here, with the hope of the figure represented by the biblical story of Noah coming to her rescue. His "boat that was supposed to save everybody" failed her, however, as did the powerful Napoleon of Card VII who was finally impotent in a state of exile. Her hopes were met with disappointment wherever she turned in her attempt to find a suitably idealizable selfobject to compensate for defective mirroring. Powerful figures were of little use to her; they become like her "cute as a button" Beethoven.

She continued valiantly forward with a percept of bears climbing a mountain, but these normally vigorous, burly animals were also "sickly." Ms. T. finally resorted to the mythical figures represented by unicorns. Like her Dumbo on Card II who was a "freak" and the mythical animal of Card V who had trouble "taking off," her unicorns quickly changed to inanimate rocking horses. Apart from the possible connotation of a wondrous or noble unicorn that is reduced to a child's simple toy, her unicorn, together with

her Dumbo figure, offered little more than minimal comfort as she continued to experience considerable desperation in her effort to repair an enfeebled self.

Card IX

28. *Two witches over a big pot,
    throwing all sorts of stuff in.
    It's all poison. (D3)*

    *A looking up shot so you can't see
    what's in there, but everyone knows
    witches always make poison.*

v29. *A pelvis area. (D11)*

    *Its shape. Now I can see the organs
    and muscles (points to D6 area).*

30. *The back view of somebody's
    shoulders with a real pretty
    fancy evening gown. But you
    can't see the rest of her head,
    but it's a very nice hair style.
    (Dd99: lower half of D3 and
    upper projection of D1 area)*

    *From the back. [Pretty?] The ele-
    gance, fanciness. Wealth.*

31. *Two women with long
    dresses. The wind is blowing
    their hair and dresses.
    (DdS99: two larger white
    space areas on either side of
    Dd30)*

    *The two white things. Like a myth
    where the people weren't supposed
    to do something and they turned to
    stone and got petrified. That was
    their punishment.*

The percept of witches introduced something not noted previously:
malevolent figures up to no good. Although not a surprising response in
this blot area, there had been no previous indication in the protocol to
prepare the examiner for a response of malevolent figures intent on
creating harm. The percept of a pelvis that followed did not help to clarify
matters.

Ms. T.'s subsequent response, flowing evening gowns, was in sharp
contrast to the witches' robes often seen in this D1 area. The witches'
poisonous brew percept may be construed in several ways. Its meaning
in regard to hostile wishes is clear; it may also be another manifestation
of a vulnerable self struggling to preserve cohesion in light of forces that
undermine this effort. Witches may further represent an aspect of self-
depreciation.

What, then, of the elegant gown of the woman whose face cannot be seen?
The fancy quality can be considered to represent Ms. T.'s need to feel proud

of herself, perhaps even to be seen as beautiful or admirable by others. That she could not, in effect, show her face, represented either shame or the inability to feel proud and worthy of admiration. The response was reminiscent of this patient's earlier response of a headless manikin used only to display the special dress not meant for her. Although headless, "but it's a very nice hair style" she tells us: Is one really to believe her? Is Ms. T. not, after all, the one with the "icky" hair of the depreciated, enfeebled drawing of the woman she described earlier on the human figure drawings? Laudable as it may be that Ms. T. still manages to sustain some hope for mirroring, it should not be forgotten that she is also skeptical that the realization of her need may be "fanciful."

The reference to wealth is consistent with the few other expressions of selfobject needs for idealization, needs that also have not materialized. Therefore, the reference may be consistent with the previous percepts of Napoleon in exile, the petrified Noah's ark, or the king's crown that is merely pomp and circumstance and that people can see through. The percept may represent the wish for admiration, and in its absence, the attempt to turn to an idealized selfobject to compensate for defective mirroring.

The final response to Card IX, women in long, flowing, white dresses, became in the end another fanciful myth. She appeared to convey the sense that any hopeful attempt, however tentative in her imagination, was still ill-fated. She imagined that her longing for the admiration that comes with empathically attuned mirroring would be punished. For this patient, the punishment of petrification was once again that state of devitalization of the self from which she found little relief.

Card X

v32. *Bugs, like in a movie I saw. They ate the brain out. The Wrath of Khan. Could transmit their thoughts. They didn't have any control of their actions when the bug's in their ear. (W)*

The colors and squishiness, like a caterpillar that crawled and slithered. I clean my ears twice a day because I don't like icky things.

33. *The Fontainebleu and seafood restaurant in Paris. The Eiffel Tower is nearby. (D2 + D11)*

The way there's statues around the fountain. When I used to go on vacation, I went wherever I wanted and did what I wanted.

34. *Crustaceans. (D1)*

The shape they have here.

35. *Disneyland. When the Magic*   *That's how it looks. Everyone has*
    Kingdom comes out at night.   *to clap their hands for Tinkerbell so*
    (D10)   *they wouldn't die.*

36. *Two pterodactyls. They kiss*   *The bodies, their fancy tails. They*
    and there's a blue heart. But   *kissed and their heart grew.*
    they're extinct, so it doesn't   *They're prehistoric birds. Like a*
    make any difference. (D6)   *cartoon thing. The heart means*
                                       they kissed.

Ms. T.'s opening response on Card X sounded ominous at first glance. It resembled the "rotting brain" of Card VIII and her "balancing on their brains" comment on Card VII. It also followed from her response of the witches' poisonous brew on the previous blot. Perhaps the chromatic cards triggered a previously concealed or effectively defended layer of this patient's pathology, but the reference to a horror movie somewhat minimized this concern.

The primitive quality of a percept with mention of eating the brain or bugs in the ears, together with Ms. T.'s overpersonalized comment about cleaning her own ears, nevertheless suggested that at least momentary loss of distance occurred. Whether or not an examiner may regard a response such as this as psychotic-like, its meaning can still be empathically understood from the vantage point of psychoanalytic self psychology. Even psychotic productions contain indications about the self state.

From this viewpoint, Ms. T. managed to vividly convey that she experienced herself as depreciated, with an intensity not previously seen in the protocol. Here, Ms. T. presented herself as so devalued that she felt herself without any means to restore even minimal self-esteem. The chromatic blots indicated that the depths of the self disorder reached deeper than previously recognized. The percept of the rotting brain and the petrified Noah's ark on Card VIII provided the first signs of this degree of psychopathology, but not until Card X did this level emerge in its most profoundly devalued form.

As profound a picture of a depreciated self state as these responses indicated, Ms. T. did manage to recover sufficiently to produce a grand Parisian scene. This quasirecovery occurred immediately after the Card X percept of bugs, a percept that would probably be considered her most regressed depiction of the self state. Her associative comment recalled a time when she felt herself to be in greater control. This comment indicated that the self, as embattled or beaten down as it became, still held some possibility, however unlikely, of being restored to a hardier or more robust and resilient state.

This configuration recalls Kohut's comment, made on a number of occasions, that there is no self without a selfobject. However devitalized the experience of the self may be, the possibility that a revivable selfobject can still be sought points to the means for treating the narcissistic injury or underlying self disorder. The prognostic implication of such projective test responses or inquiry elaborations is useful for specifying treatment indications or recommendations. Some clinicians may dismiss this interpretive view as merely mistaking an instance of hypomanic denial, but this criticism overlooks the important point about the repair of the self. Regarding this sequence of responses on Card X as simply an attempt at denial is shortsighted.

Ms. T. followed her Parisian scene response with the magical wonder of a Disneyland image, complete with a reference to having to clap hands "so they wouldn't die." Although this response could be understood as magical thinking and hypomanic denial, in another sense it is one more indication of what has to be done to preserve a faltering sense of self-cohesion. To conclude, this patient described a myth about a prehistoric animal and its needs for the "heart to grow" and therefore to sustain the self to forestall its extinction.

Summary

In Ms. T.'s Rorschach findings, a consistent picture emerged of a diminished self, unable to sustain a robust state of vigor to enable the patient to turn pridefully to others in anticipation of being admired or understood. Again and again, Ms. T. appeared to experience the depletion of a self that could not hold itself up to the world. She could not expect the selfobject responsiveness that she required to assist her in preserving self-esteem and was easily devastated as her efforts to seek admiration went unheard. As a result, assertive selfobject-seeking attempts at restoring self-cohesion were driven underground.

Ms. T. attempted to turn to idealizable figures for their imagined strength to buoy the chronic selfobject failures of mirroring to which she was continually re-exposed. Persisting disappointment and disintegration products permeated this protocol. Her attempt to establish idealization as an alternative pathway to self-cohesion was Ms. T.'s effort to revive faltering self-esteem. In this way, she tried to build a compensatory structure that might lead to the restoration of the self. That her attempt characteristically led to her sense that idealized selfobjects were impotent, immobilized, or illusory only further undermined

Ms. T.'s self disorder and intensified the prevailing beaten-down adaptation at the core of her experience of the self. She was unable to emerge from this state sufficiently revived.

A compensatory structure to take the place of chronic, ongoing, deficient mirroring is not the same thing as filling a gap. The goal of selfobject responsiveness, or optimal treatment for that matter, is structure formation rather than feeding, sustenance, or any other variation of supplying temporary palliatives. None of these is particularly therapeutic as far as analysis or intensive psychotherapy is concerned. The repair of empathic failure is accomplished by creating a new, efficacious pathway through which the self becomes firmed up. For this patient of poor or marginal prognosis, the outlook for repair of the self cannot be particularly optimistic. This guarded outlook leaves little room for the hopeful indicators on her Rorschach protocol to survive strongly enough to help her very much. Her protocol results offered a picture of chronic, unrelenting mirroring selfobject failure with far more defensive than compensatory structures. Despite her insightful and richly productive percepts, the nature of the psychopathology and the impoverishment of self-cohesion that characterize this patient's personality structure cannot sustain an exploratory treatment effort beyond support. To attempt much more is arguably misguided and clinically ill-advised, although she could derive benefit from a cautiously supportive treatment.

Thematic Apperception Test

Card 1.

It's time for the boy to practice his music lesson. He doesn't want to but he knows he's supposed to or he'll get in big trouble. He didn't want to play but his parents decided he would play. Everyone else is having fun playing outside. [Outcome] He sits there for 3 hours and stares at the violin. He gets so disgusted, and he puts in his 1 hour of practice. So he didn't get to play with his friends, and wasted 3 hours just staring at the thing. He doesn't have much say in whatever he does even if he's miserable.

The basic theme of the story is typical and the resolution of giving in to the parents' demand not uncommon. Spending 3 hours staring at the violin could be either a passive-aggressive position or an attempt by the boy to assert his own desire. A better understanding is gained, however, by attending to the affect state of disgust or misery in the boy's futile effort to assert his own will. Although Ms. T. did not use the word defeated in her story, it is not difficult to imagine that she felt that way. Here is another instance, as in several of her Rorschach responses, in which she felt undermined after attempting to stand up for herself. She ultimately gave in to defeat and had no impact on the parents. In this respect, feeling "miserable ... disgusted" was a euphemism for feeling devitalized. When the self was not responded to, Ms. T. gave up in defeat.

In the story cited here, the boy appeared to seek some sense of understanding by or meeting of the minds with his parents, but there is no indication that the parents (at least in the storyteller's eyes) showed a capacity for recognizing the boy's plight. Thus, any sense of compromise, understanding of the boy's conflicting wishes, or even an awareness of his conflicts was lacking. His selfobject need was at least to be understood or to have his needs recognized. The failure at this level gave rise to a self state characterized by feeling impotent and devitalized in the face of unresponsiveness from the selfobject environment. The ensuing depletion of the self, expressed in the story by the affects of "disgusted ... miserable" resulted from this lack of responsiveness or selfobject failure.

Card 2.

You're not paying attention to me, so I won't pay attention to your cards. All these people live on the farm. She has to go away to school. It looks like she doesn't want to. He works the farm. He gets visual—he gets feedback what he's done. So everything he does has some obvious causal effect. She doesn't look happy, also her dress is crooked, so she doesn't take very good care how she's dressed. It looks sad, I don't know what she wants to do. [Led up?] These two people just figured she should go to school. [Who are they?] It doesn't really matter. [Outcome?] Even though she doesn't want to, she does what everyone wants her to do. Even though she's miserable and her sweater's on crooked.

Whatever momentarily distracted the examiner, Ms. T. showed her exquisite sensitivity to even the slightest withdrawal of attention. Her comment censuring the examiner, framed with an "eye for an eye" quality, could be viewed by many clinicians as a two-pronged expression of hostility; first, she called me "on the carpet" for my inattention, and then retaliated in kind. It is characteristic of a self psychological approach, however, to understand this remark as provoked by feeling ignored or not responded to. Thus, the anger or rage is not interpreted as the primary consideration but is secondary to the central injury.

From this viewpoint, both the beginning of the interpretation of Card 2 and the end of the interpretation of Card 1 were statements about Ms. T.'s self state: She felt that she was not taken seriously or listened to and that she was responded to in an offhand or dismissive manner. In both stories, she was asked to do something she did not want to do or that she found unappealing. She added the "eye for an eye" retaliative aspect to her outcome in which she defied the examiner's objective by withholding what I asked for. This response may also represent her attempt to master a situation that left her feeling immobilized and "miserable." Her solution was to stand in the way of what I as the offending examiner asked her to do. Perhaps standing up to disappointing selfobjects was preferable to passively (or passive-aggressively) "wasting" time, as on Card 1, and ultimately feeling defeated.

Note how Ms. T. began her story with another reference to having to do something she did not want to do. As on Card 1, she was made to do something distasteful to her. In contrast, the man of Card 2 got the better end of the deal, like the boy's friends on Card 1, who got to play. She seemed to say that other people come to feel that they are responded to ("has some obvious causal effect"), whereas she, like the boy on Card 1, "doesn't have much say in whatever he does." References to the crooked dress and to not taking good care of her appearance may be other indications of indifference to herself, indifference resulting from depression. Indifference or disinterest become, therefore, euphemisms for depression, like the boy of Card 1 who felt "miserable." The disheveled appearance reflected the devalued self-esteem she felt when what she did or wanted was treated with casual indifference, or when she was unnoticed and ignored.

When Ms. T.'s story suggested that "it doesn't really matter" who made the girl go to school, she again retaliated in kind against her family, as if to say that if she did not matter to them, they did not matter to her. This response recalls her comment to me at the beginning of Card 2. Even more important, Ms. T. conveyed the impression that selfobject needs for mirroring were submerged or given up. When she said, "It doesn't really matter" who the people are, she resembled a young child who petulantly says, "You can't hurt me." This response may reflect Ms. T.'s feelings about her unmirrored, unresponded-to self. It was her defensive rejection of her selfobject need for others to notice that she was injured.

Finally, the outcome of her story reflected her unenthusiastic compliance by going through the motions ("she does what everyone wants her to do"). She was still surrounded by the empathic failures of a selfobject environment that dismissed her need for mirroring. This fact predisposed her to the depletion depression or devitalization that typified much of her ongoing experience ("even though she's still miserable"). Although it may sound flippant when she followed this statement about feeling miserable by commenting "and her sweater's on crooked," it no longer seems so when considered from the viewpoint that her sense of herself is devalued.

Card 3BM.

I don't know. There's tons of stuff to do and so many tasks to finish. They're so tired, they put their head down for a minute. Then they'd have enough energy to finish. They'll fall asleep and won't get it done and get in trouble. [Outcome?] They'll be disappointed she didn't finish it.

The quality of being overburdened was notable in Ms. T.'s emphasis on the "tons of stuff to do" and the fact that the person is "so tired." She experienced life as requiring much effort; her fatigue and diminished energy might be associated with a retarded depressive syndrome. The strain referred to in her response can also stem from a self state stretched to its limits as she tried on her own to keep herself afloat. Her story contained no indication that someone will come to her assistance; once again, Ms. T. expected her selfobject environment to fail to notice her burden. Rather, there is "disappointment" in her inadequate functioning, disappointment that brings only "trouble" instead of the empathic understanding she desires.

Being disapproved of and found wanting were what this patient experienced from her selfobject environment. Her needs were ignored or unnoticed; she felt the effort to continue as a burden. She wished for the selfobject environment to wake her up, in effect, and to take note of her need for mirroring selfobject responsiveness.

Card 7GF.

The perspective is off on this. The little girl and the lady are both waiting for something. The little girl's distracted, looking to a spot where she hopes something will happen, but she looks disinterested like there's got to be something else better. So she obediently sits there waiting, wishing to do what she wants. They told her to just sit there and wait. [The lady?] She doesn't even know the little girl. They're just waiting for some unknown reason. She has something productive to do while waiting. The little girl's just hopelessly aimlessly waiting.

The major themes were much the same as on the previous cards. Her initial comment about the "perspective" suggested being caught off guard when presented with this card. The threat to self-cohesion by the marked selfobject failure was triggered from the start because she seemed taken aback that the "perspective is off." She proceeded to tell a story as if the two people were sitting in different spaces (the lady "doesn't even know the little girl"). The activity of waiting "for some unknown reason" remained the same for both. The two figures could hardly be more uninvolved with one another as they were described in this story. Indeed, one could almost imagine that there were two completely separate cards with the same story.

The girl was "disinterested," Ms. T.'s metaphor, like "miserable ... disgusted ... so tired," for disengagement in the face of mirroring selfobject failure. She "obediently" complied with what was asked of her, as in the previous stories of not enjoying practicing the violin or not wanting to go to school. She felt emptiness and lack of enthusiasm for what she was expected to do. These feelings arose from a selfobject environment in which parental figures were uninvolved with Ms. T.'s needs. Consequently, she revealed a self state of emptiness, unresponded to by the depersonalized mother figure referred to as just "the lady." The girl was "hopelessly aimlessly waiting" for this "lady" to come to life for her in an important psychological sense. The impersonal, psychologically bereft, and empty quality contained in this response is the sort of material that plays by David Mamet capture in a raw and gripping way by the bleakness and the starkness of their stagecraft.

Card 7BM.

It's the middle of a serious conversation. This is just a break in the topic. Either an insurance policy or money matters. [Who are they?] They're relatives. [Make up a story.] It makes no difference. Otherwise they wouldn't be that close to each other. [What led up?] Some acute situation. Now they have to band together and decide what to do. [Outcome?] They come to a consensus.

This card seemed more difficult for Ms. T. to tell a story about. It required more prompting to elicit important story features, and even with this amount of inquiry there was less specificity compared with her other TAT stories. She was reluctant to indicate exactly what relationship these relatives had. There was some degree of closeness or need to "band together" in this story, but who they were and how close they were to each other were irrelevant. Indeed, as she said, "It makes no difference." The closeness was apparently based on the consensus of equals or nearequals, without any indication of the guiding parental function frequently elicited on this card.

On the previous card, Card 7GF, the girl did not feel attached enough to consider initiating contact with the "lady" who "doesn't even know the little girl." The present card was also notable for the absence of a selfobject function characterizing the relationship between the two men. There was distance despite the fact that the men were relatives. There was also an affective estrangement to the "acute situation" that momentarily brought them together to reach a consensus. Although perhaps not totally distant, cold, or business-like, this relationship was not particularly warm, benevolent, or characterized by paternalistic concern. Ms. T. was again driving underground her need for selfobject responsiveness, which could occur only with an "acute situation."

An empathically attuned response should be one of concern or at least a sense that one party feels threatened or that self-cohesion is in danger. The response represented here is different: A dispassionate "serious conversation," even though it may lead to a resolution ("they come to a consensus"). Ms. T. might have been turning from the mother who did not know the girl (that is, the patient herself) or her need for mirroring selfobject responsiveness (Card 7GF) to the "relative" of Card 7BM. The somewhat more involved relationship between these male figures led to a more satisfactory resolution by "consensus" compared to the "hopelessly aimlessly waiting" of Card 7GF. Still, there was the perception of these men as "relatives," but "it makes no difference" just who they were. It is difficult to see this response as even a remote indication of idealization. It is also doubtful that this attempt to compensate for what was unavailable by mirroring was psychologically satisfying or that Ms. T. felt sufficiently invigorated to revive an enfeebled, understimulated self.

Card 18GF.

That's odd. Two people, a lady holding another person up. Something must have happened. It looks like something pretty sad or serious. [Led up?] The person collapsed or got sick or something. She's probably been taking care of this person for a while. [Who are these women?] I didn't say two women. I was very careful to say a woman and a person. One's a caretaker, the other one is just a person. [Male or female?] Neither. I can't tell. Maybe an old man. She's taking care of her father or a relative or something. [How does she feel?] All worn out and frazzled. He's dependent on the lady. She's pretty sad and distraught. The person's sick and needs her help. Because it's no fun to have to be responsible and take care of someone else.

Again, this patient was momentarily thrown off guard by something about the card, possibly its stark bluntness connoting distress. This reaction appeared in her opening comment of "that's odd" and later in her insistent correction of the examiner's error in thinking that both figures were women. Furthermore, her terse closing of the story much sooner than most of her other stories also required a greater degree of inquiry to elicit important details. Even at that, Ms. T. was uncharacteristically guarded about revealing too much. She grudgingly allowed that the person in distress was an old man and was surprisingly reticent about deciding whether the man was a "father or a relative or something." After that, one is still in the dark about this point. A self psychologically informed interpretation of her "worn out and frazzled ... sad and distraught" feeling indicates the same self state already revealed consistently across the TAT cards. The chronically lacking acknowledgment that she was asked to assume so much responsibility is noteworthy; she felt depleted or "all worn out."

Card 13MF.

The next morning. He just got up out of bed, got dressed and ready to go. [Who are they?] They have a steady relationship. He's nice enough not to wake her up in the morning.

Card 14.

The inside of a building. He's busy working all day, and just took a minute for time out to get some fresh air for some relief.

These two cards contributed little to the clinical picture. The responses added nothing noteworthy to what Ms. T. already said.

General Discussion of Ms. T.

This case, reported in its entirety, illustrates a number of important aspects of a self psychologically informed approach to psychodiagnostic test material. It reveals that oscillations in the self state can be detected in relation to events or affects that interfere with sustaining self-esteem. This approach, guided as it is by Kohut's theoretical formulations, revealed that Ms. T.'s attempts at restoring self-esteem were provoked by reactions to others' failures to recognize that she was in distress. She experienced self states of devitalization or anergia, which were aggravated by the unresponsiveness of the selfobject environment to her need for being heard.

Because of this deficient or unresponsive mirroring, Ms. T. turned hopefully to others to enliven her or to provide enthusiasm. Some of these manifestations took the form of an attempt to establish compensatory structure to restore self-cohesion through idealization. These efforts met with limited success and only compromised Ms. T.'s capacity to buoy up faltering self-esteem. In the end, therefore, she experienced herself as diminished and had pronounced feelings of depletion. These feelings were the basis for several of Ms. T.'s responses such as "icky hair," "awful and ugly body proportions," "an angel without her head," "Dumbo," "a special dress ... so it's not for me," on the Rorschach, TAT, and human figure drawings.

Ms. T.'s devalued self seriously compromised her capacity to sustain zest or a thriving, vibrant internal experience. This aspect of the self differs from the customary sense of thinking well or favorably about oneself, because Kohut's view of the self reached deep to capture a quality of a viable, buoyant self state. Many clinicians may not readily apprehend this aspect of the depleted or devitalized self as fundamentally different from self-esteem, but such a simplistic view about identity or lowered self-esteem is too limited.

The idea of an attempt to protect against devitalization by seeking reparative selfobject responsiveness in the form of compensatory structures was not one of Kohut's familiar concepts, and it has received virtually no attention in the psychodiagnostic testing literature. This case provides ample opportunity to observe the degree to which a chronically injured self is mobilized repeatedly in the projective test content. It also demonstrates that this patient attempted unsuccessfully again and again to repair the injury to the self or to restore some measure of enlivenment so that the depletion might be better tolerated.

This case also illustrates the patient's alternation between understated yearnings for mirroring and for idealization. This alternation is related to her efforts to revive the deadened self state and her attempts to find alternative selfobject functions when mirroring selfobject responsiveness failed her. Ms. T. made some attempts to obtain what she needed for sustaining the self through abortive attempts at idealization. That these were quickly dashed rather than pursued with hopefulness demonstrates how ultimately unsuccessful her attempts to restimulate faltering self-cohesion became. Nevertheless, this case illustrates the effort to develop compensatory structures. It also shows what happens on projective testing when that attempt is thwarted and when the mirroring sector of the self has been as chronically and seriously damaged as it has been for this patient.

As I have already indicated, it is necessary to consider the self state and attempts to repair defective self structure together with patients' experience of their external world or selfobject environment. Through selfobject responsiveness, people manage to re-establish or revive what they need to preserve self-cohesion. With Ms. T., the mirroring selfobject function necessary to respond vigorously to her need to be kept "afloat" was again and again deficient. The repeated empathic failures that she experienced left her chronically disappointed. As so many of her TAT stories and Rorschach responses suggested, she felt unresponded to in her attempts to secure mirroring, and she was ultimately defeated. Attempts at establishing another route to repair the self by forming idealizing selfobject transferences were either halfhearted or did not go far enough. She quickly abandoned hope that there was anything there for her "in the midst of this primitive stuff" beyond the "pomp and circumstance." Her confidence was undermined: Ms. T. referred to a "Napoleon ... who got where he wanted to," but he "ended in exile," or "Noah's ark ... that was supposed to save everybody" but "doesn't exist" and is "petrified." Consequently, a compensatory structure as an alternate route to repair a devitalized self failed to develop reliably for her.

Beyond her diminished self-esteem, Ms. T. indicated in her projective test protocol the central significance of the buoyancy or vitality of the experience of the self. A normal expectation of mirroring is essential for ensuring self-cohesion, and building compensatory structures protects against devitalization of the self by attempting to establish another route to secure selfobject responsiveness. This protocol shows the failure of mirroring, and it also reveals idealization as a compensatory structure. The characteristic experience or phenomenology of the devitalized unmirrored self is conveyed most tellingly in this patient's projective test content, which depicted the remains of a self so devastated by both deficient mirroring and idealizing selfobject responsiveness that it was unable to sustain itself for long. Ms. T.'s self markedly lacked a quality perhaps best denoted as resilience or hardiness.

In the next chapter, I present the projective testing protocol of a patient who demonstrated more interplay among selfobject functions than did Ms. T. Like Ms. T., this patient showed a basic mirroring deficiency, and he also attempted to establish compensatory structures centered on idealization and, to an extent, twinship. Ms. T.'s self disorder was more severe; as a result, her feeble attempt to establish an idealizing selfobject transference quickly failed. Thus, her protocol illustrates a more predominant mirroring selfobject disturbance than does the protocol discussed next. The patient whose projective test findings are presented in chapter 8 repeatedly attempted to seek idealizing and twinship selfobject functions, although in the end he too was unable to secure them with any greater success than did Ms. T.

The contrast between the two cases demonstrates the differences in level of psychopathology of the self (despite comparable overt symptomatic disturbances), differential utilization of selfobject functions and attempts to establish compensatory structures, and approximately similar outcomes as far as the success of these efforts.

8 Mr. L.: Idealization and Twinship

A CASE OF ADMIXTURES OF SELFOBJECT FUNCTIONS

The second case that I present in its entirety is of interest for several reasons. This psychodiagnostic protocol has elements of the three major selfobject functions that Kohut identified, and therefore represents a typical clinical presentation of selfobject functions. Not a textbook case of clear idealization or twinship, it shows the difficulty in distinguishing these selfobject transferences from each other. The patient, Mr. L., alternated among selfobject functions to find a viable pathway for the repair of self-cohesion and like many other patients, attempted to establish a compensatory structure in the face of chronic mirroring selfobject failures.

Mr. L.'s case illustrates a point that Kohut came to see over time as his work progressed: Selfobject functions are not entirely independent of each other. With the possible exception of mirroring needs, which occur most often, other selfobject transferences predominate at different times. They come forward at some points and recede at others, often when an attempt at restoring self-esteem is either blocked or unsuccessful. Such vacillation is not an instance of inconsistency or failure to establish a predominant selfobject function; selfobject functions do not represent *formes frustes*. Admixtures frequently appear.

The case reported here is a good illustration of this clinical situation. I discuss it by considering all three selfobject functions and emphasize idealization and twinship as efforts to repair self-cohesion when mirroring has become unavailable or unsuccessful. The patient showed a degree of overt psychopathology comparable to Ms. T.; the degree of symptomatic disturbance is approximately equal in the two cases. Mr. L., however, had a more favorable premorbid adjustment. His disorder was more reactive and less chronic than the characterologically entrenched pathology of Ms. T.'s disorder.

Mr. L. was also more resilient than Ms. T. insofar as he could seek out idealization and twinship selfobjects to somewhat better advantage than did Ms. T. Consequently, the admixture of selfobject functions in Mr. L.'s protocol may appear to be confusing, only because Ms. T. displayed a clearly demarcated or predominant selfobject need. The arrested development in Ms. T.'s self disorder testifies to the difference in degree of psychopathology in these patients' disorders. The constriction that characterized the pronounced mirroring deficit of Ms. T.'s condition produced a more pathological clinical picture and prognosis than did that of Mr. L. In the end, however, despite Mr. L.'s persistent attempt to secure selfobject responsiveness through idealization and twinship, the efficacious repair of a self disorder was no more successful for him than it was for Ms. T.

This case illustrates that the clinical identification of selfobject transferences varies according to psychological test or procedure. For Mr. L., the twinship and idealization selfobject functions appeared more distinctly on the Rorschach yet were barely evident at all on the TAT and figure drawings. Had the TAT and drawings been performed without the Rorschach, a clinician would not have detected evidence for idealization or twinship selfobject functions, and a disturbance of mirroring would have been viewed as central. Had the Rorschach been administered without the TAT or figure drawings, deficient mirroring might not have appeared to the extent revealed on the TAT and human figure drawings.

Mr. L.'s case demonstrates, therefore, that the interplay of selfobject functions, like defenses and conflicts, can frequently require an entire protocol. A complete and balanced diagnostic testing protocol becomes crucial to identify predominant selfobject patterns and central self psychological dynamics like compensatory structures, as these ideas were thought about and developed by Kohut.

Mr. L., a 45-year-old married White man, was admitted to the inpatient psychiatry service of a general hospital following a suicide attempt precipitated by family difficulties. He had been an accomplished learning disabilities supervisor and administrator, who had become enraged when his adolescent son was diagnosed with an attention deficit syndrome by colleagues at a hospital in which Mr. L. worked. He became furious with his son and argued with his wife about her overprotectiveness of the boy. Mr. L. experienced an intensification of anxiety, accompanied by shortness of breath and chest pain; the anxiety had developed in the past 2 years. He began drinking heavily, although not so much as to raise concerns about alcohol dependence, and he experienced impotence. Mr. L. expressed guilt over his outbursts towards his wife and son, and he worried about growing old.

The Rorschach protocol for this patient included a second inquiry following the formal inquiry proper, after 15 of his 40 Rorschach responses, for the purpose of testing limits. This patient's protocol was obtained before the Comprehensive System administration method was in widespread clinical use. The usual question was: "What comes to mind about a _____?" which is indicated as [Association] in the following transcript. Some clinicians may regard such questions as provocative and prefer to emphasize the problem-solving perceptual nature of the Rorschach test. Others view this manner of conducting the Rorschach inquiry as advantageous. The method is derived from examining the psychodynamic patterns that emerge on projective tests. In this approach, content analysis is regarded as equal in importance as the formal scores are in the complete diagnostic evaluation. Some may prefer the leaner Comprehensive System administration procedure for its neutrality and may combine an interpretive approach based on the empirically grounded Structural Summary codes and ratios with a judicious use of content analysis.

Not all clinicians will regard the administration of the case that follows as "true," and some will consider it "not Rorschach." I am submitting the protocol for the consideration of those clinicians who will find the content rich and revealing. The follow-up inquiry of probing for associations may sometimes be of critical significance in understanding a self psychological approach to projective test material. I chose the present case partly because it illustrates that a judicious eliciting of associations as a means of testing limits revealed dynamic material for a self psychological interpretation. I remain convinced that this interpretation might not have emerged as clearly in the absence of these associations.

Human Figure Drawings

The first drawing was that of a man, which elicited the following elaboration:

> A young person going out for a walk. He's excited that the air is clean and fresh. He's looking forward to the new things he'll find as he explores. Basically, it's the woods, nature, being alone, smelling the trees and flowers. [Describe personality][1] Very changeable, moodwise. Sometimes he's very

---

[1]Examiner's queries appear in brackets.

happy, sometimes he's very sad. When the mood changes he likes to be alone.
Basically, he's very free, left to his own thoughts. [Q] There's a contradiction
between emotional involvement and intellectual involvement. He's very
sensitive to the needs of others. It makes him drained, unable to deal with his
own needs. Then he realizes his own inadequacies, because he's very angry
and oppositional. [Q] Being able to be in total control of his environment and
himself. Wanting to do what he wants to do. He doesn't like being controlled
by authority in his job, by people who know less than he does. It bothers him
when he's unable to obtain what he wants, when he knows he's right and
he's misunderstood. When obstacles, such as money, block his goals in life.
[Goals?] Living, not wealthy, but achieving comfortable things.

This verbalization represented Mr. L.'s self state. He experienced tension
in the face of the pushes and pulls impinging on him, while trying to calm
himself. The pastoral-sounding beginning of his description of the person
suggested an idyllic, wished-for self state of a young man with few cares or
worries. This state shortly gave way either to changeable moods that were
vacillations in the self state or to ambivalence. The turning inward that he
talked about may be a withdrawal from the world when he was asked to
attend to others' needs while his own self-cohesion required him to shore up
needed reserves for himself. In this way, he attempted to protect himself from
becoming "drained" by others and "unable to deal with his own needs."

Thus, his "moodiness" is the affective vacillation of a vulnerable self that
is exposed like a raw nerve. He experienced this state as an "inadequacy
because he's very angry and oppositional." Presumably, demands placed on
him by others were irritating intrusions that conflicted with his preference
"to be alone." Mr. L. attempted to restore cohesion to a self that he felt was
interfered with and put upon. There is a question about suitable or available
selfobject responsiveness because Mr. L. turned inward when self-esteem
was threatened. He was preoccupied with his feeling undermined. This state
was far removed from the idyllic peace in the communing-with-nature
scene with which he began and suggests that a wish for calmly merging
with a secure or comforting presence was mobilized.

Mr. L. was now threatened by feeling a loss of control and feared
holding on to what he needed to feel calmed. "Achieving comfortable
things" may represent his attempt to assure himself a dependable selfobject environment that he can turn to or rely on to feel comforted. Instead,
he felt "misunderstood" and confronted with "obstacles." Mr. L. thus
described a self state of disrepair, a vulnerability to others' demands
when he himself is too much in need of the calm equilibrium that a reliable

selfobject environment ensures. He felt out of sorts and dissatisfied, if not annoyed or distressed.

The second drawing that Mr. L. was asked to supply was that of a person of the opposite sex, to which he provided the following commentary on request:

> That's a mother-like figure, sweet and gentle, calling her children in to the house. Very warm and loving. She might appear simple but is a deep thinker, she's hurt very easily but doesn't show it. She gets a lot of satisfaction from her family. The family takes advantage of her. Though she resents it, she'll always have a smile covering up the hurts, with her arms stretched. She's also there to hold the family together. [Fears or worries?] That she's not able to protect them the way she should. A lot of responsibility falls on to her. She's unable to deal with them at times. [Sad or depressed?] Failure of her children to conform the way she wants them to, because of her high expectations that's sometimes unrealistic. Failure also of her husband's inability to take over a lot of chores thrown on to her. Incomplete communication, feeling the family might be against her. They're going in different directions with different goals. So, basically she's given up. [Angry?] Very little. Disagreements with her husband as to how to deal with the children. Over money, being taken advantage of, that she has no control.

The description of this female drawing, like his male drawing, began with a picture of serenity but soon changed to an elaboration of inner distress taking the form of feeling overburdened with responsibility and failing to realistically meet obligations. This patient's elaboration of the figure drawing conveyed his feeling that other people disappointed by ignoring what the figure needed in the way of understanding or recognition. Thus, the woman failed to win adequate mirroring; "basically she's given up." The depletion or diminished enthusiasm gave way to feeling taken advantage of and lacking control.

Although drawings of same-sex figures frequently offer a good initial indication of the self state, it is difficult to interpret verbalizations about opposite-sex drawings. Should the commentary on inquiry be understood as an idealized self representation when the patient feels too undermined or depleted? Should the female drawing be taken to represent the patient's own sense of depreciation of someone important in his life, perhaps as a defensive effort to protect the self from further injury? Should this inquiry be thought of as a restatement of the devalued self continued from the previous drawing? The guidelines are rarely clear on these questions, and examiners must proceed carefully with their interpretations.

In the case at hand, Mr. L.'s description on inquiry to this drawing did not certainly indicate whom he was speaking about. Nevertheless, the overriding themes of being overburdened or unresponded to cannot be ignored. He ultimately gave up in defeat and could not sustain a sufficiently buoyed-up feeling of self-esteem. This interpretation points to the way that Mr. L. might experience both his own self state and the selfobject environment he turned to for assistance in sustaining self-esteem. Whether or not he felt himself to be faltering and diminished, he continually experienced indifference or unresponsiveness to legitimate mirroring needs. This lack deprived him of feeling capable and enthusiastic; instead, he felt devitalized.

Rorschach Content

Card I

1. *Two people sitting over a table having dinner. Discussing the events of the day. Both are coming from work. It's a pub-like atmosphere. Their discussion is based on the ineptness they came across that day. They're in disagreement, one trying to quiet down the other by the raising of the hand. (W)*

    Here's the table, their heads, rear ends.

2. *A butterfly. (W) Can I turn it around?*

    The body, the wings here.

v3. *Two people dancing around a maypole. One seems very happy, the other's very sad. When they're happy it's more energetic a movement, when it's sad, you can tell by the head being down that he doesn't want to participate. (W)*

    They're holding hands around it.

<4. *Two donkeys. Actually, one donkey with a reflection in the water. Sees his own reflection. (W)*	*Looking down, big ears, here's the reflection.*
5. *An Oriental woman right here. (D4)*	*The face, hair, standing right on the ground. Not as gentle as most. Looks hostile.*

Mr. L.'s atypical approach to the inkblot was characterized from the outset by penetrating behind the imagery of his opening response. His response was more like a TAT story than a typical Rorschach percept, and his first response most likely typifies the real-life dilemma that preoccupied him. Despite the convivial letting-one's-hair-down mood that he wished to convey by setting the discussion in a pub, the predominant themes of criticism or devaluation ("the ineptness they came across that day"), disagreement, and attempts to restore calm interfered with the congeniality he was striving for.

The predominant self state was characterized by disharmony by seeking calm to re-establish cohesion ("one trying to quiet down the other"). A specific selfobject need has not yet emerged, but the affective state of disruption or disequilibrium was clear. The need to restore a state of calm intimacy or communion is more central than is the wish to discharge a hostile or critical impulse.

The serene image of a butterfly, coupled with his asking permission to turn the card, might suggest dependency or fragility. Following the tense disagreement disrupting the initially harmonious mood of the previous response, the butterfly and the request to turn the card could also be a restatement of the need to restore calm. The next percept is dancing around a maypole, as innocent-sounding as the butterfly, but it quickly becomes associated with the bittersweet *lachen und weinen* ("laughter and tears") of an affect state that alternates between these moods but does not settle into either one. The happy affect was experienced as an "energetic" quality of movement that may connote the vitality of the self state that Mr. L. was seeking. In similar fashion, the sad affect was represented by the "head being down," metaphorically standing for the devitalization of the self that cannot hold its own, that "doesn't want to participate" or hold its head up with pride and vigor.

In some clinical conditions in which alternating mood states are prominent, such a response can imply a bipolar mood disorder. Fluctuating affect states suggested by projective test responses like these may also represent the simultaneous presence of a destabilized self state, independent of the clinical-biological indications of a bipolar or cyclothymic disorder.

Mr. L. continued with a percept of donkeys, seen as a reflection. It is tempting to regard reflection responses as manifestations of a mirroring selfobject function, but frequently no automatic equivalence or similarity is indicated. Other than the fact that mirrors give off reflections, the in-depth meaning of mirroring, at least insofar as Kohut has richly characterized this phenomenon, bears little beyond surface similarity to the idea of a mirror image or reflection.

More telling about Mr. L.'s response, however, is the imagery of donkeys, particularly as they follow the struggle that he expressed between disagreement and harmony (Response 1) and sadness and joy (Response 3), with the butterfly percept between. The depreciated donkey may convey Mr. L.'s self state when his attempt to resolve the dilemmas disposed him to feel like the ass represented by the donkeys of this response. Mr. L. may have felt himself to be an object of scorn or ridicule. The image of the donkey comes closer to capturing the experience-near self state of depreciation than do the donkeys seen in reflection indicate a mirroring need.

The clinical interpretation of this patient's final response, an Oriental woman portrayed as hostile, is unclear at this point. Perhaps seeing the woman as Oriental connoted something exotic, foreign, or otherwise alien to his life, or more crucially, his internal world or experience. The possibility of passive gentleness alternating with the unaccustomed hostility associated with Oriental women recalls the alternating moods in Mr. L.'s maypole response. The connotation of the woman as hostile could also be construed as an undoing and a projection of his own hostile wishes. The possible interpretive options are uncertain at this juncture; thus, this response must be subsequently reconsidered in the evaluation in a broader context.

Card II

6. *Two people, possibly monks, having a conversation. They're much more compatible as they're touching hands. (W)*

    The heads, bodies. Pressing hands, like they're having fun, they're in accord, pushing together.

7. *Two elephants nuzzling each other's trunks. (D6 + D3)*

    The same place without the top red. Their trunks and ears here.

<8. A rat, down flat, sprawled out. Used like a rug, like a bearskin rug. (D6)

Looking down at it. A different perspective. The shape of the head. The anatomy, the fur. [Fur?] The roughness of the surface and the shading. [Sprawled out?] It's very flat.

v9. A bird, a duck in flight. I'm taking one white part with the black as background. (DS5 + D4)

The beak, head, the wings. Like looking down from an airplane. [Association] Running away. Freedom. The softness. Escape.

v10. Two birds, like little hummingbirds. Taking nectar from a flower. (W)

The little beaks. The rest of the card is the flower. Stamen, pistils, the petals. The stem. [Association] Very cheery. Free.

The response of monks on the first chromatic blot of the Rorschach cards may be surprising, all the more so because the all-red color on Card II frequently elicits percepts about blood. It is always questionable to assume that examiners' preconceived ideas about the meaning of specific cards parallels patients' responses. Schafer (1954), P. M. Lerner (1991), and most commentators on Rorschach interpretation stressed this point, which was discussed in detail in chapter 4. With that in mind, it is advisable to de-emphasize interpreting this response of monks seeking compatibility as a defensive denial or reaction formation against hostile wishes. The relatively serene percept of monks as gentle figures, touching hands in a gesture of accord or compatibility, can be construed as an excessive effort to portray a conciliatory or cooperative relationship.

This interpretation follows from a drive theory view about the underlying hostility suggested by the red color presumed to be the driving force behind the response. This line of thinking applies regardless of whether a reference to red color or blood is articulated. Although this assumption is understandable, most responsible projective testing clinicians probably concur with the need for caution about this interpretation, regardless of whether the impression is supported by corroborating evidence throughout the entire projective testing protocol. The hypothesis-generating potential of this form of interpretation, at this stage in the workup, must be viewed as tentative.

One need not be similarly cautious about making a self psychological interpretation of the response of monks in conversation because this interpretation is not based primarily on the red-blood–aggression link.

An interpretation derived from Kohut's interpretive strategies emphasizes the cohesion-restoring quality of the selfobject function represented by the cooperative gesture as a central or salient feature of the patient's psychological state. This self psychological interpretation does not ignore the defensive implication of the patient's protecting him- or herself from experiencing aggressive impulses. Kohut more likely would have emphasized seeking communion with or establishing a bond between these figures as the patient's primary concern.

In his monks response, Mr. L. was apparently seeking either an idealizing or a twinship selfobject function. Twinship is suggested by the bond of understanding or accord as the primary mechanism influencing this percept. The possibility that either an idealized or twinship selfobject function arises at this point can be examined by considering this response in the context of Card I. He began Card I with a depiction of a convivial conversation in a pub-like atmosphere that faltered. This response may represent the need for an atmosphere of cooperation in which he could be understood in depth by a like-minded person. The atmosphere might allow the merging or connectedness to occur, if the twinship selfobject function in which "one trying to quiet down the other by the raising of the hand" permitted the self state he wanted to recapture.

This possibility is consistent with the still tentative interpretation of the compatible monks touching hands, now retrospectively applied to the response to Card I. Regardless of the theoretical framework, sequence analysis may proceed in both forward and reverse directions. The alternative interpretation of an idealizing selfobject function suggests that the monks represent a selfobject that Mr. L. turned to for vigor or for a sense of calm strength or reassurance, or possibly for admiration.

The percept of the monks was followed by one in which elephants nuzzled each others' trunks. Nuzzling connotes intimacy, however incongruous this sensation may appear in connection with an anything-but-cuddly large animal like an elephant. Elephants, however, may also be seen as playful, interesting to watch, approachable and gentle, despite their imposing size. Yet the overriding image was the nuzzling, despite its incongruity, similar to the gentleness of the Oriental woman who was hostile and perhaps, therefore, unavailable or unapproachable. The image was in keeping with the monks' desire to press their hands together in accord, a percept suggesting a wish for closeness, intimacy, or mutuality of the type possibly understood as a twinship selfobject function.

The next percept, of a rat sprawled out like a rug, was all the more unusual because Comprehensive System criteria were satisfied for coding both texture and form dimension. Thus, the psychological significance of affectional longing and self-awareness was suggested in this response of a furry rat. The incongruity of a rat as a decorative rug, with its distasteful qualities rarely associated with warmth and furriness, suggests that Mr. L. looked in far-flung places for what he needed to restore either a sense of psychological connectedness or the calm reassurance to buttress faltering self-cohesion.

These responses are a further indication of incongruity between what Mr. L. needed and what was possible for him. Was he indicating that he searched in the most remote places (furry rat rugs, elephants nuzzling) for what the self needed for its viability? Did he feel that his efforts led nowhere? Most of his responses to this point, on both Cards I and II, converge on this possibility. Unremarkably, the rat percept was followed by a bird in flight, in which his associations of "running away, freedom, softness, escape" suggest that protecting the self from injury or threat was as much as he could manage. His association of "softness" recalls the textural quality of the furry rat, and the softness embedded among associations about escaping to safety may also indicate the fate of his needs for intimacy or closeness.

In the matter of eliciting associations following the formal inquiry, it is often difficult to decide when a judicious use of testing limits for select responses is appropriate. Although advising caution in this regard, Exner (1993) did not exclude the possibility of testing the limits after the formal Comprehensive System inquiry but advised against eliciting associations as an appropriate use of testing limits, as is the case for the response now being considered, as well as for several others following. Although Exner's reasons are compelling, there are arguments in favor of testing limits by eliciting associations. Mr. L.'s references to escape and softness would not have emerged without what can be seen as a provocative question that specifically elicited associations.

Without the associations, the bird in flight would have been thought about as calm or serene, like the following percept of hummingbirds taking nectar. It remains to be determined whether one impression was more accurate than the other or whether these images represented different, conflictual aspects of the personality structure. Ultimately, the issue of administration procedure is one consideration in the risk–benefit balance involved in this test administration decision. Whether the dynamic of escape or safety would have emerged in the absence of obtaining associations as a form of testing limits must also be determined.

Mr. L.'s final response to Card II, hummingbirds taking nectar from a flower, also has connotations of gentleness and oral dependency. It follows the hostile Oriental woman, his closing response to Card I, and the furry rat; the incongruity of these images can suggest the unavailability of a deeply experienced need state. From the viewpoint of self psychology, frustrated or interrupted mirroring responsiveness is a probable candidate for what was amiss. Hostility or anger is less likely; this picture is not so much one of a drive seeking discharge as it is of a need state that is profoundly blocked or closed off.

Card III

11. *Two men. They appear very stagnant even though their bodies are very free flowing. They seem stiff and formal. (D9)*

The bodies here. They appear just to look formal there.

v12. *Two African natives with their backs toward each other. Doing a religious dance. (D1 + D3)*

The shape of the head: negroid. Doing some type of ritual around a fire.[Fire?] The red. The color suggested fire. [Association] Values, rituals, tradition. [Q] Conformity.

13. *Very segmented parts. Parts of rats, monkeys, butterflies. Nothing is coming together, though. (W)*

The red is the butterfly, the other red is little monkeys. Fish here, also two birds like eagles. It could also look like the abominable snowman. Or a polar bear. [Association: abominable snowman] It's unknown. Does it exist? But also the softness and power.

The stiffness denoted in the initial response contrasted with the reference to the bodies as "free flowing." It is yet another inconsistency or incongruity emerging with increasing clarity as a central feature of Mr. L.'s personality makeup. First glances, he seemed to tell the examiner, do not convey the full intensity of what he experienced in depth. Free-flowing people are stiff, birds in flight run away, a rat is characterized by its furriness, and the convivial atmosphere of a pub-like, intimate conversation or dancing around a maypole gives way to disagreement or disharmony. From the point of view of the predominant self state, it grew increasingly clear that Mr. L.

felt keenly that the world was out of kilter for him. His opening response to Card III of stagnant people revealed that he felt that way himself and that he needed to recover. He wanted to feel "free flowing," that is, more psychologically enlivened or connected, both to others as well as to the depths of his own internal experience.

Mr. L. craved the ability to feel vibrant or allied with what was important to him. He felt repeatedly rebuffed or shut out from what he wanted and had to escape from unpleasant situations with his psychological wounds exposed like a raw nerve. He struggled to get the psychological oxygen he wanted even if he seemed to return to the same devitalizing experiences (expressed in all the incongruous percepts previously noted) that ultimately undermined the self.

Unlike Ms. T., this patient was able to seek out either an idealizing or twinship selfobject function to help repair the self. For both patients, however, the attempt came with considerable difficulty. Ms. T. retreated almost immediately from the possibility of acquiring compensatory structure through attempts at idealization. Mr. L. continued to try, however, rather than giving up in defeat that might lead to the devastation of self-esteem that was so prominent a feature of Ms. T.'s record.

Mr. L. initially attempted to see himself as psychologically alive ("free flowing") on Card III but quickly became "stiff and formal." His next response aimed to restore some bond or connection in the form of a religious ritual, although the figures had their backs toward each other. The color used to indicate the fire could stand for the vibrancy or enlivened feeling he hoped to establish through the psychological connection of the ritual. It faded, ultimately, into a routine of conformity and perhaps left him feeling emotionally flattened.

This self state in which the psychological oxygen or enlivenment he sought was insufficient, evoked his third response to Card III, segmented parts of animals with "nothing coming together." Starting with rats and monkeys, he managed to end with the possibility that one of the animal species is an eagle (soaring and majestic by implication, although not actually stated by Mr. L.). The oscillation again represents his resiliency in bouncing back after an injury to the self and attempting to restore self-cohesion.

His final associations evoked the additional response of the abominable snowman. Again, this powerful image is "unknown," and Mr. L. asked: "Does it exist?" When the reference to softness reappeared, it probably denoted a longed-for calming or soothing to help repair the self state.

Soliciting associations generated the interpretive yield of the natives' ritualized conformity, suggesting devitalization. In addition, questioning the existence of the abominable snowman, as well as its soft, powerful quality, indicated his feeling estranged from a self whose reality he questioned. These features might well have been obscured without this form of provocative or vigorous inquiry. Detecting these features contributed to a greater understanding of these characteristics of Mr. L.'s personality.

Card IV

14. *The head of a dragon. Bending over, his head's touching the ground. As if sniffing out something. Ready to spurt fire. (W)*

The head, long neck, end part and back legs. [Sniffing?] I don't know. Something dangerous.

v15. *Two dogs, like puppies. Each is on top of a cliff, looking down into the valley. (D2)*

The dark shaded area is the cliff. Looking down, giving you height. [Association] Just overlooking everything. The vastness. It's very comforting, peaceful.

16. *Part of a giant, half a part. From the waist down. Almost like Jack and the Beanstalk. Walking toward Jack, with his boots on. (D7)*

Here's the boot. [Jack and the Beanstalk?] Being chased by something frightening but able to get away from it. Running, trying to get away, to find something, trying to manipulate, outsmart. Going into the unknown.

17. *Now I see the whole giant. The head's small, distorted. Accentuated on the feet, the boots. He's carrying the goose that laid the golden eggs, you see the head of the goose. (W)*

The whole thing is the giant. Carrying the goose here. [Goose ... golden eggs?] Being able to monetarily afford everything you want. Money growing on trees type of thing.

Card IV not only elicited the common imagery of a strong towering figure but appeared so compelling that Mr. L. was unable to let go of it throughout three of his four responses. By now it is clear that idealization is a central selfobject need for Mr. L. The percepts of giants should also be considered in relation to the people in the pub comparing notes about the ineptness of others, the monks, and the religious ritual. These powerful or awe-inspiring figures (giants, monks, the abominable snowman) suggested that this patient was inclined to turn to strong, idealizable figures for firming up the self when it was undermined. Likewise, imagery connoting communion, such as the religious rite or the people in the pub, tentatively suggested a twinship or companionate selfobject function. The feeling of being at one with or like others can bolster self-cohesion when the sense of the self is experienced as weakened, injured, or vulnerable.

Mr. L.'s idealizing and possibly his twinship selfobject needs were revealed in ways that indicated that these selfobject functions were not operating effectively. His initial response to Card IV was a dragon, but he described it in an atypical way as bending over with its head touching the ground, as if it were investigating a potentially dangerous situation. His dragon was like a detective, "sniffing out something," and it was ready to attack ("spurt fire") should the danger be confirmed. Rather than standing up straight, exposing its powerful size for all to see and admire, Mr. L.'s dragon was in a potentially threatened or vulnerable position from which it must be vigilant and ready to protect itself.

This image of a dragon was not likely to be experienced as vigorous or admirable in its great size, nor could it give this patient the comforting feeling that there is someone in his corner to whom he can turn for protection or strength. Mr. L. designated the idealized selfobject as an imposing dragon, which does not exist in reality; he characterized his dragon as threatened and consequently needing to be watchful ("sniffing out"). Recall his additional percept of the previous card, the soft but still powerful abominable snowman, which he also noted to be an imaginary reference. Did he harbor concerns about whether idealized selfobjects were really there for him in a sufficiently reliable or dependable manner?

This patient reported puppies perched on top of a cliff, seen with the benefit of the shading on the blot. The puppies were overlooking a vast terrain, and the response carried a serene affective tone. These diminutive puppy dogs, themselves in need of being protected, were depicted as safe. Before too quickly concluding that this percept connoted vulnerability that can be calmed or soothed, the following two percepts of giants, the first of which was "half a part, from the waist down," were disquieting. One association included a spontaneous reference to the Jack and the Beanstalk tale, in which the boy is chased by the giant, tries to run away to safety, but is "going into the unknown." The danger of the dragon's "sniffing out something" has returned and re-exposed Mr. L. to the dangerous "unknown." That the giant was headless and the boy of this percept tried to "outsmart" the giant highlighted Mr. L.'s reliance on intellectual defenses or resources to protect himself. He therefore turned inward to his own abilities or talents to safeguard a vulnerable sense of cohesion of the self. Strong, idealizable selfobjects are vulnerable, weak, nonexistent, or endangered; he must be the strong person with his wits about him.

Idealizable selfobjects may be too unreliable for him to trust that they can protect him. He thus saw himself once more as the small, powerless boy, like the puppies of the previous response, who turned to a responsive and dependably available selfobject environment. Mr. L. found such help either lacking or too uncertain to last long enough to ensure a sustained calming, as may be seen when the danger of the giant returned immediately after the puppies on the cliff who felt comfortable. Note that the selfobject need (in this instance, idealization) was revealed by its faltering or malfunction.

Mr. L. concluded Card IV with a second giant, this time with the benefit of a head, but a head compromised by being "small and distorted." This giant, bearing the goose with the golden eggs, represented Mr. L.'s hope for everything he wanted. His hope for the reassurance of an idealizable selfobject might be illusory, insofar as it expressed the misdirected notion that whenever the self felt endangered, he needed only the goose that laid a golden (that is, protective) egg. The giant of this percept, who bore the magic goose, distorted head notwithstanding, was another reminder that the golden eggs that Mr. L. hoped to secure for himself probably fail him in the end. Unlike Ms. T., however, he continued to search for a responsive idealizing selfobject.

Unsuccessful mirroring selfobject responsiveness may have set the stage for the readiness of the self to feel itself undermined or threatened. This patient's figure drawings had already indicated that Mr. L. felt devitalized and experienced his existence as out of kilter and lacking equilibrium. Thus, it is not difficult to understand this patient's desire for a strong, resilient figure to emerge as an idealizable selfobject, to assist his overtaxed capacity to preserve self-cohesion. Puppies overlooking the peaceful expanse of land and the association to money growing on trees are characteristic indications of his need for calm security. Mr. L. was trying to find a way to keep a vulnerable self sustained or afloat.

Card V

18. *A bat, flying. (W)*   *The wings. The body of it.*

v19. *A bush. The legs on two sides*   *The dark area is the bush. Leaping*
      of two animals, rabbits. Run-   *in for cover. [Q] They jump, hop,*
      ning behind the bush. They   *and they're swift. They run fast.*
      escaped from something,   *They're usually hunted.*
      possibly a hunter. (W)

20.   *A ballerina. Arms raised, and*   *The head, chest, arms raised as in*
      leaping into the air. (W)   *a swan. Flight into the air. Freedom*
                                                of flight. The body's very graceful.

v21. *A person diving into a swim-*   *The body, legs here, and the head.*
      ming pool. Right in the midst   *[Association] Being swallowed up.*
      of the dive. Both arms and   *Encompassed by the water.*
      legs extended. (Dd99: W ex-
      cluding D6 area)

After the conventional bat, Mr. L. returned to what has been emerging as the predominant theme of seeking safety from threat. In his response of a scared rabbit, he commented on the swiftness of the rabbits, perhaps another indication of his resiliency at times of danger or anxiety, reminiscent of his percept on Card IV of the boy who used his skills and talents to "outsmart" the foreboding giant. Mr. L. knew what his resources were, and did not feel as defeated and defenseless as Ms. T. By this point, however, it was becoming clear that it was a great strain for Mr. L. to sustain this effort. There was hardly a moment's respite, and he constantly needed to be watchful and vigilant, like his rabbit "leaping for cover ... they're usually hunted."

There followed another serene image, this time, a ballerina. Also portrayed as a leaping figure, the ballerina was not leaping like the rabbit to save her life from a hunter. Rather, she had "freedom of flight." This pattern was seen previously, on Card IV, on which the dragon spewing fire when he sensed danger led to a puppy overlooking a peaceful terrain. Now, on Card V, a rabbit using its wits by leaping quickly and agilely to save itself was followed by a serene percept of a graceful ballerina calmly and freely leaping. This calmness, however, was again transitory. The following response represented a graceful dive, but on a probing association on inquiry, Mr. L. confirmed the resurgence of threatened self-cohesion in his comment about the diver's being swallowed up. The incongruous furry rat, hostile Oriental woman, and nuzzling elephants percepts, with their connotations of closed-off affectional need, are also relevant in the present context.

Card VI

22. *An insect coming out of a co-*   *The wings. Freedom.*
    coon, trying to fly. (W)

<23. *A man lying down. Along a*   *The nose, arms raised, his legs.*
    pool of water. The image be-   *[Association] Restful, peaceful,*
    ing reflected, too. (D1)   *but he knows he shouldn't be be-*
        cause of the rigidity of the arm
        extended. He's doing it but knows
        he shouldn't be.

24. *Two monkeys back to back.*   *Just their bodies.*
    They're very happy. (D1)

<25. *A bird's nest. The heads of*   *The nest is over here, and the*
    birds. Chirping, waiting to be   *birds are in it.*
    fed. (D4)

26. *Two little boys, trying to*   *The legs here, they're unable to*
    reach or grab something.   *get what they want on the coat*
    Their hands are extended up.   *rack.*
    Possibly from a coat rack.
    One foot on the ground, one
    foot up trying to reach what-
    ever's on the coat rack. (D1)

Despite the rich productivity of Card VI, it revealed little new. The significance of an insect emerging from a cocoon and attempting to fly is familiar enough to clinicians, and hardly requires much discussion. In consideration of the self psychological view of the emergence of an invigorated self, it is useful only to point out that this self materializes through transmuting internalizations in small increments, such as the percept of a cocoon represents. Therefore, projective test imagery such as a cocoon is misleading for an interpretation of genuinely firmed-up or stabilized self-cohesion. There is little in Mr. L.'s record to suggest anything different. The image's appearance now was merely a hope or wish that a strengthened or cohesive self might still develop.

The image of a cocoon developing wings may also express this patient's need for a reliable selfobject to help consolidate more than a fleeting sense of self-cohesion. That Mr. L.'s last response on the previous card involved a diver being swallowed up emphasizes how crucial this need had become. His response certainly indicated nothing about feeling that he was close to reconstituting self-esteem.

The following response was notable first for its indication about passivity. Moreover, this water scene captured the disparity between the theme of peacefulness conveyed by the restful figure and the rigidity of the arm position suggesting tension and distress. This incongruity is consistent with several similar responses examined thus far in Mr. L.'s Rorschach record. He seemed to grasp how little the serenity of the pool image indicated about his internal self-experience. His comment about "he's doing it but he knows he shouldn't be" may convey this experience.

Happy monkeys back to back, his next response, seemed relatively innocuous and diagnostically noncontributory as well. This response was followed by the bird's nest with the young waiting to be fed, another passive reference, with no further associative elaboration. Mr. L. seemed to want to take a break on Card VI, to yield to passivity and to convey the impression of not wanting to get too worked up or provoked by this Rorschach blot. At the same time, he recognized that the picture of calm or peaceful images did not reflect his actual internal state. His closing percept, describing two little boys' inability to get what they want, was in contrast to the nesting birds being fed. This response suggested the association between passive dependency and frustration of need, but it added little to what has already been noted about the self state and predominant selfobject functions.

Card VII

27. *Two little imps looking at each other. Very mischievous. Planning what to do to have some fun. (W)*

The heads, hands, rear ends. [Imps?] The shape of the face. [Association] Childish-like, fun. Devil-may-care. Sitting on rocks.

v28. *Two women doing the Charleston. (D2)*

The movement or positioning of the body. [Association] Devil-may-care.

v29. *A mother dog and two baby dogs. (W)*

The head and body. Nuzzling one baby dog and the other one coming toward her.

v30. *Two dogs, pulling, tearing some material. Fighting over it, pulling it apart. (W)*

Instead of this as the mother from before, it's like a washcloth or something. They're tearing it. It's not a whole anymore, it's being torn.

Playful imps may be a continuation of the childlike, mischievous responses from Card VI. That he also attributed a devil-may-care quality to the imps, which he then repeated in the next response of two women dancing, suggests that he desired to throw caution to the wind, to disengage from responsibilities and adult cares, and generally to give in to a passive, uninhibited, even hedonistic life. The passivity and dependency of being cared for emerged most clearly in the percept of the mother dog with her pups. This theme continued in his last response to this blot, the playful, carefree activity of the puppies, which is as important as, if not more important than, an interpretation based on oral aggression.

Some of Mr. L.'s previous responses on other cards may be understood as clearly belonging with this aspect of the personality as it was now emerging. For example, the hummingbirds drinking nectar from a flower (Card II) suggested dependency and passivity, as did his references to the abominable snowman on Card III as both powerful and soft, the elephants nuzzling on Card II, and the free-flowing bodies on Card III.

Note, in addition, the contrasts in these responses, in which references to vigorous images alternated with softer qualities. Thus, nuzzling and the free-flowing furry rug made from a rat both appeared on Card II, and previously, the at-first gentle Oriental woman (Card I) was described as hostile. Earlier in the protocol, when these responses were originally discussed, their incongruous elements were noted but their meaning was uncertain. Perhaps these elements indicated ambivalence or an aspect of the self starting to emerge or break through. A crucial part of the remaining workup centers on the question of why there appears to be, at this point, an apparent surge of passivity, dependency, and a generally disinhibited attitude toward responsibilities and concerns. The central underlying issue has to do with Mr. L.'s moving to this position from one based on eliciting idealization selfobject needs.

Cards VI and VII have established an aspect of Mr. L.'s personality previously only subtly foreshadowed, particularly in the context of his responses about danger, outsmarting malevolent forces, escaping to safety, and being swallowed up or enveloped. In particular, the self psychological connotations of the references to passivity and dependency of Cards VI and VII became a major focus of the continuing investigation and analysis.

Card VIII

31. *A group of animals going in circles, like ring-around-a-rosy. (W)*   *It's circular. They're all holding hands.*

32. *I'm blocking. Cow's heads.* *How they're shaped here. [Asso-*
    (D2)   *ciation] Milk, food.*

33. *A rat. (D1)*   *The body, its shape.*

34. *A parrot.*   *I can't find it now. [Association]*
                                   They're talkative, imitative. Stable
                                   on his perch, staying in one place.
                                   I also see two birds within a nest.

It's all fragmented, doesn't go
together.

Mr. L. experienced difficulty on this card, possibly because of the introduction of the multiple colors. Most patients do not experience this degree of distress on Card VIII. Indeed, some patients often seem to welcome its introduction and spontaneously comment on the pleasantness of the soft colors after the drab black–white–gray tones and the blood-red color of the seven preceding blots. In view of the passivity and dependency that emerged on Mr. L.'s responses to Cards VI and VII, the soft, muted colors of Card VIII might have been expected to evoke further passivity. Instead, Mr. L.'s opening response to Card VIII was "going in circles," which then gave way to his comment about blocking. He proceeded to deliver a percept that he failed to locate on inquiry, and his closing remark conveyed just how lost he was by this point. He appeared to be in a state of distress. Presumably, the disequilibrium of the self state, foretold earlier, now returned with great urgency.

This patient's customary defensive operations eluded him because he never reconstituted despite four responses to this blot, and he failed to recover his composure. This pattern represents an example of a disintegration product, even though it does not approach the severity of a transient psychotic lapse. Nonetheless, the failure to achieve a stabilization of self-cohesion depicted a self state characterized by the experience of feeling without an anchor. Mr. L. attempted to hold onto his bearings, although with limited success. The association to ring-around-a-rosy, a children's game, leading to the passive-dependent oral association of feeding linked to the percept of the cow's head, and the birds in the nest, all suggested a regressed quality in the midst of his attempt to anchor himself by being "stable on his perch." The significance of the response of a rat in the midst of all this is unclear.

Of four responses to Card VIII, none produced a scoreable color code, notwithstanding the administration procedure of eliciting associations on two of these four responses. Perhaps the color was destabilizing, and Mr. L.'s avoidance of its mention represented his adaptive defense to minimize the apparent distress that this blot provoked. Consistent with this interpretation favoring a self-protective dampening down of disturbing affect was Mr. L.'s description of the parrot as "stable on his perch" as an effort to prevent an affective breakthrough. A quiescent parrot was preferable to sudden eruptions of loud, angry squawking, not unlike the equivalent of a pure C response.

Thus, the parrot was reined in, dampened down, and in control. In this respect, from the standpoint of the psychology of the self, color (or its notable absence) can be understood as a manifestation of a self state in varying stages of cohesion. The optimal form-dominant (FC) response might imply good or at least reasonable self-cohesion, whereas progressively less stabilized degrees of self-cohesion or infirmity of the self might be associated with the CF and C codes.

Absence of color might be understood as this patient's attempt to find a tolerable level of affective experience compatible with preserving optimal self-cohesion. Avoidance of color could be understood as protecting a vulnerable self state. Mr. L. might have too easily yielded to the overstimulating pull of color by giving in to the less well-integrated CF and C manifestations of color on the Rorschach blots. The price that he paid was a damping down of affect, a process that drove the self into hiding, as it were. This reaction resulted in a lack of enthusiasm or vigor and captured the affective deadness or mechanical plodding through life seen in many patients with prominent pathology of the self. In this view, the absence of color does not signify the defensive withdrawal from drive states but the self-protective attempt of an injured or vulnerable self to ensure whatever degree of cohesiveness it can manage to preserve.

Mr. L.'s overall protocol has not been characterized by affective emptiness suggestive of depletion. The record revealed distancing from disruptive affects threatening to undermine his attempt to preserve self-cohesion. Being "stable on his perch" in the midst of a world that was "all fragmented" was the best that this patient could manage. Responsiveness to color was disruptive to his effort. This degree of minimization of color may also suggest that Mr. L. experienced the selfobject environment around him as unavailable or unresponsive to his needs and thus failing to serve as a source of assistance to buttress a vulnerable self in the face of threat or disrepair.

Mr. L.'s breakdown or loss of composure on Card VIII needs to be understood in the contexts of the emergence of the passive-dependent manifestations indicated on Cards VI and VII as well as the clinical picture of the self and its selfobject needs that had characterized the protocol during the first half of the Rorschach. I already noted that his responses to the early blots showed his floundering around, feeling depreciated or underpowered. He seemed to be searching for idealizing selfobject responsiveness to enable the self to become invigorated or buoyant. Incongruous responses interspersed with percepts characterizing a vulnerable self state created the impression that Mr. L. was casting about at random to restore the needed level of self-cohesion, however unresourceful these efforts appeared. He sometimes found himself searching blind alleys and felt disconnected or lost; the need to escape from potentially dangerous or misdirected object choices never dissipated.

On Cards VI and VII, a shift or realignment of selfobject functions emerged. He began to show a pronounced passive-dependent orientation, possibly resulting from searching for what he needed but looked for in the wrong places. From this viewpoint, the distress on Card VIII might be understood as another indication that even his passive-dependent position failed to sufficiently stabilize the self. Giving in to a regressive adaptation characterized by passivity did not get him what he needed. Despite the risk of overinterpreting the sequence of responses and associations seen on Card VIII, Mr. L. apparently never managed to get beyond a position of "going in circles" in seeking "milk ... food," failing to "stay in one place," and feeling "it's all fragmented, doesn't go together." He was attempting to repair a self in disequilibrium by resorting to a wholesale regressive dependency. From the standpoint of the psychology of the self, however, the essential problem was the difficulty in relying on the selfobject responsiveness needed to buoy up an injured self state.

Card IX

<35. *The color's hard to deal with. A family. The father, sitting at the table eating dinner. He doesn't seem happy, he seems very tired and angry. (D1 + D4 + area adjacent to D4 up to the midline)*

The father, with a moustache, nose, the eyes. These objects make it look like he's not alone, but encompassed by the other figures.

36. *Animals grabbing a fish in their mouth. (D12)*

A dog who grabbed it for food. The image of it looks like a reflection.

v37. *Two ladies having a conver-*   *The heads, pony tails, the bodies.*
     sation together, dressed to-   *Standing nose to nose. [Nose to*
     tally alike. (W)   *nose?] That's why they're dressed*
                                        alike, like they're in some type of
                                        disagreement, like "Why are you
                                        wearing this same thing?" [Asso-
                                        ciation: dressed alike] Imitation,
                                        trying to be different and unable to
                                        do so.

v38. *An owl. Staring straight*   *The white area with the shading.*
     ahead. (DS8)   *The eyes, the tail. [Association]*
                                        Wise, watchful. Just seeing every-
                                        thing but being very watchful,
                                        questioning. Being noncommittal.

As on Card VIII, there was a productive yield of four richly elaborated responses to Card IX, despite the fact that it is the most difficult blot for generating responses. Once again, none of the responses produced a score-able color response, despite the well-embellished descriptions of the per-cepts and the vigorous inquiry on two responses. His spontaneous comment at the outset ("the color's hard to deal with") may indeed be telling, despite this patient's limited use of the color on Cards II and III.

Having noted that color is present, although difficult for him to integrate, Mr. L. delivered, in effect, a portrait of his chief complaint in the apparent form of a Rorschach response. In referring to himself as the unhappy, tired, and angry father, Mr. L. described his self state of depletion. His use of the term *encompassed* on inquiry should perhaps have been pursued; it is not clear whether he meant to connote feeling encompassed in the sense of embraced and included or surrounded and possibly intruded upon. The dominant affect state, however, was not depicted as warm or inviting. The selfobject environment in which he was most closely "encompassed" did not invigorate the self. Instead, he felt depleted and worn down.

Wherever Mr. L. turned (reflected, coincidentally, in the frequent card turning), he found more dissatisfaction in obtaining relief or selfobject responsiveness from any source. In his second response of an animal grabbing food, the grabbing is more psychologically salient than is the reflection response, with its less relevant connotations of mirroring or egocentricism. The animal apparently grabbed the food because it was not easily available in a nonaggressive way; Mr. L. seemed to suggest that one's needs must be met aggressively or with force. Mr. L. did not anticipate that his needs would simply be recognized as legitimate and responded to. He must demand, struggle, or fight for all he got. His selfobject milieu was therefore unresponsive and depriving and seems to have turned its back on him.

By this point, he appeared to feel that there was nothing out there for him to use to repair an infirm self and so he must grab for what he needed. Grabbing is not seen by self psychologists, at least in Kohut's view, primarily as a manifestation of hostility or aggressiveness. The response is understood as what the patient must do to secure a needed selfobject function in the absence of an available or responsive selfobject.

This patient turned next to the figure of women dressed alike and in disagreement. In this way, Mr. L. expressed friction in association with similarity. It is tempting to consider that the similarity or "imitation" referred to a twinship selfobject need; this interpretation might be the case but equally plausibly might not. His association was derived from a failed attempt to assert a difference (and by inference, autonomy), but he had to resort to imitation. The similarity constituted an irritant, a source of "disagreement" as the patient perceived the matter. Thus, the similarity represented by the women's style of dress does not sound like the shared alikeness or mutuality of finding oneself allied in under-standing. Rather than linking this response with the disappointment of a twinship selfobject need, it is more prudent to regard this response of imitation, ultimately leading to disagreement, as simply a further aspect of the patient's problem in locating a source of selfobject responsiveness that he found restorative or enlivening.

Mr. L.'s final response to Card IX was that of an owl, seen in a stance of vigilance and not committing to (or perhaps trusting) anything it saw in the immediate surround. This response recalls the watchful dragon percept of Card IV. The connotation is not that the world is unsafe, but rather that the patient was cautious about judging who was friend or foe. This position is appropriate after having been burned by a hurtful or, more typically, disappointing selfobject environment. Once burned, twice shy: Avoiding color, his caution after coming down from his "all fragmented" experience of Card VIII, the sense that "color's hard to deal with" on Card IX, and now the worldly-wise and thus vigilant owl all represent Mr. L.'s need to protect himself from the potentially disruptive effects of a world that did not recognize or respond attentively to his devitalized self-esteem.

Card X

39. *A king and his court. His sub-*
    jects are looking at him. (W)

The king, his cape like the King of Siam. The crown, his hair. All the way around are his subjects. His arms are outstretched. [Associa-tion] Total control as if he'll grant unto thee what he wants to grant unto thee. Very powerful. Very decadent and ostentatious. His sub-jects are very plain and ordinary.

v40. *A group of sea horses.*
     There's fish swimming
     around them. Each one is
     separated by the fish as if
     they're captive. And crabs,
     but again I see things in iso-
     lation, nothing together. Like
     the crabs alone, the animals
     alone, nothing together. (W)

Fish swimming here, fast enough to keep each one in its place. [Associa-tion] Nothing really. They also carry around their young, protect-ing its young.

Again, Mr. L. reported no scoreable color responses. His benevolent king quickly turned into a "decadent" monarch concerned with dominating his depreciated ("plain and ordinary") subjects and watching them grovel for whatever the king was willing to "grant unto thee." This grandiosity was little more than defensive bravado, especially as at this point in the protocol Mr. L. saw himself as no grand figure. In view of his beginning on Card IX with the devitalized father, Mr. L. may now on Card X be attempting to continue his theme of needing to revitalize the self. The victory may be hollow, however; the repair to self-esteem occurred by dominating others so as to make them feel depreciated.

His association to the King of Siam should probably have been pursued further; thus, it is not possible to know whether Mr. L. had in mind *The King and I* as the basis for his association. Accordingly, one can not know whether his association to the well-known gruffness and domination of the king in that popular musical might also have contained a reference to the king's hidden, vulnerable inner nature.

Although this notion must remain speculative, the theme of strong-armed control continued in Mr. L.'s next response to Card X, that of the larger and potentially more powerful sea horses held captive by smaller fish surround-ing them by swimming rapidly. He seemed to feel held captive by his own family, represented here metaphorically as the smaller fish, who are powerful enough in their resourcefulness to keep the sea horse immobilized. Many parents do indeed feel just this way about their adolescent children, particularly if the children are in trouble. Coupled with the need to be "protecting its young," this patient seemed to express here his own conflict about asserting his control and being protective of his "subjects," but feeling undermined and impotent in the struggle.

In the end, he felt "in isolation" (like his monks of Card II); "nothing is together." Again, Mr. L. conveyed the self state of an injured, devitalized, and immobilized man doing whatever he can to preserve self-cohesion. He was "in isolation" in a selfobject environment that seemed to frustrate him, and consequently, he experienced himself and his world as one in which "nothing is together." This isolation is not that of schizoid detachment.

The course of the Rorschach protocol shows the progressive devitalization of the self. Beginning with two people on Card I attempting but ultimately failing "in disagreement" to establish a viable self-selfobject unit, Mr. L. came to the end of the protocol with a family in disarray, two women "in some type of disagreement" over looking alike, and finally feeling captive by his conflict between "protecting his young" and dominating them in a powerful yet controlling manner.

Rorschach Synthesis and Clinical Discussion

This Rorschach protocol captures in rich detail the way that Mr. L. experienced what happened to him psychologically and the way that he perceived events intruding on the peace of mind he sought to preserve. I begin my discussion of Mr. L.'s protocol with this phenomenologic statement because it directs attention to an important aspect of this patient's psychological life. It lends itself to an investigation of selfobject functions as conceptualized by self psychology. I attempt to maintain this focus on the patient's psychological experience of faltering self-cohesion as I proceed to illustrate the technical aspects of the thematic analysis portrayal of the devitalized self state. It is important to understand Mr L.'s attempt to manage faulty mirroring by securing idealization and to some extent twinship as part of his attempt to acquire a compensatory structure to repair the injuries to self-esteem.

Mr. L. found himself adrift in a world that has stopped working right for him. Over and over, he conveyed that wherever he turned, his efforts to secure a stable or familiar anchor were thwarted. This perception was foreshadowed in his opening figure drawings, as his initial exuberant, joyful anticipation quickly gave way to a mood of disquietude. He felt drained by inadequacies, loss of control over his environment, and feeling misunderstood. This basic theme persisted on the Rorschach as well.

The mood of a bubble bursting emerged at the outset on Card I, in which the convivial dinner conversation turned to disagreement. The dance around a maypole was spoiled when the person's sadness prevented him from enjoying the event. After the initial revival of joyful hopefulness, he proceeded to experience the devitalization of a selfobject environment that did not respond to his normal-enough animation. Thus, the downturned head of the sad person dancing around the maypole was the dispirited, devalued self that cannot hold its head up in a joyful or proud way. The figure "doesn't want to participate" because the self was depleted.

He delivered several more responses that added to the impression that Mr. L. legitimately sought affection (no excessiveness comes through on this Rorschach about what he seemed to ask for), but he encountered either encumberances or disappointing outcomes. Thus, a furry rug was made from a rat, birds in flight were escaping, and people appeared "free flowing" but then stiff and formal. His references to segmented parts showed that his search for contact far too often met with off-putting or unavailable responsiveness.

These experiences provided the backdrop for what may be inferred as insufficient mirroring. The evidence for the phenomenon is clear across many Rorschach blots; the mirroring deficit is based on an empathic understanding of how Mr. L. reacted to the disappointments of unresponsive selfobjects. For example, a person who was diving was swallowed up (Card V) and little boys grabbed for something they could not reach (Card VI). Against this background, the examiner can begin to see and attempt to understand that Mr. L. sought other selfobject functions to restore self-esteem. Mr. L. first indicated his needs, showed that they were ignored or rebuffed, and turned to mobilize idealizing and twinship selfobject functions to help fortify self-cohesion in the absence of adequate mirroring.

This differentiating among selfobject functions demonstrates that mirroring underlies almost all selfobject functions. Kohut pointed out that deficient mirroring in early development may have been so extensively asynchronous with a patient's need for empathic responsiveness that it can no longer be trusted as a reliable means for repairing injuries to a vulnerable self. For Mr. L, its pervasive failure, easily seen throughout his projective protocols, made it all the more important to identify other selfobject functions to repair self-esteem and to secure what he hoped for to revitalize self-cohesion.

Other routes, often in the form of compensatory structures, need to be developed for that purpose, just as coronary bypass surgery secondarily supplies sufficient arterial circulation to critically diminished regions of heart muscle. In respect to projective testing, the identification of defective mirroring does not imply that it is the only selfobject function present, even though it is frequently the impetus for summoning forth idealization and twinship functions. It is a starting point or a basic substrate that should signify to examiners to look for compensatory structures.

Mirroring is sometimes the central or predominant selfobject need (as in the case of Ms. T., despite her fleeting or halfhearted idealization attempts that were quickly abandoned). Mr. L., in contrast, showed a generally sustained effort to search for idealizing selfobject functions, compared to Ms. T. Therefore, the response contents or elaborations of his Rorschach percepts may point to other selfobject functions that were more central than was mirroring. These alternative means to repair the self were compensatory structures he attempted, albeit unsuccessfully when mirroring was too unrevivable for that purpose. The evidence for idealization, particularly during the first half of the Rorschach, is generally persuasive.

At certain times, Mr. L. turned to powerful, idealizable figures. At other times, the imagery of several of his responses suggests that he turned to companionate twinship selfobject functions for firming up the self when it was undermined or vulnerable. The evidence indicating that idealizing selfobject needs were mobilized is more compelling than that suggestive of twinship selfobject needs. Relying on strong, powerful figures or seeking to feel at one with others appeared at different times. Both selfobject functions were intended to stave off devitalization of the self when the self state was dominated by its vulnerability to injury, weakness, or inability to sustain itself with sufficient and consistent vigor.

The most definitive statement about selfobject functions depicts the extent and pervasiveness of the injured self state and typically points to an absence or deficiency of mirroring. This fact appeared repeatedly and consistently throughout Mr. L.'s protocol. Thus, the underlying mirroring selfobject needs were almost always apparent. Neither idealization nor twinship functions appear as clearly. They may alternate without one clearly overshadowing the other, as the case of Mr. L. demonstrates. Therefore, admixtures of selfobject functions are the norm; clear demarcations among selfobject functions or textbook-style pure forms rarely occur. Pure forms

also exist infrequently in life, and intensive treatment is also characterized by admixtures of selfobject needs. Much of the work of psychodiagnostic testing centers on identifying these compensatory structures,
which must be strengthened in treatment.

As in the case of Ms. T., Mr. L.'s Rorschach record permits a comparison
between drive theory and self psychological viewpoints. Although neither
theoretical conceptualization is necessarily superior, the clinical material
still lends itself to several interpretive possibilities. For example, as early
as Card II, the response of "monks ... touching hands ... they're in accord"
introduced the idea that this patient was looking for a calming function or
a degree of cooperative understanding. He was self-protectively cautious
of exposing his need; thus "they're having fun." Kohut considered that
people are cautious about expressing legitimate needs because of their
vulnerability to having these needs rebuffed. He did not regard the appearance of defensiveness as a true defense (in the technical sense). Mr. L.
expressed the wish to feel buoyed up or connected with someone, out of
which the possibility of being understood might emerge.

Sidestepping the possibility of a defensive minimization of hostile
aggressive wishes that might be suggested by this response of monks on
this card, I have chosen to highlight instead Mr. L.'s expression of a wish
for contact or communion with a benevolent or soothing figure. A monk
also connotes someone more elevated or principled than the average
person. Monks are respected not so much because a person may turn to
them at times of need, but rather for their dedication to deep reflection
or contemplation. Their dedication occurs even at the cost of some
withdrawal from the rest of humanity. The percept of monks stands for
these characteristics and thus represents either an idealizing or twinship
selfobject function.

Examiners should not discount the possibility that a percept of monks
also connotes the wish to retreat into a protected existence, free of complexity and problems. To some fearful schizoid personalities, such a percept can
represent a safe haven. This view, however, is not likely to apply to Mr. L.:
He wanted something from his life, not to turn his back on the world. The
reference to touching hands suggests seeking a connection in depth, in
which a merging based on similarity or commonality was desired. The
selfobject function might be one of twinship. Mr. L.'s responses of people
trying to engage in intimate conversation with one quieting the other (Card
I) and of elephants nuzzling (Card II) are somewhat consistent with an
interpretation of twinship selfobject needs.

The evidence is perhaps thin or at least equivocal, and is not adequate enough to convincingly sustain this interpretation to every examiner's satisfaction. I am nevertheless discussing the twinship implications of the monks response because the response demonstrates the distinctive qualities of a level of psychological contact that is deeper or more intimate than a casual interaction. A response such as monks is clearly closer to the in-depth meaning of twinship as an intimate level of understanding compared with a response such as people dressed alike (Card IX) and its association about imitation (rather than depth of involvement or understanding).

This quality of merging need not imply a boundary disturbance. Kohut regarded merging as a normal need for being like or part of another, without necessarily implying a severe loss of distance. Although he recognized that prominent boundary disturbances involving merging could occur, the merger associated with a twinship selfobject function was typically not of this kind.

It is also possible that the percept of monks stands for a calming or soothing presence without necessarily representing similarity of thinking or feeling. In this case, idealization may be the basis for the selfobject function in question. It is often difficult to make such a relatively precise differential diagnosis or determination of specific selfobject functions from Rorschach responses alone. Therefore, the projective test battery is almost always essential for specifying distinct selfobject needs, even though the Rorschach can readily reveal the existence and severity of the underlying self states.

Two other noteworthy features about Mr. L.'s protocol deserving comment are the manifestations of passivity and dependency, and the apparent disruption of ego functions on Card VIII. Both characteristics are common events on many Rorschach records. They are all the more interesting in the present case because they afford an opportunity to conceptualize these phenomena from the self psychological point of view. Thus, dependency and passivity have their own unique psychological significance when approached from the standpoint of the psychology of the self. Passivity represents the failure of the self to sustain its buoyancy or autonomy: Prominent dependency and passivity are reactions to being unresponded to, injured, or chronically undermined. The patient has given up hope. This state is not unlike a disintegration product such as rageful outbursts or panic-like states, although certainly a far more subdued and barely noticeable reaction in comparison to prominent anxiety or rage.

Dependency of sufficient magnitude represents an excessive or pathological breakdown of the capacity of an invigorated self to put itself forward as firmly present or assured. Along with theorists from an ego psychological or object relations position, one with a self psychological framework also understands passive longings to be embedded in the character structure rather than being a symptomatic complaint. From the ego psychological standpoint, however, dependency is considered either a defense against aggression or an entrenched characterologic position marked by prominent oral wishes.

Kohut did not apparently discuss dependency as a form of disintegration or as a breakdown product such as rage, and he might not agree with this conceptualization of passivity as dynamically similar in this respect. Whether significant dependency or passivity can be considered in the same light as aggression, and so represents a disintegration product, its dynamic significance as a manifestation of a beaten-down or defeated self state is not far off the mark.

The second feature I want to highlight is the self psychological attempt to understand fragmentation phenomena as seen on the Rorschach. Of course, patients can display varying degrees of fragmentation, ranging in severity from acute psychosis to momentary lapses of clear or orderly response production in otherwise well-compensated, relatively healthy people. Mr. L. displayed a degree of severity on the better-adjusted side of a midpoint of this continuum. This impression is based on the fact that his difficulty on the Rorschach was not widespread across most of the blots and his loss of composure remained generally circumscribed and well-contained. His disorder is a good example of temporary fragmentation phenomena of a nonpsychotic nature, often seen in outpatient adults with a moderately intense self disorder. Mr. L.'s fragmentation began to appear on Card VIII; thus its possible provocation by the color cannot be discounted.

Mr. L.'s fragmentation reflects a self state characterized by the failure to maintain stabilization. By this point in the protocol, a nearly intolerable tension state was evident, whether or not influenced by the introduction of the multiple chromatic colors. The patient was practically unable to reconstitute throughout the entire sequence of responses to Card VIII. Card IX was barely improved, and he finished the card with an owl staring straight ahead, watchful and vigilant, at the cost of finding himself "noncommittal."

Although he recovered and became "stable on his perch," the repair he settled for was to feel affectively shut down. He may have restored a tolerable equilibrium to a self state "going in circles ... it's all fragmented, doesn't go together," but this state is not a restoration of a self characterized by zest and vitality.

Mr. L.'s Rorschach protocol showed that even relatively modest degrees of fragmentation of the self can be detected. His protocol was typical of that in outpatients with symptomatic disturbances superimposed on a chronic self disorder. Aspects of this protocol also resembled rapidly reconstituting acute reactions that occur in disruptive states, including psychoses. Rather than representing a breakdown of defense operations or ego resiliency, fragmentation phenomena on the Rorschach may also be understood as the reaction of a vulnerable self threatened by diminished cohesion. This reaction represents disintegration states such as those that Kohut identified. The absence or temporary empathic unavailability of a restorative or calming selfobject environment is often implied by the appearance of fragmentation. The experienced destabilization may be exacerbated by the diminished selfobject responsiveness that accompanies such states of distress.

Still another issue in this extended case example is the fact that the testing of limits in expanded Rorschach inquiry was conducted so as to encourage the production of fantasy material beyond the perceptual problem-solving task. Because the primary function (if not the *only* real function) of the inquiry often yields banal records, it is important to consider the unique value of a rich, elaborative record such as that produced by Mr. L. The issue is not one of productivity; the number of responses that Mr. L. produced was not influenced by the style of the subsequent inquiry. It is even arguable whether the procedure of requesting associative elaborations appreciably affected the resulting clinical interpretation because the association phase was richly elaborated to begin with.

The interpretation of the Rorschach material bearing on the self state would almost surely have been elicited regardless of the administration procedure. The multiple indications of depreciation and compromised self-cohesion were sufficiently abundant in this record were an examiner favorably disposed to attend to the content in that way. The basis for the interpretations of Mr. L.'s unstable hold over his faltering selfobject world would, however, only have been hinted at, but probably not fully clarified without some additional associations. For example, consider the response of the abominable snowman and Mr. L.'s wondering whether that creature actually existed (Card IV), the person diving and being swallowed up (Card V), the devil-may-care associations on Card VI, and the "stable on his perch" comment on Card VIII.

Thematic Apperception Test

Card 1.

That's a young boy looking at his violin, very confused. He didn't know what to do with it because it's broken. He thinks it through and decides to repair it. He has to get glue and glue it together so no one would realize it was damaged. [Led up?] He was playing around, it didn't belong to him, and he was too rough, so he broke off the top part. [How does he feel?] Puzzled and unhappy. [Outcome?] He's relieved. No one would find out.

Stories pertaining to the violin as broken and in need of repair are somewhat less common, but Mr. L. continued the themes that characterized his Rorschach and figure drawing protocols to this point. Thus, the broken violin seems to represent the self in a state of disrepair. As on the Rorschach, his initial reaction was one of confusion as he attempted to understand why the violin was broken. By inference, this patient wondered how he could reconstitute himself. The focus of his story is the injury and his concern that it should be repaired.

The comments that he was confused and that the violin did not belong to him need not be thought of as a derealization phenomenon. From the viewpoint of the psychology of the self, they represent instead his affective reaction to the experience of an injury to the self. He appeared perplexed at this threat to the cohesiveness of the self; it did not "belong to him." The affective state of surprise represented the sudden or acute nature of the recent disruption in his life, as if to say: "Is this really happening to me!" This disruption in turn provoked, or more likely reactivated, the underlying threat to self-cohesion.

It is tempting at this point to quote a comment from a recently published lecture by Kohut. In explaining his ideas about the repair or restoration of the self, Kohut (1996, p. 387) paraphrased a line from the play *The Great God Brown* by Eugene O'Neill: "Man is born broken; he lives by mending. The grace of God is glue." Kohut noted that the characters in the O'Neill play wear masks; they sometimes wear one another's masks, and they become uncertain about their identities "so there's a great uncertainty about the cohesion of their selves" (Kohut, 1996, p. 387). In Mr. L.'s story about the boy's confusion over whether the violin was his, the metaphor of glue in Kohut's example from the O'Neill play provides a useful link to understanding Mr. L.'s story to Card 1. The need for glue to repair the broken instrument represented something vital and central to Mr. L.'s disrupted self-cohesion, just as repairing faulty self-cohesion was the core problem that required mending in the O'Neill example as reconceptualized by Kohut.

The secrecy about the boy's having damaged the violin seemed important to Mr. L. It may be considered alongside his comment about the top part of the instrument having broken off, as well as related material seen previously on the Rorschach, notably on Card IV. In view of the phallic appearance of the scroll of the violin, the references to wrongdoing and secretiveness could very easily lend themselves to a drive theory interpretation centered on oedipal concerns. In this view, clinicians may be persuaded to emphasize the libidinal and aggressive aspects of the psychodynamic conflict. These aspects also take into account the prominent defenses and the nature of the resolution of the core conflict indicated by the response.

Before proceeding to present an alternative interpretation from self psychology, I note that Kohut had not intended to discard or disparage central tenets of the theory of the interplay of drives in ego psychology. He did become increasingly convinced, however, that the traditional oedipal interpretations were not useful clinically in understanding and treating not only the self disorders themselves, but disorders based largely on neurotic conflict.

Rather than emphasizing the conflictual interplay of competing drive states, Kohut focused his attention on the devaluation of self-esteem which young children may undergo while experiencing oedipal urges. This devaluation can occur if parents fail to recognize a child's healthy libidinal and assertive steps at this period of development. In chapter 2, I mentioned that oedipal children feel that their longings are unwelcome and shameful. Ultimately, their basically healthy wishes for admiration are driven underground rather than coming forward with vitality as a developmental step toward affectionate intimacy or sensual closeness.

What bearing does this reiterated reconceptualization of the oedipal situation have on Card 1 of the TAT? The answer may lie in the boy's concern about keeping his "wrongdoing" a secret. The violin was not his, and he had to cover up the fact that he broke it; he hoped that the repair conceals his damage. The need for secrecy, therefore, may not represent the patient's fear of wrongdoing, superego guilt, and punishment. Rather, his concern may center on his need to protect the self from the criticism he anticipated at being found out. Mr. L. is worried that whatever he did to damage the violin was not understood, and an empathic failure precipitates a fall in self-esteem. The boy was actually resourceful in trying to repair the violin, but he cannot feel pride in making the repair because he was intent on concealing what he felt was misunderstood as wrongdoing.

The self psychological view of Mr. L.'s story to Card 1 recast the oedipal theme as a concern that more or less normal inquisitive or exploratory urges may go awry. He needed to summon the resourcefulness to quietly restore the situation to normal by himself. Most important, this patient felt that others failed to understand his wishes and faulted him for them or in some manner showed displeasure toward him.

Card 2.

An everyday occurrence on a farm. A mother and father working in the field, the daughter is going to school. The mother is dreaming about the possibility of selling the farm. She's rugged, dowdy, thinking about going off to the city where her life would not be as difficult. [Difficult?] No hard labor, the hours. She's worked hard all her life. [Father?] He's nebulous. No feeling that it's a part of everyday life, it's daily routine. [Daughter?] Uncaring. Although nostalgic, but she's accepted her whole lot in life. [Lot in life?] To grow up like mama. To be a part of the same thing. [Her relationship with mother?] One of pity. This is her mother's lot in life, but she pities her. [Mother's relationship with daughter?] Total isolation. No contact. She knows what her daughter thinks about her, but she ignores it. [Father's relationship with daughter?] Nil. He's unaware of the daughter. The family's in total isolation, each one has their own life.

Mr. L. returned here to the theme of a disjointed, indifferent family. His response was reminiscent of his initial response to Card IX of the Rorschach and his elaboration on the drawing of a female. By now, all these depictions of the family engaged together created the clear impression of people who went their own way and showed little or no concern for one another. Most tellingly, this family appeared to represent a selfobject environment deficient in the capacity for empathic understanding. The patient experienced life in the family as lacking even a basic awareness that some recognition of need was in order when someone was in a state of disequilibrium. In this TAT story, the father was practically not a part of the family at all, at least psychologically. Moreover, the mother–daughter relationship could hardly be imagined to be any more remote or indifferent than that represented here.

As with both figure drawings and many of Mr. L.'s Rorschach responses, the initial indications of hopefulness quickly receded to reveal an undercurrent of depression characterized by a lack of enthusiasm. For example, Mr. L.'s first drawing was that of a young man stimulated by nature, and Card I of the Rorschach began with the pub-like atmosphere for a congenial talk, leading up to two figures dancing around a maypole. These responses soon became dominated by the emerging need of protecting self-esteem. These enthusiastic openings very shortly dampened down, to be replaced by feelings of being misunderstood and having to surmount obstacles. On the previous TAT card, the boy of Card 1 was able to repair the violin and was "puzzled and unhappy"; his sense of relief came only from escaping detection rather than from satisfaction. Now, on Card 2, people accepted their lot in life, ignored one another's needs, and existed in "total isolation." The emptiness and devitalization were certainly palpable, but so too was the glimmer of what Mr. L. needed in selfobject responsiveness to find some way out of his dilemma. Like his monks of Card II, Mr. L. did not seek an isolated existence apart from a selfobject milieu; rather, he asked only that his environment should be responsive to his mirroring and idealization needs.

That mirroring has been deficient or undermined was rather evident by this point, but how Mr. L. attempted to get what he needed to sustain self-cohesion was not entirely clear. It is important to determine whether stable compensatory structures became established or whether idealization or twinship were viable alternatives to restore his self-esteem. It is critical to see how the selfobject environment materialized for him as the TAT continued, in view of indications from the Rorschach about tentative attempts to secure either idealization or twinship selfobject functions.

Card 3BM.

A young person, female I believe. Some tragedy just happened. She's totally distraught, not knowing what to do. A solution won't be found. [Led up?] A death. Her husband. [How does she feel?] Distraught, she doesn't know what to do next. "How can I take over, everything's unmanageable." [Outcome?] She picks up after awhile and life goes on. She fits the pieces of her life back together and possibly remarries.

After the initial reaction to the inability to find a solution, the patient showed a capacity to regain composure. This resourcefulness was seen previously, most tellingly following Card VIII on the Rorschach. Moreover, the figure on Card 3BM recovered from a state of distress by herself, without any indication that a particular selfobject function was involved in the repair of the self state. The memory of the deceased husband or the prospect of a remarriage was not compelling enough here to form the basis for a potential selfobject function. Even a memory might qualify, because as Kohut emphasized, a selfobject is not synonymous with a person; it is the function of the object that is crucial, whether or not it takes the form of an existing person. No one was available or remembered or sought to help the person. Rather, the person was left alone with her despair.

In a similar fashion, on Card 2, all the figures went their own way, oblivious to and unconcerned about one another. Previously, on Card 1, the boy who broke the violin was left to his own devices to find a way out of his dilemma. Mr. L. seemed to go it alone, but not from a masochistic need or feeling of unworthiness. Instead, this patient did not expect someone to become available to whom he could turn to bolster self-esteem. By itself, this indicates some measure of resiliency or self-sufficiency and suggests what might be a psychological asset. In a self psychological view, this apparent strength was simultaneously a liability insofar as it indicates that the patient existed in a less-than-optimal selfobject environment. Why did the patient present a picture of "toughing it out" of this magnitude?

One answer to this question is derived from the advantage of a test battery in which findings across several tests combine to highlight a fuller picture of the personality compared to isolated aspects on single test measures. Thus, one knows from Mr. L.'s Rorschach that he withdrew from reaching out to his selfobject environment when he experienced disappointment or empathic failure. As a result, he felt alone too often with his own distress to risk seeking self-restorative selfobjects.

As with the dragon sniffing danger (on Card IV from the Rorschach) when he reduced a powerful image to one that is itself threatened and needs to protect itself, Cards 3BM and 1 of the TAT showed Mr. L. left to his own devices to find his way out of difficult straits. The dragon on Card IV was followed by a boy needing to outsmart a giant to protect himself from potential harm; on TAT Card 1, the boy thought of a solution by gluing the broken violin himself; on Card 3BM, the despondent figure also reconstituted by fitting the pieces of her life together on her own.

Mr. L. seemed to indicate that he has managed to rebuild self-cohesion by either gluing broken pieces or by slowly fitting pieces of a shattered life together. Thus, the violin of Card 1 and the distraught situation on Card 3BM represented an injured and diminished self state. One pathway to repair was through idealization or twinship, as noted previously from this patient's Rorschach. Failing at that, Mr. L. had to pull himself up by the bootstraps.

The affective tone of Card 3BM, understood now in this context, reflected less the restored self-cohesion resulting from a responsive selfobject environment than a defensively self-sufficient external portrayal of himself to the world. This patient's response to Card 3BM was notable not for its indication of resilience, but for the way Mr. L. shut out his need for empathic responsiveness to recover from the despair he described on the card. Perhaps his somewhat arch comment at the outset ("a young person, female I believe") was another indication of minimizing or distancing himself from affective involvement. The subtlety lies in what was concealed or not said rather than in the superficial story outcome of rebuilding or of carrying on. In O'Neill's metaphor for repairing a damaged self state, "the grace of God is glue" adheres much more durably when there is an affectively responsive or empathic selfobject environment behind it to back it up.

I have already pointed out that on all three cards examined thus far, the principal figures had to resolve their problems by themselves. The boy of Card 1 was mostly concerned with avoiding the shame or criticism of being discovered at fault. There is no indication that he turned to anyone for assistance. On Card 2, all the figures went about the unsatisfying business of their lives in isolation from each other. They acted as if their existence depended on turning their backs to their affective states, including the anger or disappointment they felt toward one another as unresponsive selfobjects.

Now, on Card 3BM, a figure was in great distress and had experienced a major loss. Once again, the person was alone with the depleted affect state and compromised self-cohesion. There was nowhere to turn to attempt to restore self-esteem. The person was left with only the empty sentiment similar to saying "get on with your life," which people invariably experience as little more than dismissive or unempathic and ultimately nontherapeutic. This state of affairs appears to be the affective picture that Mr. L. conveyed about his life and the state of his injured and depleted self. The TAT captured this picture in his interpersonal life, and more important still, internally in depth, as well as extending what was already seen on Mr. L.'s Rorschach.

Card 4.

A woman is trying to hold her husband back from fighting a person who insulted her. She tried to do it through reason, but reason's no longer there.

He's too angry. [Outcome?] He breaks loose and ends up in a big brawl, but he comes out on top.

On Card 4, for the first time thus far, one figure depicted in the picture appeared willing to come to the aid of another. The paradox, however, was that the woman whose honor was being defended was unable to make a sufficient psychological impact on her protector because "reason's no longer there." This response is not appreciably different from Mr. L.'s response to Rorschach Card I in which two people tried to talk in a congenial atmosphere but ended in disagreement. Card 4 resembles other Rorschach responses, notably the family with the tired and angry father (Card IX), two ladies in conversation but also in disagreement (Card IX), and the decadent and ostentatious king surveying his subjects (Card X). As Mr. L. developed his story to Card 4, it became evident that the woman was quickly forgotten and receded into the background, whereas the man was consumed by anger, unreasonableness, and the need to be victorious.

It is difficult to know whether the figure representing the central object of identification for Mr. L. was the woman whose needs were ignored or the man whose needs for winning were central. People were not seen as on his side or acting truly out of concern for his best interest. Previously, on Card 2, other people were indifferent, if not actually withholding; on Cards 1 and 3BM, other people were unavailable or unempathically responsive. Mr. L.'s story to Card 4 again showed that he expected little beneficial concern from others. Even the appearance of coming to his aid was not, in the long run, truly real or genuinely expressed for him. As conceptualized in the self psychological framework, Mr. L.'s response revealed a self experience in which he was ignored. Those selfobject functions, such as mirroring or idealization, that could help a flagging self, ultimately disappointed because they fail to take account of what he needed to restore self-cohesion, submerged as they were by others' needs for power, vindication, or "coming out on top."

Card 6BM.

A woman is thinking about something. The man is an investigator who just told the woman her son was killed trying to commit a crime. The mother's staring out thinking about what ways she went wrong. [Relationship with son?] It's very close yet she really didn't know her son. Very protective, nurturing. [Didn't know her son?] He never let her. He'd hurt her if he did. There's differences in values or ideals.

The woman's first concern was her own failure that contributed to the son's wayward behavior. A picture of estrangement was emphasized reminiscent of the family scene of Card 2. Although the mother was not depicted as indifferent to the son's death, neither was her concern the central emphasis of Mr. L.'s story. The mother asked what she did wrong and conveyed herself as being nurturant, but the tone of the story suggests that the problem lay with the son who did not permit the mother to know him intimately. Once again, the focus is on protecting her self-esteem, just as the man of Card 4 was more concerned about his self-esteem in "coming out on top" rather than about protecting the woman.

Did Mr. L. function in a world in which he saw others as too self-absorbed to notice him, or was he himself so greatly in need of protecting his own self-esteem that he has little interest in others? An examiner can identify a need or feeling state, but cannot always tell whether the need is either experienced internally or externalized in the form of a projection. The question is fundamental to the clinical workup of psychodiagnostic testing, regardless of the theoretical persuasion that any examiner brings to the interpretation of this material. This element of interpretation has been stressed by Schafer (1954), Schachtel (1966), and P. M. Lerner (1991).

Regardless of the uncertainty about the answer to this question, the indications in the clinical material of being unresponded to, ignored, or depreciated frequently convey salient features about the patient's self-esteem. In the example at hand, one can at best guess at Mr. L.'s capacity for interest in others, but it is possible to conclude that he very much feels himself to be ignored or forgotten about.

It is perhaps no accident that references to protective nurturing appear more directly on Card 6BM than on the previous TAT cards; maternal responsiveness was strongly evoked on this card. Mr. L. seemed to be dispassionately wondering aloud: Where did the maternal care go wrong, or where was it lacking? The theme of the death of a child is powerful, rarely portrayed more vividly than in Mahler's *Kindertotenlieder*, his setting of haunting elegies to dead children. This extremely rare theme on Card 6BM is even more gripping than the story about the death of the husband on Card 3BM, which was dealt with nonchalantly. Granted such a powerful theme, what is it about a mother who sees herself as nurturant that leads a child to turn away to the extent that there appears to be so little internalization of the mother? On Card 6BM, the story ended simply with the comment about the difference in values between the mother and son and how their lives diverged as a result. This remark is defensive, of course, but also affectively distanced.

The story outcome recalls the key dynamic of Mr. L.'s story to Card 2, most notably the marked deficiency of mirroring selfobject responsiveness. As with Card 2 and the ensuing TAT responses, the central issue is not so much the question about defective mirroring but about the potential for compensatory structure, such as idealization or twinship, to take over as a viable pathway for repairing and restoring self-esteem.

Card 7BM.

A young man totally rejecting the opinion of his father who is very stern, hard, and very rigid, uncaring. [Led up?] They never saw or understood each other. No real interaction. The boy turned his back on his father. [Outcome?] The father dies, and the son goes his own way. [Why a rift?] The father didn't have time for his son. He has no concern. He never wanted children.

It is not difficult to see that this father–son relationship was fundamentally characterized by callous disregard. If the family represented on Card 2 could be viewed as ambivalent at best, there can be little doubt that the near-total indifference on the part of both father and son pictured here revealed an unusual degree of mutual rejection. The appearance of disinterest might obscure deeply submerged longings and the ensuing anger at their frustration, which could only be guessed at from the available material. It is nevertheless difficult to imagine that the son missed anything from what was experienced as an unresponsive and indifferent parent.

The appearance of an unavailable object is more than just an absent person or an underdeveloped psychological function. From the standpoint of psychoanalytic self psychology, a deficiency represents a problematic threat to self-cohesion. It can appear in the form of interfering with the development of a selfobject function as a primary psychological structure, notably idealization in the case of a paternal relationship. Alternatively, a self disorder may be characterized by interrupting the formation of compensatory structures to strengthen other defective sectors of the self.

It is not possible to determine with certainty which of these instances applies to the state of Mr. L.'s self-cohesion or to his need for available selfobject functions. There is good evidence that defective mirroring compromised this patient's attempts to acquire either idealization or twinship as compensatory structures. This conclusion is clearly noted from the Rorschach protocol, which revealed that his attempts at idealization, and possibly even twinship, ultimately failed to provide the adequate "glue" he needed to buoy flagging self-cohesion. Mr. L.'s difficulty in solidifying idealization as a means for repairing self-esteem may be understood further in light of what was revealed on Card 7BM. On this card, an impoverished paternal relationship undermined any potential strengthening that might otherwise have provided for solidifying viable selfobject functions.

Card 12M.

A woman just died. A priest comes to give her the last rites. She died alone, with no one around her. The priest was her only friend.

Mr. L.'s story to Card 12M was atypical. Usually, a man is said to be lying on a bed, and the intention of the figure hovering above becomes the focus of the story. Here, the figure was mistaken for a woman, and instead of being ill or asleep, as customarily, the woman was dead. The priest represented the "psychological oxygen" needed to revive a depleted self, if it is understood that the figure of the dead person stood for a self in a state of devitalization. The image of a priest giving last rites recalled Mr. L.'s Rorschach percept of monks touching hands, from Card II.

Here the priest was cast in the role of supreme comforter. This percept contrasted with the benign communing of the withdrawn monks, an order characterized by extreme self-denial and turning away from the world. Although not quite the same as a savior, here the implication was that the potentially idealizable priest could not revive the dying person. This patient's attempts at idealization or twinship as seen on the Rorschach became too undependable to adequately do the job.

In some respects, therefore, Card 12M may be viewed as a continuation of Cards 6BM and 7BM. On Card 6BM, the son has died and the mother was turned away from; on Card 7BM, the father was emotionally indifferent and unavailable for genuine responsiveness. Now, on Card 12M, the figure died alone and without support; her only comfort arrived too late.

The stories for these three cards considered in succession suggest that the self lacked adequate mirroring of the need to be seen as valued, important, or as a source of pleasure. The mother of Card 6BM was a figure who turned away from the unmirrored self, as if to say "You are not my child; your values are alien to me." Subsequently, an attempt to revitalize the self through some other potential selfobject function, such as idealization or twinship, was spurned by the father of Card 7BM who showed no interest or availability for that purpose. Thus, the possibility of the father's serving a protective or revitalizing selfobject function was virtually obliterated. Accordingly, there was little hope of restoring self-esteem by developing a viable compensatory structure. As a result, the self was left in a devitalized state, in effect bereft and dying as on Card 12M, with its only means of sustaining itself too late to the rescue.

On Mr. L.'s Rorschach, the hope for idealization or twinship as a means to sustain flagging self-cohesion ultimately became too unreliable. This state gave rise to the passivity and "going in circles" that emerged there. Modestly reconstituting the self allowed him to hold his own, "stable on his perch," albeit at some cost to firmly secured self-cohesion. It may be anticipated that Mr. L. will find a way to emerge from the bleak picture of a self in ruin, because this capability was previously detected on the Rorschach.

Card 13MF.

After making love, a man realized that in the act of love he killed her. He is totally distraught in what he did, and the passions that led up to it. So he kills himself.

Mr. L. seemed to say here that strong passions or needs can, in effect, kill. It is well known that Card 13MF is an emotionally provocative card for all but the most affectively distanced individuals. That Mr. L. could find a way for the mother to emotionally wall off the death of her son on Card 6BM points to this patient's adept way of keeping emotions in check. The same emotional distance appeared in the marked coldness in Mr. L.'s story on Card 7BM about a father–son relationship. There, he managed to change lack of support and emotional indifference to a near virtue, as he did earlier on Card 2. Now, on Card 13MF, the stimulus may be too overpowering and may cost him more effort to withdraw affectively. He seemed able to accomplish this withdrawal only by killing himself off. It is really the intensity of his affective arousal that was killed off or obliterated.

These responses alongside the passivity and affective flattening seen on his Rorschach protocol indicate that Mr. L. needed to go to great lengths to keep himself "stable on his perch." The self psychological implication, however, of this degree of emotional withdrawal is that this man was left with a self state that was killed off or driven underground. There seem to be few real available selfobject functions for him to draw on to sustain a cohesive self without having to dampen it down to this extent.

Card 18GF.

A mother nurturing her child who's been hurt by falling down the stairs.

At first glance, this response seems to be unexpected, but it is not so surprising if it is a revival of something that Mr. L. had been looking for all along: Mr. L. had experienced an injury and wanted to be responded to by someone who noticed that he has been hurt and that his need for attention was reasonable and understandable. Only when such normal needs go unattended do self disorders begin to emerge, at least in Kohut's view about how pathology of the self destabilizes normal developmental urges. Card 18GF is a simple expression of exactly this point, and in its simplicity, it expresses all that a self in a state of injury requires to be sustained.

The selfobject function was clearly stated as well: When the self is threatened, all that is required is that its vulnerability should be recognized and responded to empathically, that is, in the more or less normal way that most people expect to be responded to when undermined. In his simple story to Card 18GF, Mr. L. said that when a child is hurt, someone must step forward to tend to the injured child.

This very simple, direct statement shows how patients find a way to tell us just exactly what they need. In view of all that has preceded this response, the message of Card 18GF needs only to be listened to at face value and understood for what it is worth. To reiterate a deceptively simple statement made by Kohut (1996, p. 208):

> From very early on, what a child needs is empathic responses to him as a self (or at least as an anticipated self). Not to his drives. Every time a mother gives milk to the baby, she is feeding her hungry child—she is not feeding a drive. A mother, an empathic mother, an empathic mothering environment never responds to a drive; it responds to a child.

Discussion of Mr. L.

This patient presented for treatment with a depressive syndrome clinically similar to that of Ms. T. The chief complaint and mental status findings revealed a comparable degree of severity of symptomatic distress. The precipitant was more identifiable in Mr. L.'s case and, in addition, he had a somewhat more favorable premorbid psychosocial adjustment in comparison to Ms. T. In generally similar clinical syndromes of comparable severity, the productive responses that these two patients gave illustrate similarities and differences in psychodynamic makeup. Both cases illustrate that a self psychological viewpoint may be applied to projective test interpretation as an alternative to classical drive theory or ego psychological theory.

Devalued self-esteem with ensuing disruption of cohesiveness of the self was a prominent feature throughout the projective test protocols. The ways that these patients attempted to repair a devitalized self centered on the differential capacity to make use of selfobject functions of idealization or twinship. These selfobject functions operate as potential compensatory structures to assist in recovery from a self disorder. They represent alternative pathways to repair self-esteem in the face of pathogenic unempathic responsiveness to normal mirroring needs.

Whether or not one follows a self psychological theoretical position as a basis for interpretation, it is not difficult to see that Mr. L. experienced almost constant rebuffs or disappointment wherever he turned. One distinctive contribution of self psychology to understanding the experiences of a patient like Mr. L. follows from the theory's emphasis on empathic failure or unresponsiveness leading to feeling undermined and devitalized. Diminished or devalued self-cohesion was the basis for Mr. L.'s depression. It is not difficult to discern how this mechanism operates from the content analysis of Mr. L.'s projective test responses.

I previously pointed out that several of Mr. L.'s projective test responses could be conceptualized from the standpoint of an ego psychological approach to drive theory. In particular, defensive and adaptive aspects of oedipal dynamics are clear from the patient's references to strong, overpowering figures on Card IV on the Rorschach, for example, and from his preoccupation with secrecy on TAT Card 1. Even the oral wishes previously noted after Mr. L.'s breakdown on the last chromatic cards on the Rorschach could be viewed as an oedipal regression. I have attempted to show in my discussion of this material, however, that the same themes may be conceptualized from the viewpoint of Kohut's psychology of the self, specifically, the relation between the oedipal situation and devitalization of the self.

Kohut thought that oedipal children expect parents to admire or affirm them; the children's desires are not primarily drive dominated or sexualized. If a parent of the opposite sex is capable of resonating with the child's wish for acknowledgment in an empathically attuned way, the experience echoes or mirrors the child's primary need. If the parent is unable to provide this response to the oedipal child's essentially normal developmental assertive or prideful urges on a regular basis, the child again and again is re-exposed to the empathic failures of the unresponsive parent. This experience interrupts maintaining a buoyant or joyfully expectant self and sets the stage for chronic injury to self-cohesion. This experience forms the substrate for diminished self-esteem and predisposes to a self disorder, and as a result, the child may feel crushed or insignificant. This process is evident in the sequence of Mr. L.'s anticipation of a welcoming or exuberant response, which is then followed by confusion, disappointment, and the sense that the bottom has dropped out. This feature is more telling than the more usual interpretation of oedipal material.

For example, the design of Card IV was initially elaborated as powerful and vigorous, but this response was soon undermined and ultimately became linked with danger. Some caution is necessary before one assumes that the towering percepts on Card IV represent a disguised oedipal conflict. In a similar fashion, an interpretation of superego conflict might be preferred on the basis of phallic-oedipal wishes, such as those suggested on TAT Card 1 by the broken instrument and the need for secrecy. A genetic reconstruction based on the oedipal situation is not even uncritically accepted as a necessary or universal psychodynamic configuration in contemporary psychoanalysis.

Without attempting to argue the issue of the fate of the oedipal situation in psychoanalytic theory, I want to point out that although some clinicians interpret contents about simultaneously threatening and powerful phallic-sounding imagery, wrongdoing, or the need for secrecy as derived from oedipal dynamics, these same contents might also be conceptualized from a self psychological interpretation of the oedipal situation. Feelings of shame, smallness, or the inability to stand up for oneself may result from parents' inability to enjoy or applaud an oedipal child's assertive urges, perhaps because of the parents' empathic limitations, depression, or vulnerability to feeling threatened by assertion. Thus, reactions of devitalization and depletion depression may be what an oedipal child is left with after his or her developmentally appropriate stirrings are misunderstood, criticized, or otherwise undermined. As a result, feelings of wrongdoing or secrecy might represent what is more accurately the shame or humiliation of someone who is made to feel insignificant or worthless.

The more important question, however, centers on Mr. L.'s attempts to repair frequent rebuffs to self-esteem. What did this patient attempt to effect in his world and with others to recover from the injuries to the self? Identifying the interplay between available selfobject functions and compensatory structures is one way to answer this question.

This approach is not that different from the ego psychological approach that conceptualizes defenses as attempts to protect the person from anxiety resulting from superego conflict related to drive discharge. The psychological objective for adaptation may differ in the ego psychological and self psychological viewpoints, in which either the self-reparative or defensive function becomes a primary focus of the diagnostic study. In the ego psychological framework, the emphasis is on the identification of defenses and evaluating their effectiveness or resiliency. From the point of view of the psychology of the self, the question becomes one of identifying selfobject functions in the service of restoring self-esteem.

This central question forms the basis for the balance of my discussion about Mr. L. The essential feature of this patient's self disorder began with his attempt to turn to others with the expectation of being responded to; instead, his efforts were ignored. Mr. L. saw himself like the disjointed family members of Card 2 on the TAT; they went their own ways, unaware of and unconcerned about one another. As on Cards 1 and 3BM, Mr. L. had to make his way through life under his own power. He must pick up the pieces of emotional disarray in whatever way he can and with little anticipation of emotional support.

It was difficult for Mr. L. to depend on a selfobject environment to provide affirming or empathic recognition when he was injured. He could not expect to receive admiration for his accomplishments or attributes in a reliably empathic manner. Consequently, mirroring selfobject functions were driven underground. The hints of budding mirroring longings are best understood as tentative attempts to secure this function, but these are at best fragments or glimmers of a selfobject need probably long abandoned. Any vestiges of mirroring selfobject needs are best construed as remnants of, or undermined efforts to achieve, sustained mirroring. These needs were not an established or viable part of Mr. L.'s psychological orientation to the world.

This fact clearly appeared on the first Rorschach card. After the initial revival of joyous hopefulness, there followed the re-emergence of the devitalization he evidently experienced at the hands of a selfobject environment that failed to respond to his animation. Thus, his needs were unmet and were empathically misunderstood. For the same reason, the boy of Card

1 on the TAT never turned elsewhere for guidance or direction; he had only his own resources to rely on to find a way out of his dilemma.

Against this backdrop of insufficient mirroring perpetuating a devalued self, one sees the attempt to seek other selfobject functions to restore self-esteem. Thus, Mr. L. first indicated his needs, the ways that these were ignored or rebuffed, and his feeling that mirroring selfobject responsiveness was not there for him. He conveyed that his attempts to achieve idealization and twinship selfobject functions might help him fortify self-cohesion in the absence of adequate mirroring. At first, he invoked images that provided either a calming function or a degree of cooperative understanding. In this way, Mr. L. expressed the wish to feel buoyed up or connected with someone, out of which the possibility of being understood might emerge.

The patient's urgent wish to feel himself psychologically enlivened repeatedly met with frustration or rebuffs from the selfobject environment as seen most clearly on the early Rorschach blots. He continued to turn to potentially strong, idealizable figures as well as to figures providing a companionate function, and mirroring selfobjects appeared as a distant memory from which he has withdrawn. Their chronic failure to operate reliably led Mr. L. to instead attempt to secure idealization and twinship selfobject functions that have evidently not become so totally shut off for him.

His effort was an uphill struggle, and he turned hopefully to idealization and twinship selfobjects, but had to retreat from these as well. Mr. L. did not, however, abandon the possibility that either twinship or idealization could serve as potential routes to repairing the devitalized self state. And so it went, beginning with Card II and oscillating back and forth in this way until at least Card VIII.

This process is the way by which, if successful, compensatory structure is built up, as an alternative pathway to sustaining a cohesive self that is injured or whose stability becomes compromised. This point is also the most critical difference between Mr. L. and Ms. T. Unlike Ms. T., who was probably too damaged to be able to maintain the effort to acquire compensatory structure through idealization, Mr. L. showed a relatively less severe degree of devitalization resulting from inadequate mirroring. He had more resilience and attempted to seek idealization or twinship selfobject responsiveness. Ms. T., in contrast, could make only the most tentative and short-lived attempt at idealization. Passivity appeared increasingly as Mr. L. experienced rebuff or empathic failure at nearly every turn. Although better able than was Ms. T. to stay the course, he had only marginal success in his effort to secure this type of compensatory structure.

By the time he reached Card VIII, this patient showed the first significant psychological testing indication of what Kohut described as a disintegration product. He was sufficiently destabilized to abandon the effort to seek idealization or twinship selfobjects. As a result, he had diminished ability to continue pursuing the vigor that he sought in a responsive selfobject to revive a flagging, devitalized self. The disappointment that the selfobject environment did not respond empathically drove the self, in effect, into hiding and disposed him to a joyless, mechanical plodding through an existence in which expecting to be understood, affirmed, or responded to was considerably diminished.

This deadening of affective arousal produced the ennui or listlessness that impeded Mr. L. from enthusiastically taking part in life. It appeared superficially as depression, signifying the failure of selfobjects to function optimally. It foreshadowed the depletion of the self and its protective shutting down or withdrawal. The passivity and increased dependency indications seen before Card VIII did not therefore represent features of depression or even the ingrained characterologic predisposition to a depressive personality. Rather, the passivity can be understood as this patient's best effort to be "stable on his perch."

Mr. L. briefly revived the effort to sustain self-cohesion, but it led him nowhere and he ultimately returned to a position of being undermined and immobilized. He was "in isolation" from a selfobject environment that has not functioned well for him. When he said "nothing is together," it became his metaphor for feeling depleted and worn down.

Failing to restimulate a viable selfobject environment through compensatory structures of idealization and twinship, he grew increasingly adrift, passively withdrawn, and consequently trying to get by in whatever way he could manage. With a markedly dampened-down affect life, Mr. L. experienced the joylessness and understimulation of someone defeated and had little reason to struggle in an unresponsive selfobject environment.

It is hardly surprising that Mr. L.'s TAT responses were dominated by stories in which relationships were characterized by puzzlement and indifference. The predominant feeling tone was one of being alone with his problems, without considering that someone else could be sufficiently understanding. The figures in Mr. L.'s stories solved problems alone, without anticipation of support. The most striking feature of these interactions was not that others failed to comprehend or disappointed in their availability, but rather that nobody ever expected anyone to come to another person's assistance.

The main indications about the interplay of selfobject functions appeared in Mr. L.'s Rorschach responses. Although evidence for faulty mirroring was consistent throughout all the projective protocols, the emergence of idealization and twinship occurred predominantly on the Rorschach. There does not seem to be an affinity between selfobject functions and particular projective tests. In general, the fact that an injury to self-esteem has occurred defines the self state. It is the self state that is consistently detected on projective psychological tests. There may be less regularity regarding the appearance of idealization and twinship selfobject functions on one or another projective test.

Twinship and idealization selfobject functions were weakly apparent in the previous case of Ms. T., but were more vigorously pursued by Mr. L. in an effort to establish compensatory structures, at least until he became too undermined to sustain this effort with any success. Regardless of the viability of idealization or twinship as durable selfobject functions, these functions do not seem to be characteristically associated with any specific projective test instrument.

POSTSCRIPT:
SUMMARY AND REFLECTIONS

In *The Future of an Illusion*, Freud (1927/1961) wrote: "The voice of the intellect is a soft one, but it does not rest till it has gained a hearing" (p. 53). He was describing how drives can overwhelm, but not totally silence, the rationality that comes about when internal self-control predominates. Such internal control is one therapeutic result that marks the strengthening of that psychological function the ego psychologists would subsequently term the *observing ego*. In the language of Rorschach psychology, it can be represented by acquiring the resilience to produce a sufficient number of *M* responses of good quality to compensate for, if need be, impinging determinants suggesting potentially disorganizing affect states.

Notwithstanding Freud's pertinent observation, there is also a number of conditions (many of which are character disorders and sub-clinical forms of character pathology) typified by hypertrophy of rationality and intellect. Not all of these states necessarily signify psychological health; some denote obsessions or related characterologic disturbances typified prominently by isolation or distancing defenses such as intellectualization. Conditions that are dominated by overintellectualization are frequently associated with smoothly operating or efficient deployment of defenses. There is characteristically minimal distress, although chronic low-grade dysthymia may be present. It is a form of defense that appears, on the face of it, to turn pathology into a virtue.

The disorders of the self sometimes appear this way, often accompanied by diminished zest or vigor, boredom or ennui, or aimless life paths lacking in goals or a clear enough sense of direction. The improved efficacy of the newer generation of antidepressant and anxiolytic compounds effectively treats the symptomatic manifestations of some of these disturbances, leaving the remaining ingrained characterologic adaptations as the residual stamp of the personality.

For these conditions, it can be argued, it is the voice of the unconscious that is soft but persistent. This restatement of Freud's comment cited

earlier reflects the maladaptive consequences of chronic boredom or anhe-
donia, directionless career paths, and unsatisfying, joyless relationships
with other people. Further, it is a view that highlights one of the most
refined, sophisticated uses of diagnostic psychological tests.

This subtle characteristic is an indication of one way the dynamics of
human personality and its deep psychological layers do not yield their
secrets easily. For this reason, psychodiagnostic testing is typically re-
quested when a clinical interview or early treatment sessions do not sufficiently clarify a patient's problem. Clinicians hope that psychological
testing will reveal submerged aspects of a patient's personality; therefore,
testing that merely replicates the clinical diagnostic interview is rarely
useful. If testing does not augment what has been obtained on interview, the
testing has probably failed. Diagnostic psychological testing can be compared to the use of radiologic procedures in clinical medicine when the
history and physical examination are suggestive but not definitive. Test
findings should attempt to reveal what cannot be seen with the naked eye
on clinical examination or by history. Diagnostic psychological testing can
be a more or less invasive procedure, not unlike the difference between a
routine electrocardiogram and a cardiac catherization study.

Regarding the psychodiagnostic evaluation, some clinicians are of a
temperament that remains predominantly if not even inflexibly faithful to
conducting strict logically-driven inquiries on all projective tests. Although
frequently emphasizing obvious details that any layman would have no
difficulty understanding, this particular clinical temperament reflects an
examiner's view of personality that advances the field in important ways in
its demand that explanations must be logical, internally consistent, and
reproducible. When practiced as a single-minded rigid pursuit of this form
of evidence, however, this approach retards understanding, coming as it
does at the cost of compromising psychological curiosity about discerning
personality dynamics in depth. Although few psychologists regard themselves as so dogmatic that they would not even consider an impression based
on less than ideal empirical evidence, there are varying degrees of psychological depth, nevertheless, that clinicians are willing to examine and
attempt to understand.

The differences in conceptual approaches are at the core of what defines
the meaning of psychological understanding for clinicians. If a clinician
wishes to know if anyone is "at home" (a popular metaphor for the meaning
of the human movement (M) response), the clinician can focus his or her
investigation on determining whether the criteria for scoring M have been

satisfied, or the clinician can probe the associations that (dare I say it) remind patients or make then think of such responses containing an *M* code. It is the difference between ringing someone's doorbell to see whether the person is visibly at home and examining the person's diaries or personal papers to understand what "floats his boat."

None of what I have said is new. Of course, it goes without saying that any psychodiagnostic testing examiner needs to understand which method or combination of methods is compatible with his or her temperamental makeup. Like inspecting TAT cards or Rorschach blots, there is no right or wrong answer to this problem; it is largely a restatement of the age-old question about how clinicians understand what is inside the black box of a person's psychological existence. All that is new about restating this controversy is that examiners who are interested in understanding the interior life of self states and self disorders will need to probe for a degree of depth with sufficient intensity and persistence. For the moment, scales of narcissism or self-esteem simply do not pass muster.

If a clinician seeks answers to questions about problems that are fairly close to the surface, a probing examination may be unwarranted. If the problem is deeply concealed, the investigation may need to be aggressive. I have selected clinical examples that lead to straightforward inferences about self states. Understandably, the interpretive value of records that are less well elaborated is not as evident. Indeed, most Rorschach records are more banal and frequently not as distinctive as many of those reproduced in these pages.

Thus, there is a difference in kind between the quality of responses or verbalizations obtained from rich, productive protocols, and those obtained from ordinary or banal records. This difference can be reduced, however, if examiners are so inclined, by obtaining carefully elicited associations about motivational states at appropriate points in the inquiry. Examiners must be diligent in following up salient comments. For example, ascertaining a beginning, middle, and outcome to TAT stories usually does not suffice; provocative comments about the story must be pursued cautiously but vigorously. The reserve necessary to conduct a careful, unobtrusive Rorschach inquiry need not be regarded as a model when applied to the TAT or figure drawings.

Lest my intention be misunderstood, I am not arguing to supplant the unobtrusive Rorschach inquiry. Rather, I argue that something can be added by augmenting the standard Comprehensive System inquiry and moving beyond a perceptual problem solving function to permit the unfolding of the predominant self state. Admittedly, not all clinicians are disposed to use inquiry data in this way. In the final analysis, the techniques of administering projective tests ultimately remain a matter of clinical and theoretical persuasion. Likewise, clinicians need not fear that conducting probing inquiries inevitably contaminates clinical findings any more than they should feel they must artificially guard against influencing patients' responses by looking patients in the eye and thereby revealing the examiners' reactions to the clinical material. Being well-trained means that clinicians have the necessary internal self-discipline to control their reactions without having to resort to playing "musical chairs" or other contrived devices to do this for them. Examiners who have difficulty with this fundamental clinical temperament might find greater satisfaction in other endeavors. In this context, it is worth remembering that the reason Freud advocated using the couch was not primarily to stimulate regression or to facilitate free association. The real reason is because he could not stand being looked at or scrutinized searchingly throughout the day by his patients.

I argued the case for conducting a detailed and vigorous inquiry at some length in chapter 4. The extended case study of Mr. L. (chap. 8) demonstrated this clinical situation compellingly, in a relatively well-compensated patient. On the other hand, severely disorganized patients, many with borderline personality disorder, more readily reveal their psychological distress, which can include states of profoundly disturbed self-cohesion. Such patients characteristically lack the defensive resilience to protect themselves effectively. Thus, their painfully experienced affect states and compromised reality testing emerge in a seemingly uninhibited way, leaking or oozing out, because they cannot prevent this discharge. The case of Ms. T. (chap. 7) illustrated this form of psychopathology.

Many people have less pronounced self disorders than did Ms. T. and Mr. L. Many show a level of resilience, despite pronounced disorders of self-cohesion, intermediate between severe and mild self disorders. These patients not infrequently manage to elude themselves, the clinicians who treat them, and the psychodiagnosticians examining their personalities. Their disturbances are often manifested in subtle nuances and require a sufficiently probing inquiry.

In chapters 5 and 6, I discussed a number of clinical examples of devitalized self states that were derived from subtle indications. These examples require appropriately rigorous restraint to avoid overinterpreting their meanings. Schafer's criteria are a helpful guide in this effort. Nevertheless, figures described as standing or looking around with nothing to do, waiting for someone to come by when nobody is there, or looking empty can characterize devitalization experiences. Similarly, selfobject failure, absence, or under-responsiveness may be detected in TAT stories such as the boy with the violin that no one showed him how to play or a person who cannot take decisive action, trust someone's advice, or solve a problem alone. Drawings of human figures that are small or confined to a corner of the page or that otherwise suggest a vulnerable appearance (such as a person with crutches, missing a limb, or nude) point to the possibility of a devital- ized self state. Inferring such self states from the details of the drawings is suggestive rather than definitive, and a vigorous inquiry to elaborate the fantasied inner nature of how the drawn figure thinks and feels is usually critical to substantiate this type of clinical interpretation.

The thrust of most of the examples I have discussed is that impaired self-cohesion appears in the broad class of projective test responses denot- ing experiences of feeling depreciated. On one side of this range of self states are manifestations of an unmirrored self, usually characterized by affect states of being rebuffed, slighted, or ignored. A painfully experienced manifestation of a similar self state is characterized chiefly by a person's being made to feel depreciated or humiliated. Accordingly, projective test responses of this type depict figures such as clowns, hoboes, or other ignored or stepped-on figures on the Rorschach test, and comparable imagery from the TAT or projective drawings might contain figures de- scribed as small, insignificant, or unimportant.

Kohut observed that the selfobject need is best seen clinically when self-cohesion is threatened. The self seeks a level of responsiveness that restores a sense of stabilization. What the injured self needs for its repair is central, not the unique characteristics of the person whom the patient enlists in that effort. Some patients have built entire lives around conceal- ing feelings of depletion, and projective testing does not easily penetrate this defense. The standard unobtrusive inquiry fosters this defense and may assist patients whose vulnerable self states require concealment.

As a result, vulnerable self-esteem in the form of self-depreciation, shame, pronounced disappointment, and devaluation do not easily emerge from patients' projective test responses in the absence of a sufficiently probing inquiry, just as people may hide an injured or diminished self on clinical interview and in treatment. This self-concealment of an injured or undermined self state is both a measure of the preserved ability of many well-compensated patients to protect themselves as well as the very prob- lem that potentiates the illness and the ensuing need for treatment. For this reason, projective tests that permit a wide-ranging in-depth inquiry become all the more necessary. In addition to revealing such self states, a probing inquiry also rewards examiners with a more complete understanding of selfobject needs (and sometimes, their differentiation from one another) and the success or failure of compensatory structures.

How unfortunate it is when clinicians, while pursuing reliability, unwittingly contribute to what patients can ill afford. I do not dismiss or disparage reliability, logical thinking, and the scientific method; I have devoted the major part of my career to research that values and appreciates these ideals. My point here is simply that an approach that stubbornly refuses to see beyond empirically documented evidence deprives itself of the opportunity to at least heuristically open itself to what is most true and important about human personality. Some of what Freud could only have guessed about at the end of the 19th century has proved to be true, but much of it has not. Similarly, some of what we may only guess about now, at the end of the 20th century, will stand the test of time, and some will not. In the logical inquiry of a clinical science, it is usually more important to pursue possible explanations to advance the field than to settle for the comfort of the tried and true and the superficial.

In my closing remarks, I wish to emphasize that no agreed-on theoretical approach has achieved supremacy in understanding character pathology. The same symptoms, associations, and projective testing findings can be examined from multiple viewpoints, none of which has the last word. Without advocating an atheoretical position on the subject, I want to stress that clinical material can be conceptualized from several viewpoints. A self psychological framework makes no more claim to being the most appropriate theoretical position than does an ego psychological, psychoanalytic object relations, behavioral, or social learning approach. All these represent alternative ways of conceptualizing clinical material. My overriding premise throughout this book has been that one useful way to think about psychological testing material in a logical and consistent manner is from the viewpoint of psychoanalytic self psychology.

As always, clinical interpretation remains an exercise in disciplined, logical thinking, regardless of the data that inform clinical inferences. Even empathic understanding, as Kohut described it, is not a loose, undisciplined, feeling-dominated mental activity but a carefully applied and rigorously self-monitored psychological activity of well-trained clinicians. Thus, my main point remains that fantasy elaborations can regularly augment empirically derived, objective clinical findings in the understanding of personality. The appreciation of self disorders and selfobject functions, in fact, requires the use of empathically understood data obtained from projective diagnostic tests. These data expand the richness of the in-depth understanding of self states.

REFERENCES

Abraham, K. (1927). Psycho-analytic studies on character-formation. In: *Selected Papers on Psycho-Analysis* (pp. 370–417). London: Hogarth Press. (Original work published 1921)

Akiskal, H. S. (1980). External validating criteria for psychiatric diagnosis: Their application in affective disorders. *Journal of Clinical Psychiatry, 41,* 6–15.

Alexander, F., & French, T. M. (1946). *Psychoanalytic therapy: Principles and applications.* New York: Ronald Press.

Allison, J., Blatt, S. J., & Zimet, C. N. (1968). *The interpretation of psychological tests.* New York: Harper & Row.

American Psychiatric Association. (1952). *Diagnostic and statistical manual of mental disorders.* Washington, DC: Author.

American Psychiatric Association (1994). *Diagnostic and statistical manual of mental disorders* (4th ed.). Washington, DC: Author.

Arnow, D., & Cooper, S. (1988). Toward a Rorschach psychology of the self. In H. D. Lerner & P. M. Lerner (Eds.), *Primitive mental states and the Rorschach* (pp. 53–70). Madison, CT: International Universities Press.

Aronow, E., Reznikoff, M., & Moreland, K. (1994). *The Rorschach technique: Perceptual basics, content interpretation, and applications.* Boston: Allyn & Bacon.

Athey, G. I., Jr. (1986). Rorschach thought organization and transference enactment in the patient–examiner relationship. In M. Kissen (Ed.), *Assessing object relations phenomena* (pp. 19–50). Madison, CT: International Universities Press.

Bacal, H. A. (1985). Optimal responsiveness and the therapeutic process. In A. Goldberg (Ed.), *Progress in self psychology* (pp. 202–226). New York: Guilford Press.

Bacal, H. A. (1994). The selfobject relationship in psychoanalytic treatment. In A. Goldberg (Ed.), *Progress in self psychology: Vol. 10, A decade of progress* (pp. 21–30). Hillsdale, NJ: Analytic Press.

Bacal, H. A., & Newman, K. (1990). *Theories of object relations: Bridges to self psychology.* New York: Columbia University Press.

Balint, M. (1968). *The basic fault.* London: Tavistock.

Basch, M. F. (1983). Empathic understanding: A review of the concept and some theoretical considerations. *Journal of the American Psychoanalytic Association, 31,* 101–126.

Basch, M. F. (1984). Selfobject theory of motivation and the history of psychoanalysis. In P. E. Stepansky & A. Goldberg (Eds.), *Kohut's legacy: Contributions to self psychology* (pp. 3–20). Hillsdale, NJ: Analytic Press.

281

Basch, M. F. (1994). The selfobject concept: Clinical implications. In A. Goldberg (Ed.), *Progress in self psychology: Vol. 10, A decade of progress* (pp. 1–7). Hillsdale, NJ: Analytic Press.

Beebe, B., Jaffe, J., & Lachmann, F. (1992). The contribution of mother–infant influence to the origins of self- and object-representations. In N. Skolnick & S. Warshaw, (Eds.), *Relational perspectives in psychoanalysis* (pp. 83–118). Hillsdale, NJ: Analytic Press.

Beebe, B., & Lachmann, F. M. (1988). Mother–infant mutual influence and precursors of psychic structure. In A. Goldberg (Ed.), *Progress in self psychology: Vol. 3, Frontiers in self psychology* (pp. 3–25). Hillsdale, NJ: Analytic Press.

Bellak, L., & Abrams, D. M. (1997). *The T. A. T., the C. A. T., and the S. A. T. in clinical use* (6th ed.). Boston: Allyn & Bacon.

Bowlby, J. (1969). *Attachment and loss: Vol. 1, Attachment.* New York: Basic Books.

Curtis, H. C. (1986). Clinical consequences of the theory of self psychology. In A. Goldberg (Ed.), *Progress in self psychology* (Vol. 2, pp. 3–17). Hillsdale, NJ: Analytic Press. (Original work published 1986)

Eagle, M. N. (1984). *Recent developments in psychoanalysis.* New York: McGraw-Hill.

Elson, M. (1987). *The Kohut seminars on self psychology and psychotherapy with adolescents and young adults.* New York: Norton.

Erikson, E. (1950). *Childhood and society.* New York: Norton.

Exner, J. E., Jr. (1991). *The Rorschach: A Comprehensive System. Vol. 2, Interpretation* (2nd ed.). New York: Wiley.

Exner, J. E., Jr. (1993). *The Rorschach: A Comprehensive System. Vol. 1, Basic foundations* (3rd ed.). New York: Wiley.

Exner, J. E., Jr. (1995). *A Rorschach workbook for the Comprehensive System* (4th ed.). Asheville, NC: Rorschach Workshops.

Fairbairn, R. (1941). A revised psychopathology of the psychoses and psychoneuroses. In *Psychoanalytic studies of the personality* (pp. 28–58). London: Tavistock.

Fosshage, J. L. (1989). The developmental function of dreaming mentations: Clinical implications. In A. Goldberg (Ed.), *Progress in self psychology: Vol. 5, Dimensions of self experience* (pp. 3–11). Hillsdale, NJ: Analytic Press.

Freud, A. (1936). *The ego and the mechanisms of defense.* New York: International Universities Press.

Freud, S. (1955). Group psychology and the analysis of the ego. In J. Strachey (Ed. and Trans.), *The standard edition of the complete psychological works of Sigmund Freud* (Vol. 18, pp. 65–144). London: Hogarth Press. (Original work published 1921)

Freud, S. (1959). Inhibitions, symptoms and anxiety. In J. Strachey (Ed. and Trans.), *The standard edition of the complete psychological works of Sigmund Freud* (Vol. 20, pp. 87–172). London: Hogarth Press. (Original work published 1926)

Freud, S. (1961). The ego and the id. In J. Strachey (Ed. and Trans.), *The standard edition of the complete psychological works of Sigmund Freud* (Vol. 19, pp. 12–59). London: Hogarth Press. (Original work published 1923)

Freud, S. (1961). The future of an illusion. In J. Strachey (Ed. and Trans.), *The Standard edition of the complete psychological works of Sigmund Freud* (Vol. 21, pp. 5–56). London: Hogarth Press. (Original work published 1927)

Gabel, S. (1994). The development of a self-psychological theory of dreams: Historical and clinical considerations. In A. Goldberg (Ed.), *Progress in self psychology: Vol. 10, A decade of progress* (pp. 183–196). Hillsdale, NJ: Analytic Press.

Galatzer-Levy, R. M. (1988). Manic-depressive illness: Analytic experience and a hypothesis. In A. Goldberg (Ed.), *Progress in self psychology: Vol. 3, Frontiers in self psychology* (pp. 87–102). Hillsdale, NJ: Analytic Press.

Gedo, J., & Goldberg, A. (1973). *Models of the mind.* Chicago: University of Chicago Press.

Glover, E. (1955). *The technique of psychoanalysis.* New York: International Universities Press.

Goldberg, A. (1978). *The psychology of the self: A casebook.* New York: International Universities Press.

Goldberg, A. (1988). *A fresh look at psychoanalysis: The view from self psychology.* Hillsdale, NJ: Analytic Press.

Goldberg, A. (1990). *The prisonhouse of psychoanalysis.* Hillsdale, NJ: Analytic Press.

Goldberg, A. (1995). *The problem of perversion: The view from self psychology.* New Haven, CT: Yale University Press.

Goodenough, F. (1926). *Measurement of intelligence by drawings.* New York: World Book.

Greenberg, J., & Mitchell, S. (1983). *Object relations in psychoanalytic theory.* Cambridge, MA: Harvard University Press.

Guntrip, H. (1969). *Schizoid phenomena, object relations, and the self.* New York: International Universities Press.

Handler, L. (1996). The clinical use of figure drawings. In C. S. Newmark (Ed.), *Major psychological assessment instruments* (2nd ed., pp. 206–293). Boston: Allyn & Bacon.

Harrower, M. (1965). *Psychodiagnostic testing: An empirical approach.* Springfield, IL: Thomas.

Hartmann, H. (1939). *Ego psychology and the problem of adaptation.* New York: International Universities Press.

Henry, W. (1956). *The analysis of fantasy: The Thematic Apperception Technique in the study of personality.* New York: Wiley.

Holt, R. R. (1978). *Methods in clinical psychology: Volume 1, Projective assessment.* New York: Plenum Press.

Isherwood, C. (1935). *The Berlin stories.* New York: New Directions.

Jacobson, E. (1964). *The self and the object world.* New York: International Universities Press.

Kernberg, O. (1975). *Borderline conditions and pathological narcissism.* New York: Aronson.

Kissen, M. (1986). Object relations aspects of human figure drawings. In *Assessing object relations phenomena* (pp. 175–191). Madison, CT: International Universities Press.

Kissen, M. (1986). *Assessing object relations phenomena.* Madison, CT: International Universities Press.

Klein, A. (1996, December 8). Baitz and Rifkin: A substantive friendship. *The New York Times,* p. LI 17.

Klein, M. (1930). The importance of symbol formation in the development of the ego. *International Journal of Psycho-Analysis, 11,* 24–39.

Klein, M. (1975). A contribution to the psychogenesis of manic-depressive states. In: *Love, Guilt and Reparation, 1921–1945* (pp. 262–289). New York: Free Press. (Original work published 1935)

Klopfer, B., & Kelley, D. (1942). *The Rorschach technique.* Yonkers: World Book.

Kohut, H. (1959). Introspection, empathy, and psychoanalysis: An examination of the relationship between mode of observation and theory. *Journal of the American Psychoanalytic Association, 7,* 459–483.

Kohut, H. (1966). Forms and transformations of narcissism. *Journal of the American Psychoanalytic Association, 14,* 243–272.

Kohut, H. (1968). The psychoanalytic treatment of narcissistic personality disorders. *Psychoanalytic Study of the Child* (Vol. 23, pp. 86–113). *New York: International Universities Press.*

Kohut, H. (1971). *The analysis of the self.* New York: International Universities Press.

Kohut, H. (1977). *The restoration of the self.* New York: International Universities Press.

Kohut, H. (1979). The two analyses of Mr. Z. *International Journal of Psycho-analysis, 60,* 3–27.

Kohut, H. (1984). *How does analysis cure?* (A. Goldberg & P. Stepansky, Eds.). Chicago: University of Chicago Press.

Kohut, H. (1996). *The Chicago Institute lectures.* (P. Tolpin & M. Tolpin, Eds.). Hillsdale, NJ: Analytic Press.

Kohut, H., & Wolf, E. (1978). The disorders of the self and their treatment: An outline. *International Journal of Psycho-analysis, 59,* 413–425.

Kwawer, J. S. (1979). Borderline phenomena, interpersonal relations, and the Rorschach test. *Bulletin of the Menninger Clinic, 43,* 515–524.

Kwawer, J. S. (1980). Primitive interpersonal modes, borderline phenomena, and Rorschach content. In J. S. Kwawer, H. D. Lerner, P. M. Lerner, & A. Sugarman (Eds.), *Borderline phenomena and the Rorschach test.* (pp. 89–105). New York: International Universities Press.

Kwawer, J. S., Lerner, H. D., Lerner, P. M., & Sugarman, A. (1980). *Borderline phenomena and the Rorschach test.* New York: International Universities Press.

Lacan, J. (1978). *The four fundamental concepts in psychoanalysis.* New York: Norton.

Lachmann, F. M. (1986). Interpretation of psychic conflict and adversarial relationships: A self-psychological perspective. *Psychoanalytic Psychology, 3,* 341–355.

LaFemina, K. (1996, February). *Twinship: Who it defines and how it is defined.* Paper presented to the Society for Advancement of Self Psychology, New York, NY.

Lerner, H. D., & Lerner, P. M. (1988). *Primitive mental states and the Rorschach.* Madison, CT: International Universities Press.

Lerner, P. M. (1988). Rorschach measures of depression, the false self, and projective identification in patients with narcissistic personality disorders. In H. D. Lerner & P. M. Lerner (Eds.), *Primitive mental states and the Rorschach* (pp. 71–93). Madison, CT: International Universities Press.

Lerner, P. M. (1991). *Psychoanalytic theory and the Rorschach.* Hillsdale, NJ: Analytic Press.

Levine, F. J. (1979). On the clinical application of Kohut's psychology of the self: Comments on some recently published case studies. *Journal of the Philadelphia Association for Psychoanalysis, 6,* 1–19.

Lichtenberg, J. D. (1991). What is a selfobject? *Psychoanalytic Dialogues, 1,* 455–479.

Loewald, H. W. (1980). *Papers on psychoanalysis.* New Haven, CT: Yale University Press.

Lovett, C. G. (1988). The Rorschach assessment of internalization mechanisms in depression. In H. D. Lerner & P. M. Lerner (Eds.), *Primitive mental states and the Rorschach* (pp. 107–153). Madison, CT: International Universities Press.

Machover, K. (1949). *Personality projection in the drawing of the human figure.* Springfield, IL: Thomas.

Mahler, M. S. (1968). *On human symbiosis and vicissitudes of individuation: Vol. 1. Infantile psychosis.* New York: International Universities Press.

Malin, A. (1988). A short history of the psychoanalytic approach to the treatment of psychotic disorders. In A. Goldberg (Ed.), *Progress in self psychology: Vol. 3, Frontiers in self psychology* (pp. 81–86). Hillsdale, NJ: Analytic Press.

Mayman, M. (1967). Object-representations and object-relationships in Rorschach responses. *Journal of Projective Techniques and Personality Assessment, 31,* 17–24.

Mayman, M. (1970). Reality contact, defense effectiveness, and psychopathology in Rorschach form level scores. In B. Klopfer, M. Meyer, & F. Brawer (Eds.), *Developments in Rorschach technique,* (Vol. III, pp. 11–44). New York: Harcourt Brace Jovanovich.

Menninger, K. (1958). *Theory of psychoanalytic technique.* New York: Harper & Row.

Morrison, A. P. (1984). Shame and the psychology of the self. In P. E. Stepansky & A. Goldberg (Eds.), *Kohut's legacy: Contributions to self psychology* (pp. 71–90). Hillsdale, NJ: Analytic Press.

Murray, H. A. (1938). *Explorations in personality.* New York: Oxford University Press.

Murray, H. A. (1943). *Thematic Apperception Test: Manual.* Cambridge, MA: Harvard University Press.

Ornstein, P. H. (1978). The evolution of Heinz Kohut's psychoanalytic psychology of the self. In P. H. Ornstein (Ed.), *The search for the self: Selected writings of Heinz Kohut: 1950–1978.* (Vol. 1, pp. 1–106). New York: International Universities Press.

Ornstein, P. H. (1987). On self-state dreams in the psychoanalytic treatment process. In A. Rothstein (Ed.), *The interpretation of dreams in clinical work* (pp. 87–104). Madison, CT: International Universities Press.

Ornstein, P. H. (1990). The unfolding and completion of Heinz Kohut's paradigm of psychoanalysis. In P. H. Ornstein (Ed.), *The search for the self: Selected writings of Heinz Kohut: 1978–1981.* (Vol. 3, pp. 1–82). New York: International Universities Press.

Pine, F. (1988). The four psychologies of psychoanalysis and their place in clinical work. *Journal of the American Psychoanalytic Association, 36,* 571–596.

Rapaport, D. (1951). The autonomy of the ego. *Bulletin of the Menninger Clinic, 15,* 113–123.

Rapaport, D., Gill, M. M., & Schafer, R. (1945). *Diagnostic psychological testing.* Chicago: Year Book.

Rapaport, D., Gill, M. M., & Schafer, R. (1968). *Diagnostic psychological testing: Revised edition.* (R. R. Holt, Ed.). New York: International Universities Press.

Rorschach, H. (1981). *Psychodiagnostics: A diagnostic test based on perception* (9th ed., P. Lemkau & B. Kronenberg, Trans.). Berne, Switzerland: Hans Huber. (Original work published 1921)

Rotter, J. B. (1947). The scoring and analysis of the Thematic Apperception Test. *Journal of Psychology, 24,* 319–330.

Rowe, C. E., Jr. (1994). Reformulations of the concept of selfobject: A misalliance of self psychology with object relations theory. In A. Goldberg (Ed.), *Progress in self psychology: Vol. 10, A decade of progress* (pp. 9–20). Hillsdale, NJ: Analytic Press.

Schachtel, E. G. (1966). *Experiential foundations of Rorschach's test.* New York: Basic Books.

Schafer, R. (1948). *The clinical application of psychological tests.* New York: International Universities Press.

Schafer, R. (1954). *Psychoanalytic interpretation in Rorschach testing.* New York: Grune & Stratton.

Schafer, R. (1967). *Projective testing and psychoanalysis.* New York: International Universities Press.

Smith, B. L. (1992). An American in Paris. *Bulletin of the International Rorschach Society, 2,* 5–6.

Stern, D. N. (1985). *The interpersonal world of the infant.* New York: Basic Books.

Stolorow, R., Brandchaft, B., & Atwood, G. (1987). *Psychoanalytic treatment: An intersubjective approach.* Hillsdale, NJ: Analytic Press.

Sugarman, A. (1986). Self-experience and reality testing: Synthesis of an object relations and an ego psychological model on the Rorschach. In M. Kissen (Ed.), *Assessing object relations phenomena* (pp. 51–75). Madison, CT: International Universities Press.

Summers, F. (1994). *Object relations theories and psychopathology.* Hillsdale, NJ: Analytic Press.

Tolpin, M. (1978). Self-objects and oedipal objects—A crucial developmental distinction. *Psychonanalytic Study of the Child* (Vol. 33, pp. 167–184). New Haven, CT: Yale University Press.

Tolpin, M. (1983). Corrective emotional experience: A self-psychological reevaluation. In A. Goldberg (Ed.), *The future of psychoanalysis.* (pp. 363–379). New York: International Universities Press.

Tolpin, M. (1993). The unmirrored self, compensatory structure, and cure: The exemplary case of Anna O. In B. Magid (Ed.), *Freud's case studies: Self psychological perspectives* (pp. 9–29). Hillsdale, NJ: Analytic Press.

Tolpin, M. (1995, October). *Compensatory structures: Pathways to cure.* Paper presented at the 18th annual International Conference on the Psychology of the Self, Chicago, IL.

Tolpin, M., & Kohut, H. (1980). The disorders of the self: The psychopathology of the first year of life. In S. Greenspan & G. H. Pollock (Eds.), *The course of life: Psychoanalytic contributions toward understanding personality development. Vol. 1, Infancy and early childhood.* (pp. 425–458). Washington, DC: National Institute of Mental Health.

Tolpin, P. (1983). Self psychology and the interpretation of dreams. In A. Goldberg (Ed.), *The future of psychoanalysis* (pp. 255–271). New York: International Universities Press.

Tolpin, P. (1988). Optimal affective engagement: The analyst's role in therapy. In A. Goldberg (Ed.), *Learning from Kohut: Progress in self psychology* (pp. 160–168). Hillsdale, NJ: Analytic Press.

Wallerstein, R. S. (1995). How does self psychology differ in practice? In A. Goldberg (Ed.), *Progress in self psychology* (Vol. 2, pp. 63–83). Hillsdale, NJ: Analytic Press. (Original work published 1986)

Winnicott, D. W. (1953). Transitional objects and transitional phenomena. *International Journal of Psycho-analysis, 34,* 89–97.

Wolf, E. (1988). *Treating the self: Elements of clinical self psychology.* New York: Guilford Press.

Zubin, J., Eron, L. D., & Schumer, F. (1965). *An experimental approach to projective techniques.* New York: Wiley.

AUTHOR INDEX

SUBJECT INDEX

293